It is a curious situation that the United States of America prisons hold more inmates than any other democracy in the world.

If you believe various statistical data collection sites the ratio is anywhere between eight times higher and 10 times higher.

The obvious question to ask then is: Do we have that many more criminals in this country? Do we really have eight times the number of criminals than comparable democracies?

And if we do, is it because we created the best law enforcement agencies in the world? Do other countries just lack the proficiency, competence or determination to pursue criminal activity?

There are a lot of questions on this subject and the most relevant one is and always has been, if we can do anything about it. And if we can, how do we go about it? What would be the first step?

These pages provide an insight look into the current situation and list viable remedies to get out of it.

I lived in the State of Oklahoma and have worked within the Corrections setting for 10 years. Since every State has its own rules and laws and statutes to battle its criminal elements, I used the policies of this State to demonstrate how things could get better. The main ideas are certainly applicable to all other States.

Why should anyone care?

I can only answer that question for myself.

1

I care because I see a tremendous workforce being dormant, just lying around doing nothing and I not only pay for them lying around doing nothing, but I also pay for all the landscaping and cleaning work they could do, for which we now don't have the money for because we need to pay for people doing nothing.

I also care because teachers in this State haven't seen a raise in years

I care because I think it is better to invest our taxes in education and training instead of creating yet another record in mass incarceration.

I can think of much better ways to spend the taxes of the productive workforce of this State and of other States.

Somebody should have written this book a long time ago, maybe things would be better already. Some law professor should have sat down with a bunch of his students and worked out a system which could replace or improve upon the current system.

A veteran of the Department of Corrections should have formulated and submitted step by step formulas and procedures which would have been based on his extensive knowledge and experience of this subject matter.

This book is certainly an attempt to improve things. But the fact that somebody wrote a book with some ideas doesn't improve anything just yet. For now, it is just an assembly of words printed on paper.

Time will tell so to speak. The prove is in the pudding.

The Author

Content

2   Remedies

The Current Prison System

The Good - the employee

With about 2 million American citizens currently incarcerated and the costs to both State and Federal Government rising to levels not before seen or envisioned, it might be difficult for the uninitiated to find areas within the system of incarceration, which any sound minded person could deem "good". To speak of anything which is good within the current prison system seem to be more of a conundrum than anything else. The word itself doesn't seem to match with the state of affairs at all. What in the world could be deemed being good when somebody gets locked up?

So, I set out and started to talk to prisoners and staff alike. I am rather familiar with the environment, having worked as a prison guard for the better part of ten years. Naturally I had my own opinion about the bad and the good aspects of prison life. But I thought to myself, it's not good enough to portrait my own opinion, I intended to tackle the subject like a journalist would go about an assignment by his editor in chief, talking to people who spend time within the system. I tried to assume a neutral ground on this subject.

To my surprise, employees within the Department of Corrections (DOC) didn't seem to have too much of an opinion at all. That was the first surprise. Everybody has an opinion about his place of work, so I thought. And the DOC is just another place, where people work thus, they should have a distinct and articulable view on the matter. My exact approach was, to ask some people, what was good or bad about the DOC. I guess nobody ever did that because I didn't get far with that approach. I mean, you get the usual, safe, unassuming responses you basically would get from any other place of employment.

8

The job has good benefits, the job is easy, the job is secure to some extent, because people will always be locked up and no matter where you move or to which places your life will take you, you always would be able to be hired in some form of correctional setting.

Let's face it, several factors greatly increase the likelihood of being able to support yourself and your family for an extended amount of time as an employee of the DOC:

1. There are prisons everywhere,

2. People will always be locked up,

3. The custody of prisoners is not likely to be taken over by less expensive, illegal immigrants nor will inmates be transferred to another country with less expensive labor (not yet anyways),

4. The benefits are decent. Provided you work for a State or Municipality, you would normally get good health benefits and in most cases a pension,

5. A uniform is provided for Security personnel,

6. There exist the possibility to receive awards and recognition. Like in many other work environments, there exist programs to award employees. Of course, this has to be backed up by law since the DOC is a state-run agency, but Operating Procedure (OP) 110221 includes the following:

III. Additional Local Awards

Each facility/district/unit may develop local procedures to establish awards for their location including, but not limited to, the following:

A.   Safety Award

This award may be presented to any individual employee or to members of a work unit whose efforts resulted in a verifiable reduction in the frequency or criticality of injuries or illnesses in the workplace, for exceptional or improved safety records, or for any other significant contributions to the achievement of safety related goals.

B.   Other
Each facility/district/unit head may establish additional work related awards and awards criteria as outlined in their local procedures.

And on page 9 of the same reference, it reads:

V. Awards funding
Oklahoma Statute 74 § 4121 and Merit Rule 260:25-23-3 authorize the use of available monies in the agency's operating funds for awards which recognize outstanding performance or other significant contributions to the agency, and for ceremonies, banquets, or receptions where awards are presented. The cost of recognition awards may not exceed $ 150.00 for each recognized employee each fiscal year when utilizing agency operating funds.

7. The career advancement opportunities within the Department of Corrections are as good as in many other work environments I have observed. Of course, if a particular prison only has 35 positions in total, you might have to be willing to move to another location for the next available, higher position. I have observed that many DOC employees tend to stay in their position for a very long time. If you have mastered the peculiars of your job and plan to stay in that location, it is a fairly secure work environment. And the longer you stay, the better your retirement pay will look like. On top of that, DOC provides longevity incentives. The longer you stay with the DOC, the higher it will be.

At least 2 years to 4 years $ 250

At least 4 years to 6 years $ 426 etc.

At 20 years or longer, you will get a lump sum payment of $ 2 000 per year.

Let's put these points down as being good as far as employees are concerned. There is a relative high level of job security and the pay is fairly competitive, compared to the surrounding environment since there is a definite need to have a certain number of staff working inside a prison. Factories may close down, restaurant chains may decide that to keep that particular store in that specific location is no longer viable, but long-term prison closures are still a rare occasion. Prison facilities might get re-structured and prison populations might get shuffled around a little bit, but the amount of square footage to keep inmates is not likely to go down in the near future.

It was surprising to me that many co-workers met me with a somewhat blank stare when I brought this question up. I had to realize that apparently, jobs in prisons are not unlike any other jobs. I always had the idea, working in prisons demands a certain human quality or attitude, which is quite different from other jobs. And the reason for that idea is, because in prisons, you are dealing with people, your product are people. You don't go to work and move matter around, you don't go to work and push buttons, drive vehicles or operate machinery. You don't do any of these things, at least it is not a major part of your job description. One of the first things they will tell you when you enter a program to become a Corrections Officer is, that this job is not for everyone. You deal with a high level of human emotions and reactions. The time an inmate spends in prison greatly depends on his own ability to stay out of trouble. As his time behind bars progresses, so does his options increase to move up to higher levels, which translates into less time he has to spend in prison. And Corrections Officers being on the front lines and constantly being in contact and communication with inmates have the ability and the responsibility to affect their levels, into which I will get in a minute. As a Corrections Officer (CO) can be the cause to decrease an inmate's time behind bars, so can he be the cause to increase the time. And if the time increases, emotions will flare up as to why and how and that the inmate is innocent and didn't do anything wrong, etc. This is all part of the job and the application of the rules and regulations within a correctional setting is crucial to the success of a CO. In other words, the decisions a CO makes has a direct and irreversible effect on the inmate's life, in real time so to speak. As a CO, you have to be neutral, fair, firm and consistent. And simply put, not everybody can do that.

The Good – the inmate

Ask any inmate if there is anything good being an inmate and you will be hard pressed to receive any response. You will more likely receive a shrug with the shoulders or a blank smile, which is understandable. Prison life is not supposed to be good; it is supposed to serve as a punishment. You are under the care and supervision of the DOC. Your entire life is regulated not by your own decisions, but by the schedule of events others determine. So naturally I had a hard time with this subject. What more complicated my search for answers was the built-in wall you encounter between captives and captors, between the guards and the inmates. You have to understand that there is no trust between these two opposing groups. It is almost impossible to have a decent conversation with an inmate, because you are considered an enemy. A conversation can only go so far and no further. Every blue moon an inmate might come up to you in a secret fashion and complain about the noise in his cell at night, because the people he shares the room with are constantly on a cell phone, laughing and giggling all the way for whatever reason. But that is a rare occasion.

There are however a few things I distilled out of my ten years with the DOC, which I would deem positive as far as the inmates are concerned.

1.Lack of responsibility.

If you are not in prison, you have to work, pay your rent, drive your kids to school, do homework with your kids, worry about birthdays and holidays, fix the house, get a car, take care of a car, go to the doctor, send your family and kids to the doctor, pay the bills from the doctor, shave, be presentable etc. etc. Factually we are looking at an enormous number of tasks and responsibilities. In other words, there is a price for freedom. You also have an enormous number of possibilities and opportunities. For a certain number of inmates, all these things we normal people consider part of life never really appealed to them. They

13

wanted to do whatever they wanted to do and it didn't matter if it was legal or not. These types of people sometimes welcome the opportunity to be free of responsibilities and tasks. And besides that, they are lazy as well. If you find yourself in that state of mind, prison time can have a certain, appealing ring to it. Yes, you have to get up at one point to go to the chow hall and eat, you have to somewhat keep your living area clean and orderly, but that is easily accomplished in 10 minutes. In certain prison blocks, 300 inmates are locked up in double cells and only can look forward to enter the day room to sit on bolted down tables and play cards. If weather provides, every other day they will be escorted outside to say hello to the sun. That is pretty much all they can and will do all day. They will get three meals a day, they will get medical care, they will get soap and a toothbrush.

In minimum prisons and community corrections centers, inmates may have a daily job on center or off center, but still not much responsibilities. The only thing really an inmate needs to know is, to do what he gets told. As long as he follows simple rules and regulations, which are not hard to understand, he will get in no trouble and in most cases, is free to do whatever he sets his mind to. That's one reason why there never really will be any measurement against the introduction of contraband. An inmate has nothing to do but to figure out, what is the best way to get hold of some tobacco and telephones, but that is another story, which I will get into later.

For lazy people who in real life never had somebody to look up to or for whatever reasons, prison life can be a way of life. Even if you don't have a job of any kind, you will get paid a few pennies a day, which amounts to something like $ 10 dollars a month. This also varies by qualification and whether or not the inmate is employed by OCI, the Oklahoma Corrections Industries, an organization which supplies products to the DOC and other state agencies.

And some inmates who are incarcerated in Halfway Houses or Community Corrections Centers are of course eligible to be employed by

14

any business which will employ them. They are however required to give up to 50 % of their pay to the DOC. This is covered in DOC policy OP-090110

Community corrections assignment provides eligible inmates with opportunities for work release and continuing education. These programs are designed to assist inmates with Section-09 Programs OP-090110 Page: 2 Effective Date: 07/17/2017 reentry and successful reintegration into the community. Work release provides eligible inmates the opportunity to seek, obtain and maintain employment in the community prior to release from incarceration. Inmates assigned to work release status may also be eligible to pursue the opportunity of continuing their education through colleges, universities or vocational/technical centers. (4-ACRS-5A-14)

As far as leveling the earnings of the inmates towards the cost of incarceration, the following formula is applied according to the same policy:

B. Program Support

1. From inmate wages, a mandatory program support fee will be assessed. The fees for participants will be calculated for the first through the last day of the pay period inclusively.

2. The total amount of program support may not exceed 50 percent of the net wages received for any given pay period; nor will it exceed the daily contracted cost per inmate of the community contract facility or the operating cost per inmate (OCPO) of the community corrections center.

3. Net wages consist of gross pay less FICA, Medicare, federal and state income taxes and court mandated garnishment for child support. Section-09 Programs OP-090110 Page: 14 Effective Date: 07/17/2017

4. No other deductions will be given consideration in calculating net salaries for the purpose of program support.

15

5. Inmates receiving 100% VA disability benefits on work release status will be required to pay program support fees.

In other words, an inmate can have a normal job while still incarcerated to build up his earnings and depending on the time he still has to serve, can acquire a substantial amount of money before he gets released. And he doesn't have to worry about a demanding wife and screaming children. He doesn't have to worry about paying rent, keeping up his dwelling, the cost of gas, insurance or any of that. If his job pays a decent amount of money, it shouldn't be a big problem to save $ 750 on a monthly basis, because he still will be provided food, shelter, a bed to sleep in, heated and cooled air and everything else other inmates get as well. And not all of us can easily save that amount of money. Thus, it is understandable how a few privileged inmates can find this situation rather alluring. An inmate who works of course doesn't only help himself. It helps pay for the cost of the DOC as well as mentioned before. We shouldn't forget that factor. And as far as re-integration is concerned, it is a good thing.

2. The Class level system

Before I got into Corrections, I always wondered, how convicted felons got out of prison so fast. Whenever I saw stories on TV about somewhat famous people, who served time, the only clue given was "good conduct". Due to good conduct he/she only had to serve five out of 8 years or any such thing. And for someone who never was involved with anybody who spent time behind bars or knew somebody, who spent time in prison, it is not surprising. If you don't know, you don't know.

Of course, if you dive into this subject, it becomes abundantly clear, what this is all about. It's basically the Department of Corrections equivalent to the invention of apple pie. If the Judge decided that the inmate had to serve ten years, the inmate can determine by his own accord and behavior to shorten that term. It is called the Credit level

16

system and is part of the system of incarceration. The better the inmate behaves over time and doesn't commit new crimes and infractions while in prison, he can acquire higher levels, of which there are several. He starts with level 1 or 2 and can move up to level 4. Depending on the type of crime however and the year the inmate started his prison term, Class level 3 and 4 have additional criteria.

All this is not an idea of the DOC, but state law. It is worthwhile to take a closer look at this section of the law to gain a better understanding how incarceration works and what criteria inmates must meet to move up the levels.

§57-138. Earned credits - Eligibility.

A. Except as otherwise provided by law, every inmate of a state correctional institution shall have their term of imprisonment reduced monthly, based upon the class level to which they are assigned. Earned credits may be subtracted from the total credits accumulated by an inmate, upon recommendation of the institution's disciplinary committee, following due process, and upon approval of the warden or superintendent. Each earned credit is equivalent to one (1) day of incarceration. Lost credits may be restored by the warden or superintendent upon approval of the classification committee. If a maximum and minimum term of imprisonment is imposed, the provisions of this subsection shall apply only to the maximum term. No deductions shall be credited to any inmate serving a sentence of life imprisonment; however, a complete record of the inmate's participation in work, school, vocational training, or other approved program shall be maintained by the Department for consideration by the paroling authority. No earned credit deductions shall be credited or recorded for any inmate serving any sentence for a criminal act which resulted in the death of a police officer, a law enforcement officer, an employee of the Department of Corrections, or an employee of a private prison contractor and the death occurred while the police officer, law enforcement officer, employee of the Department of Corrections, or employee of a private prison contractor was acting within the scope of their employment. No earned credit deductions shall be credited or recorded for any person who is referred to an intermediate revocation facility for violating any of the terms and conditions of probation.

17

B. The Department of Corrections is directed to develop a written policy and procedure whereby inmates shall be assigned to one of four class levels determined by an adjustment review committee of the facility to which the inmate is assigned. The policies and procedures developed by the Department shall include, but not be limited to, written guidelines pertaining to awarding credits for rehabilitation, obtaining job skills and educational enhancement, participation in and completion of alcohol/chemical abuse programs, incentives for inmates to accept work assignments and jobs, work attendance and productivity, conduct record, participation in programs, cooperative general behavior, and appearance. When assigning inmates to a class level the adjustment review committee shall consider all aspects of the policy and procedure developed by the Department including but not limited to the criteria for awarding credits required by this subsection.

C. If an inmate is subject to misconduct, nonperformance or disciplinary action, earned credits may be removed according to the policies and procedures developed by the Department. Earned credits removed for misconduct, nonperformance or disciplinary action may be restored as provided by Department policy, if any.

D. 1. Class levels shall be as follows:

a.   Class level 1 shall include inmates not eligible to participate in class levels 2 through 4, and shall include, but not be limited to, inmates on escape status.

b.   Class level 2 shall include an inmate who has been given a work, education, or program assignment, has received a good evaluation for participation in the work, education, or program assignment, and has received a good evaluation for personal hygiene and maintenance of living area.

c.   Class level 3 shall include an inmate who has been incarcerated at least three (3) months, has received an excellent work, education, or program evaluation, and has received an excellent evaluation for personal hygiene and maintenance of living area.

d.   Class level 4 shall include an inmate who has been incarcerated at least eight (8) months, has received an outstanding work, education, or program evaluation, and has received an outstanding evaluation for personal hygiene and maintenance of living area.

2.   a.Until November 1, 2001, class level corresponding credits are as follows:

Class 1 - 0 Credits per month;

Class 2 - 22 Credits per month;

18

Class 3 - 33 Credits per month;
Class 4 - 44 Credits per month.

b.   Class level corresponding credits beginning November 1, 2001, for inmates who have ever been convicted as an adult or a youthful offender or adjudicated delinquent as a juvenile for a felony offense enumerated in subsection E of this section are as follows:
Class 1 - 0 Credits per month;
Class 2 - 22 Credits per month;
Class 3 - 33 Credits per month;
Class 4 - 44 Credits per month.

c.   Class level corresponding credits beginning November 1, 2001, for inmates who have never been convicted as an adult or a youthful offender or adjudicated delinquent as a juvenile for a felony offense enumerated in subsection E of this section are as follows:
Class 1 – 0 Credits per month;
Class 2 – 22 Credits per month;
Class 3 – 45 Credits per month;
Class 4 – 60 Credits per month.

In other words, one credit per month equals one day. And moving up the credit levels is neither a given nor something which stays in place once an inmate reaches it. A Level promotion needs to be earned and kept by displaying good conduct on a permanent basis. Class 4 for instance is obviously something almost every inmate strives for, but to keep this kind of privilege requires some work. Inmates can't get into trouble, they need to keep their areas clean, maintain good relationships with inmates and staff alike, show good work ethics and class participation etc. But let the text of the law do the talking. The same paragraph continues as follows:

3. In addition to the criteria established for each class in paragraph 1 of this subsection, the following requirements shall apply to each of levels 2 through 4:

a.   satisfactory participation in the work, education, or program assignment at the standard required for the particular class level

b.   maintenance of a clean and orderly living area and personal hygiene at the standard required for the particular class level,

19

c.	cooperative behavior toward facility staff and other inmates, and

d.	satisfactory participation in the requirements of the previous class level.

	4.	The evaluation scale for assessing performance shall be as follows:
a.	Outstanding - For inmates who display consistently exceptional initiative, motivation, and work habits

b.	Excellent - For inmates who display above-average work habits with only minor errors and rarely perform below expectations.

c.	Good - For inmates who perform in a satisfactory manner and complete tasks as required, doing what is expected, with only occasional performance above or below expectations.

d.	Fair - For inmates who may perform satisfactorily for some periods of time, but whose performance is marked by obviously deficient and weak areas and could be improved.

e.	Poor - For inmates whose performance is unsatisfactory and falls below expected and acceptable standards.

	Now this is all very good news for inmates, who learned how to conduct themselves and stay out of trouble, which is why this is a very effective system to get inmates to do what they are supposed to do. Of course, this system doesn't only have fans. You could argue that no supervisor of yours or your corporate HR section gives you double pay for following rules and regulations and getting along with your co – worker. These traits are obviously a given in the real world. They are a prerequisite to have a job in the first place. Be that as it may, it works in the prison system.

	But not every inmate is eligible for the class levels either. There is a long list of crimes, which disqualifies an inmate to participate in the Class level system. These types of crimes more or less all fall into the so

20

called 85 % crime classification. What exactly it is and what type of crimes we are talking about here can be located in §21 of the Oklahoma Statutes.

§21-12.1. Required service of minimum percentage of sentence – Effective date.
A person committing a felony offense listed in Section 30 of this act on or after March 1, 2000, and convicted of the offense shall serve not less than eighty-five percent (85%) of the sentence of imprisonment imposed within the Department of Corrections. Such person shall not be eligible for parole consideration prior to serving eighty-five percent (85%) of the sentence imposed and such person shall not be eligible for earned credits or any other type of credits which have the effect of reducing the length of the sentence to less than eighty-five percent (85%) of the sentence imposed.
Added by Laws 1999, 1st Ex.Sess., c. 4, § 29, eff. July 1, 1999.

To see what crimes are affected, you need not look further than DOC reference OP-060211, entitled "Sentence Administration". On page 11 of that memo, which by the way can be found on the DOC homepage like any other DOC policies quoted here, it reads:

D. Conditions Where Credits Are Restricted or Not Awarded

1. Offenses in which the law requires an inmate serve a minimum portion of the sentence before being eligible for release.

a. Effective November 1, 1988, inmates convicted of Racketeering Activities under 22 O.S. Section 1401, the Oklahoma Corrupt Organizations Act, must serve one-half (1/2) of their sentence before becoming eligible for work release, house arrest, PPCS, parole, or release from confinement on any other basis. Sentencing under this act can be identified by a Judgment and Sentence utilizing the language "racketeering" of "racketeering activity."

b. Effective March 1, 2000, 21 O.S., Section 13.1 provided that inmates who are convicted of certain crimes must serve eighty-five percent (85%) of their sentence of imprisonment before becoming eligible for parole consideration and shall not be eligible for earned credits or any other type of credits which have the effect of reducing the length of the sentence to less than 85% of the sentence imposed. Therefore inmates serving a sentence for any of the crimes listed below committed on or after March 1, 2000 are eligible to earn credits during the first 85% percent of the sentence; however, said credits will not be applied towards the sentence until the inmate has served 85% of said sentence. The affected crimes are:

Abuse (other than sexual abuse), neglect or exploitation by a caretaker, 21 O.S. § 843.1 (eff. 6/5/2001)

 Abuse of a vulnerable adult who is a resident of a nursing facility, 43A O.S. Section 10-103 (eff. 3/8/2002).

Aggravated assault and battery upon any person defending another person from assault and battery (eff. 11/1/2011).

 Arson I, 21 O.S. § 1401 (eff. 3/1/2000)

Assault and Battery with a Deadly Weapon, 21 O.S. § 652 (eff. 7/1/2001)

Assault with Intent to Kill, 21 O.S. § 653 (eff. 7/1/2001)

Bombing, 21 O.S. § 1767.1 (eff. 3/1/2000)

Burglary I, 21 O.S. § 1436 (eff. 3/1/2000)

Child Abuse, 21 O.S. § 843.5 (eff. 3/1/2000)

Child Pornography, 21 O.S. §§ 1021.2, 1024.1 (eff. 3/1/2000)

Child Prostitution, 21 O.S. § 1030; (eff. 3/1/2000)

Conjoint Robbery, 21 O.S. § 800 (eff. 7/1/2001)

Forcible Sodomy, 21 O.S. § 888 (eff. 3/1/2000)

Lewd Molestation of a Child, 21 O.S. § 1123 (eff. 3/1/2000)

Manslaughter I, 21 O.S. § 711 (eff. 7/1/2001)

Murder I, 21 O.S. § 701.7 (eff. 3/1/2000)

Murder II, as defined in 21 O.S. § 701.8 (eff. 7/1/2001)

Parental Consent to Child Pornography, 21 O.S. § 1021.3 (eff. 3/1/2001)

Poisoning with Intent to Kill, 21 O.S. § 651 (eff. 7/1/2001)

Rape I, 21 O.S. § 1115 (eff. 3/1/2000)

Robbery I, 21 O.S. § 797 (eff. 7/1/2001)

Robbery with a Dang. Weapon, 21 O.S. § 801 (eff. 3/1/2000)

Sexual Abuse by a Caretaker, 21 O.S. 843.1 (eff. 6/2/2008)

Shooting with Intent to Kill, 21 O.S. § 652 (eff. 7/1/2001)

Use of a Vehicle to Facilitate Use of a Firearm, Crossbow or other Weapon, 21 O.S. § 652 (eff. 7/1/2001)

We can see that convicts with a violent history have less chances or opportunities to earn higher class levels than inmates with non-violent offenses. And since we are talking about what inmates find good about the DOC, it might be interesting to know, what else they can do to get out of prison sooner. We are not done just yet.

23

The above refers to the 85% crimes. Yet there are many other categories, which will limit an inmate's ability to earn higher class levels. In fact, for the uninitiated, it can get quite confusing. But for the purpose of this section, it doesn't make too much sense to go into the inner workings of what crimes qualify for what class levels and why. For anybody interested in this subject shall only read the above-mentioned reference OP-060211 in full. It is mind boggling. I will get into this a little more in one of the following chapters. Again, for the purpose of this section, I only want to mention, that this entire subject of credit level assignments is a source of joy for all inmates and at least that part of their family and friends, who have interest in them coming home the sooner the better.

However, there is one other thing I should mention, since it is also something, many inmates strive for. Sometimes the Court orders the inmate to complete certain class and program assignments, before he can discharge. These programs most often have to do with some drug or addiction rehabilitation subject. Especially people with a history of drug abuse or alcohol abuse will be given the chance to go through a program, where they will or shall learn, how to better deal with their addiction, before they discharge. The idea again is to lower recidivism. Not all prisons offer the required programs or classes which is why an inmate might get transferred hundreds of miles away from his family in order to be able to participate in it. But again, it's not all bad, since the offender will also get credits for program participation.

Whatever an inmate does, if it's a course, program, class or even if he is assigned to a certain job within the prison itself, he will get credits for it. Even inmates on work release, who have a regular job outside of the prison walls in lower security prisons will get credits for program participation. Whenever possible, inmates want to participate in programs and classes, anything which gets them to a release date faster. And prison facilities of all security levels will contribute to that notion by creating these programs and work assignments. It also keeps the inmate busy and somewhat responsible. Here is a quick look at

24

credits awarded for certain type of programs and training. This is a quote straight from §57-138.

H. Additional achievement earned credits for successful completion of departmentally approved programs or for attaining goals or standards set by the Department shall be awarded as follows:

Bachelor´s degree	200 Credits;
Associate´s degree	100 Credits;
High School Diploma or	
High School Equivalency Diploma	90 Credits;
Certification of Completion of Vocational Training	80 Credits;
Successful Completion of Alcohol/Chemical Abuse Treatment	
Program of not less then four (4) months of participation	70 Credits;
Successful completion of other Educational Accomplishments	
Or other programs not specified in this subsection	10-30 Credits;

The last good thing as far as credit levels are concerned is the financial incentive. As I mentioned earlier in this chapter, inmates will earn a little money during their incarceration. It helps pay for court fines, other fines, a Ramen noodle soup every once in a while, and other items. On Level 2, you will earn $ 7.23, on Level 3 $10.84 and on Level 4 $ 14.45 (per DOC OP 060107 "Systems of Incarceration").

The facility head can approve higher pay rates than that, provided the inmate has particular qualifications, which benefit the facility. Mechanics, or journeyman licensed in their field are a few. Here is the proper quote from OP 060107:

I.   Exceptions to Level Pay Grades (4-4461)

Inmates may be paid at a higher rate of pay under the following circumstances:

1.   Inmates who are journeymen or licensed in their field and are assigned jobs at the facility to perform in that capacity, or those assigned to the agency's construction/maintenance (C&M) crew, may be paid at the same rate as a special project pay grade. Pay at this level must be approved by the facility head.

2.   The facility head may identify jobs that require a higher skill level (e.g., mechanics, inmate research assistants/law clerks, etc.) that may be paid at the rate of $27.09 per month. The ability to receive a higher pay rate will be reflected in the job description. All requests for pay at this rate must be approved by the facility head and regional director.

3.   Special project pay grades may be established as needed to accomplish difficult or extraordinary construction projects or other important projects that require special measures to accomplish.

a. Pay for a special project will not exceed $.54 per hour.

b. These special pay grades can only be established after the recommendation of the affected regional director, with sufficient justification, and a specific time period established.

c. Each request will be reviewed by senior staff and approved by the agency director.

4.   With exception of OCI and construction and maintenance programs, inmate pay will not be pro-rated.

5.   (Revision-02 10/02/2017) Inmates assigned as facility cooks/bakers and licensed cosmetologists shall be paid at a rate of $27.09 per month. This pay rate will be reflected in the job description.

There you have it. The good stuff as far as inmates and staff are concerned. Depending on who you ask I probably could have carved out the one or the other additional criteria, but this would have been more on an individual level.

You probably could talk to a lifer without parole and ask him, if he would prefer to spend his life behind bars in a state owned and operated prison or within a privately owned facility. His answer would not have anything to do with the Class level system or any work or program assignments since he will get neither. But he will sure let you know about the differences between these two. From the size of the cells, he would live in to the quality and quantity of the food items being served. How is the TV program? Did the facility contract with a local cable provider or is an over the air antenna all there is? How is the work out equipment and the access to it? Is it a 45-year-old facility with spotty A/C performance? How is the access to contraband managed? Is it more of an individual effort to get your tobacco and cell phones or is the acquisition of such items managed by certain gangs, which could make this endeavor more expensive? For a lifer without parole certain aspects of the prison system are not of major consideration. His world revolves around aspects, which makes his life more bearable and easier. And easier and more bearable can mean a lot of different things for a lot of different inmates. Some might have the tobacco smuggling operation all figured out and are in close contact with the people who bring it in. But if that contact person quits or gets fired, that source no longer is available, which requires a restructuring of the entire delivery process. And it needs to happen fast, otherwise different individuals will jump at the opportunity.

The Bad – The employee

I don't think I need to cover anything in particular. As an employee of the DOC, you deal with the same issues like in any other work environment. Either you can work with your co-workers or you can't. Either your boss is a good supervisor or he isn't. Either you get assigned the most uncomfortable jobs or you are on someone's good side. Even the 24/7 coverage is nothing particularly unusual, after all this is America and there are numerous companies and corporations, which provide around the clock service coverage, so nothing unusual about that. Equally annoying and unfortunate is the assignment of individuals to certain shifts which better suit the life of somebody with a family let's say. This and many other signs of favoritism are part of a toxic work environment as in any other company.

At one point in time, in the rather distant past, DOC however provided college tuition. At least this is what our HR Rep told me. I was way too late in the game to be able to have enjoyed it, but I need to mention it as something, which existed, thus the lack thereof now becomes bad.

Another aspect of State employment needs mentioning however. If you work in a prison environment, there is certain number of available positions. Let's say the personnel roster allows for 25 people. Some of them a regular Guards, some of them are what you would call shift supervisors, others take care of the Case Management, etc. Employees, who like a steady life, obviously don't like to move around a lot, if it is not necessary. As long as the job helps pay for your home, your family etc., you are good to go. And as mentioned earlier, you will get longevity pay and retirement, something which is not a given in many private companies. That leads to the phenomenon of employees keeping a very tight grip on their job. Why would you voluntarily move to another location, if you have everything you need as an employee right where

28

you are. Sure, other state prisons in the country might offer better pay and higher positions, but if you aren't interested in moving to another location, you get quite comfortable where you are. You have individuals who stay in their position 20 years and longer and are more or less happy with it. I call that the DOC effect. These guys just won't leave, won't retire, won't move. They stay right where they are. After they arrived in their comfortable position, there is nothing anybody can do to get them out of there. As long as they don't sexually harass anybody or get caught bringing in contraband, even DOC's hands are bound. Thus, the advancement possibilities for anybody wanting to move up the ranks in that particular facility are very limited.

Every blue moon a supervisory position will be opened up and becomes available. The race is on. This might happen every 5 years or so, depending on what level of supervisory position we are talking about. Intermediate positions are more likely to open up than higher positions, because these are clogged up by veterans with 20 to 40 years in their respective positions. If good advancement opportunities are your thing, DOC might not be the best place of work.

The Bad – the inmate

Being incarcerated is supposed to be a punishment, thus it can't be a big surprise to find a lot of negative factors. If you listen to some inmates, one prison is supposedly better than another. This is because how prisons are run, just like in a pizza parlor. You work in one location and all co-workers are nice, the supervisor on your shift is a delight to work with, all is dandy. You start to work in the location across town, because you moved in with your girlfriend, and that location still sells the same products, has identical appliances and gets his raw products from the same supplier, but your co-workers are now douche bags and your supervisor is a moron. It's a totally different work environment. The DOC has many rules and regulations and the treatment of inmates should not be so different from location to location, because especially the prison environment is tightly regulated and monitored since you are not dealing with the production of vehicle suspension parts, but with the supervision of officially grown-up adults. The DOC tried to instill some overall rule of conformity for its employees by formulating what they call the "Correctional Employee Oath". I assume it is meant to function as a guideline for how we as corrections employees are supposed to behave and carry ourselves. It goes like this:

"I do hereby solemnly affirm to support the Constitution and the laws of the United States of America and abide by the Constitution and the laws of the State of Oklahoma, as well as the policies and procedures of the Oklahoma Department of Corrections. I will treat all employees and offenders with respect and dignity. I will obey the lawful orders of those appointed over me. I will conduct myself in such a manner to enhance and establish a positive tradition of excellence for the Oklahoma Department of Corrections."

Many companies and corporations have such a fine, ethical, God-fearing credo, which formulates their overall intend and direction of how their employees shall conduct their affairs. And many employees of many companies also know that the reality can differ greatly. So, let's look at realities of prison life as I have found them.

1.   The loss of human dignity

Over the years through newspaper articles or shows on TV, by talking to relatives and friends, who have spent time behind bars, you can get the idea, how dreadful of a place a prison can be. This is so because in most cases it is. The whole idea of prison time is not to give out rewards of comfort and pleasure, but to convey the idea that you as a citizen shall attempt anything and everything to stay out of prison. And that you also should try your utmost best to not come back to prison if you couldn't help but make your acquaintance with prison life. The whole idea in most countries is, that prison is bad, prisoners are bad, the accommodations are bad, the food is bad, the guards are bad, the possibilities to enhance any positive notions or interests are bad, education or rehabilitation possibilities are bad, the location is bad, the TV program is bad, and most of them all, you lose your human dignity, which is bad as well. There is bad news all around you it seems. And my theory is that it wouldn't be all that bad, if a simple, human notion is not destroyed in the process as well.

The DOC takes custody of you, when you arrive in prison. The Judge has ordered his decree, the Court Clerk wrote a Judgment and Sentence, detailing the amount of time a person has to serve behind bars and off you go. Whomever you meet in prison from this day forward, you will be a number and you also will be no different than any other number in that system, no matter how hideous or minor your crime was, it is all the same to the prison guard, who will be your main point of contact from here on.

31

I don't know how many of you were stripped off all your cloth in front of a stranger, or in front of two strangers. You walk into a room and get told to take off all your cloth. You have to stick out your tongue so that somebody can see if you hide something in your mouth or underneath your tongue. You have to run your hands through your hair so that we can see if anything falls out of it. Lift your arms up high so it is clear, that nothing is carried from A to B under your armpits. Lift your private parts because it's easiest to conceal contraband in that particular location. Now turn around, bend over and show us, if anything is hidden in there. It is covered in OP 040110 entitled "Search and Seizure Standards".

C. Authority for Searches (Revision 08/27/14)

All searches beyond the scope of a pat-down search are conducted at the discretion of the division manager, the facility head or Inspector General as specified in the following procedures.

D. Searches of the Person (4-4193, 4-ACRS-2C-04, 4-ACRS-2C-05)

1. Offenders

Offenders are subject to pat down, frisk, strip, visual body cavity, intrusive body cavity, and property searches. If necessary for the safety and security of the facility, x-rays may be ordered in accordance with Section II. D. 1. item d. below.

In other words, every inmate is subject to searches, no matter where or when and no matter what type of facility, from Maximum Security to Community Corrections. If you are an inmate, you are subject to searches including and up to strip searches. It also says that the facility head has the discretion to issue the rules and regulations regarding searches, which in my experience basically brings us right back to paragraph D above.

The referenced policy doesn't only apply to searches of a person, but of his property as well, his living quarters and of everything he owns. Searches are an important part in a correctional setting, there can't be any doubt about that. Even if a search might not yield contraband in all cases, it is also a strong deterrent. The way facility staff conduct their searches on a regular and even on an irregular basis, gives clues to the inmates, how serious the detection of contraband is viewed. The number of guards also gives an important clue to the whole subject matter. Occasionally you will hear or read about private prison facilities and how big their problem is as far as contraband is concerned. You would be able, as an inmate, to basically purchase anything you want, if the price is right. I point out private prisons here for the simple reason, that they are managed by profit-oriented corporations. Thus, the need to have adequate staffing to control the introduction of contraband might sometimes appear secondary to the bottom line. There are limits a privately held organization has to operate within to accomplish their mission. This conundrum however became also a problem in State run prisons, because the number of incarcerated people rose over the years, but the budgets for DOC's didn't rise equally. We might get into this whole subject a little later however, for the purpose of this part of the chapter we shall stick with the subject matter at hand, the loss of human dignity.

No matter where you are housed within the facility in any particular prison, there is no privacy. About the only privacy you can get is, when you are sleeping. We have the duty to make it possible for the inmate, to get a decent amount of sleep. Even guards employed with the DOC cannot conduct searches whenever they feel like it. But we can conduct searches in an almost unlimited way. If the Director can successfully justify it, I don't think it is a big problem for any prison facility, to conduct a prison wide facility search every five days or so. Of course, this is fairly unreasonable since such an undertaking would require personnel resources which the DOC simply doesn't have. But per policy and all rules and regulations, it could be done.

If human dignity includes privacy of any sort, privacy of your person and your living area in particular, it does not exist.

If you are an inmate, all decisions are going to be done for you, including where you are going to live. This is not normally a decision, you or your family have any saying in. The assignment of housing is discretionary in the final analysis. DOC OP 060102 (M) states

This procedure does not create any inmate right. The decision where to place an inmate is totally discretionary. This procedure has been established for administrative process and guidance to staff.

In clear English it means, the DOC alone ultimately decides where to house an inmate, there is no way around it. On the other side of course it is also understood, that certain criminals cannot be housed together with others. A whole lot of circumstances need to be considered and the policies of DOC reflect that. You for instance cannot just throw together two gang rivals in the same housing unit or even the same cell. There are inmates referred to as predators, which like to victimize other inmates as established by their individual case history. You won't put these types together with old or very fragile inmates. All these factors need to be considered carefully to prevent fights or even inmate deaths.

If you have been convicted of a hideous sex crime, you probably have no other choice than being housed in a Protective Custody setting, otherwise other inmates will tear you apart. Sex crimes are the lowest level of crimes and even inmates and gang members recognize that.

2.   Protective Custody (as determined by classification committee)

Protective custody housing is available at Lawton Correctional Facility (males) and Mabel Bassett Correctional Center (females). This housing is specifically for offenders who cannot live in general population due to threats on their lives, and are classified as "protective custody" in accordance with OP-060106 entitled "Special Offender Management System" (SOMS).

For inmates who have committed sex crimes, there might not be another option than go to the Lawton Correctional Facility, no matter how far away this might be from your family and friends. For an inmate's own protection, he needs to be there. But there are other factors, which might be considered, from gang affiliations to nature of crime, to programmatic needs to treatment requirements. Consideration for family is hardly a factor in placing an inmate within the DOC prison network, after all, the DOC from here on out is solely responsible for the safety and security of the inmate, no matter the circumstances. So not only has the inmate no saying when and where his person or property is searched, he also has no saying, where he is housed. From now on he is more a number than a person. Of course, there are housing considerations, which might aid the inmate on his journey to get back to a life outside the prison walls, but few are not security related. Here is a short rundown, what DOC Case Managers and employees need to consider when placing an inmate. It is based on Security points. The more points an inmate rings up, the higher must his Security level be. The X factor mentioned in point 2 below refers to Misconduct Reports, which are disciplinary infractions done by the inmate. The letter X stands for the most serious misconduct type. The easiest way to look at these disciplinary infractions is that each type of Misconduct Reports causes the inmate to receive more security points, thus by getting more Misconduct Reports for serious infractions, the inmate can find himself with a lot of security points, which causes him to be sent to a prison with higher security measures. This by the way can be looked up in detail in DOC OP 060102 (M) entitled "Male Initial Custody Assessment Procedure".

B. Custody Evaluation Items 1 through 3 comprise the "Maximum Custody Score" and are intended to identify the inmate who presents a serious risk to the community. Inmates with a score of 9 or higher on these three items are assessed to maximum custody. Items 5-7 are intended to identify those inmates who present a risk to the safety, security, and orderly operation of a facility. The maximum custody score along with items 5-7, comprise the "Comprehensive Custody Score." All items must be scored.

1. Severity of Convictions on Current Incarceration

a. The most serious conviction on the current incarceration is to be determined, to include   all concurrent (CC), consecutive (CS), and active suspended sentences (SS) that have been rebilled, pending parole revocations, Intermediate Revocations, detainers, and warrants for the inmate using the "Offense Severity Categories" located in Attachment A (attached). The most serious offense is indicated, to include case number, and case type (concurrent (CC), consecutive (CS), detainer (DI), warrant (WA), active paroles, pending parole revocation, or Intermediate Revocation inmates, etc.) in the space provided. Suspended and paroled sentences that are still active will score in this item (To figure suspended sentence discharge dates, refer to OP-060211 entitled "Sentence Administration").

b. If a determination cannot be made on how to categorize an offense, the administrator of Sentence Administration, Inmate Records and Registries will be contacted for a disposition. Section-06 Classification OP-060102 (M) Page: 3 Effective Date: 07/01/2017

c. The number of points associated with the inmate's most serious offense is entered.

2. Prior Institutional Violence

a. One or more X, X-2, X-3, X-4 (01-4 04-1, 04-8 prior to 11-15- 15; 04-3 prior to 9-14-89) past 10 years; or

b. Predatory infractions X-2 through X-10 within 2 past years.

3.   Escape History

All escapes or attempted escapes that have occurred during the stipulated time period prior to the initial assessment are to be considered. The number of points corresponding to the most serious escape or attempted escape is entered. Escapes will be addressed in the escape section, with the following exceptions:

a. Escape from community corrections, halfway house PPCS, GPS, EMP will be assessed misconduct points if within the applicable time frames.

b. If an inmate has any escape or attempted escape from maximum or medium, county jail, juvenile institution, restricted/segregated housing unit or escape from any level of security that resulted in an injury to another or a felony conviction for a violent crime while on escape status and is not assessed points in the escape history of the custody assessment due to his age, will be assessed misconduct points if within applicable time frames.

The above is just a short quote and applies to inmates, who have a rather severe crime, who couldn't behave well or who even attempted to escape or successfully escaped in the past. All elements of an inmate's history are considered, which determines the inmate's custody level, as they call it. The basic idea here is, the more severe a crime was or is the more points are accessed. When a person has a high score based on his crime, he is not likely to be eligible for placement into minimum security facilities and so on. The above-mentioned reference is a detailed account of what elements to consider before an inmate is placed in any facility within the State or even in other States. But the whole point here is that the inmate himself is not part of the decision where he will spend his time. In cases where we are talking about violent crimes against people, that is a good thing. But I think considerations need to be taken more seriously if we are talking about non-violent crimes. If the bond to family and friends is considered a major factor in someone's rehabilitation attempts, then it must be considered, or should be at least given consideration.

2. Exposure to violence

The argument to prevent exposure to violence is simple: Don't come to prison. Don't commit crimes. Don't in other words, put yourself in a situation where you can and will be exposed to violence in one way or the other. The prison system doesn't promise a cozy existence. The prison system doesn't even promise security and safety. We as guards and administrators will do all we can to keep you out of harm's way, but we cannot give guarantees. When you enter the prison system, you will be on your own. Your protection and security will depend on the choices you will make within these walls.

Let's say, you came to prison. You didn't quite make it to a minimum-security facility or even a Community Corrections Center or any such place. Your custody assessment demanded to be placed in at least a medium security facility. Either you got too much time to serve, or you were caught a second or third time doing the same crime or any other combination of circumstances. Now you are housed along with 102 other inmates in the confines of a pod in a housing unit with a total 306 inmates. You go to dinner in the adjoining dining facility. You pick up your tray, sit along a few other inmates and try to enjoy your meal.

All of a sudden, the person who sits in front of you has a five-inch-long screw inside of his neck. Before he can react and command his hand to get hold of that screw to pull it out, the attacker retracts it and drives it into the back of his skull. Your natural instinct tells you to get up and move away. While streams of blood pour out of the victim's neck, you slowly move towards the closest wall, while the attacked makes a desperate attempt to remove himself from the place of the attack. He still doesn't know what happened. The only think he does realize is that he too, needs to move away from the pain he is experiencing. He stumbles sideways, tries to get away from the bolted down chairs and tables to give him some room to run. But he realizes that he can't run. For some reason, his legs are made out of pudding, they give in under his own weight. He only can slide next to the table and onto the floor. That is as far as he gets. The weight of the attacker jumping on his chest is nothing more than a sensation, his mind starts to wonder. His mind begins to drift, all pain is gone. The machined screw which penetrates his right eye deep into his brain makes him only wonder, what happened to his sight. Did somebody turn the lights out? What is happening? In his final moments he finds himself wondering, why it got so much more difficult to breath. This is because he now has two gaping holes in his neck. The assailant really wanted to make sure, that his victim doesn't make it. It was an exact planned attack.

The facility had just recently put a ping pong table in each housing unit pod. The inmate counsel of this housing unit had decided they wanted one to conduct tournaments and kill time. After all, there are 102 inmates and there is only so much TV you can watch on a daily basis. There was nothing else to do, they wanted to find something to entertain themselves. So, a table was approved. And in this whole process of getting the ping pong table approved, bought, shipped and finally delivered to this housing unit, somebody didn't notice the net braces, which hold the net tight and straight on either side of the table. These braces are secured by five-inch-long screws to account for different thicknesses of tables. The piece was of course delivered by inmates, so called orderlies. These chaps are inmates, who have earned a sliver of trust because they stayed out of trouble for a considerable amount of time. When they went to receiving to unpack the table, they cleverly managed to conceal the screws so no security guard would become suspicious. That part of course is more of a theory to illustrate one of the many ways, how weapons can make it into a housing unit. After the screws were mounted to the table, no security guard questioned their presence. The guy or woman just assumed that the administration knew, what they were doing. The screws stayed in place until this particular incident.

Policy 040100 states among other things:

Security Standards for the Oklahoma Department of Corrections

I.   It is the policy of the Board of Corrections (BOC) that the Oklahoma Department of Corrections (ODOC) provides security at all institutions, community corrections centers, work centers and probation and parole district offices. Security standards are established to protect the public, the employees and inmates/offenders. (2-CO-3A-01)

When the Department of Corrections receives a prisoner, they assume full and total responsibility of the safety and security of the person. There is nothing the inmate can officially buy or acquire to defend him and create a safer environment for him or herself.

40

All prison facilities are to a more or lesser degree a mirror of the outside world. The gang members, the meth cooks, the forgers, the drug traffickers, the blackmailer, etc.

In Maximum and Medium facilities, it is actually much worse than in the real world, since in the real world, criminals cannot only spread out into the areas and communities, they also can conduct their business in the private confines of their homes and clubs. They don't have that choice in the limited spaces of prisons. And despite the fact, that the Department of Corrections still calls itself that, there is hardly any Correction going on, which is not to say, there is no Correction going on at all. But you have to live with the realities of life. Many criminals in the system don't think that they are in prison, because they did something wrong. That is not the case. Their opinion is, that they ended up, where they are, because they got caught. You see, there is a major difference in attitude. The Judge, the police, the prison officials, the guards, the Case managers and all these people will tell an inmate, that he is in prison, because he broke the law, which is true. But this is not everyone's opinion. Many inmates lived their live, because they knew nothing else. It was their normal life. They were raised with guns, with drugs, with violence and with gang membership. This is their world and nobody can tell them different, only because there is some ominous law telling them otherwise. Their attitude is, that they are in prison, because they got caught, that is the only reason. So, their ways of handling life is not going to change, because in their minds, they just got caught, which is the only reason, they are incarcerated.

The same rules apply behind the prison walls as they exist in real life. A housing unit, a pod, a unit is run by the most dominant gang. Sometimes gang members share the profits from extortion and dealing drugs and general merchandise, but don't ever think for a moment, that anybody entering that environment is immune and can step out of that world, only because he wasn't part of a gang, before he got himself caught. There are rules within an inmate population, which are far more severe than any rules the authorities can come up with. The authorities

41

can threaten you with solitary confinement, they can drop your level to level 1 for years or forever so that you have to do more time. They can restrict your abilities to make phone calls, to receive visitors and to purchase food items. But they can't kill you. Only the other inmates can. And they will kill eventually if you don't adhere to their rules.

There is no protection. There is no hiding. There are no negotiations.

For instance, Protective Custody is designed to house vulnerable inmates, high profile inmates and other inmates, which might pose a threat to the security of the facility, except they don't pose a threat to the security of the facility. They really only pose a threat to themselves of getting killed by other inmates, which would reflect negatively on the facility and on the mission of the DOC.

The DOC tries to negate violence and potential conflict wherever they can, which is why there are policies in place to regulate inmate housing. DOC policy 030102:

B. Additional Considerations

1. Housing assignments will not be determined by race, color, or ethnic origin. (2-CO-3C-01)

2. The safety and security of the inmate and the assigned facility/unit will be the focus of all decisions relative to an inmate's housing assignment. Specific reasons for any security-related restrictions will be fully documented on the "Cell Assessment Form" (Attachment A, attached). (PREA 115.41)

And further down it reads:

B. Gathering of Information

During the reception process, information will be gathered which will allow the classification committee to make a determination regarding cell assignment status (Attachment A entitled "Cell Assessment Form" and the "Activity/Housing Summary" (located in the electronic health record (EHR)). (PREA 115.41(c))

This information will include, but not be limited to: family, social, sexual orientation, criminal history, military, education, institutional, employment, alcohol/drug histories and information concerning disruptive group or security threat group affiliation. (4-4312-1) However, association with any particular group does not automatically preclude an inmate from integrated housing assignments.

If an inmate needs or wants to remove him from normal prison life, his only option is to get into Protective custody. That is a housing unit where inmates live, who are either too weak to defend themselves, who have more enemies within the prison walls than associates, who snitched on other inmates or group of inmates, who committed a sex crime or a sexual motivated crime or who think their life is in danger for other reasons. DOC policy 060106 provides for that:

D. Special Management Inmates

1. Identification Special Management Inmates are inmates who display behaviors Section-06 Classification OP-060106 Page: 6 Effective Date: 06/07/2017 that merit special review and/or housing to ensure safety within a correctional facility.

Special Management Inmates will be identified during the assessment and reception process through completion of a "Special Management Inmate Notice" (DOC 060106E, attached).

Inmates who have a history of the following will be identified as special management inmates: (4-4281M, 4-4281-4)

a. Those inmates identified as:

(1) Having extreme levels of violence toward others;

 (2) Sexual predators/sexually assaultive behavior; or

(3) Highly vulnerable.

> b. Those inmates with special medical or mental health needs; and

> c. As determined by the director, chief of Operations, appropriate regional director or manager of Classification and Population.

> And a little further down it says:

B. Protective Measures Actions

 If protective measures are warranted, the classification committee will initiate the least restrictive and most appropriate protective measure to adequately address the situation.

1. If the investigation reveals the threat to the inmate is minimal or can be mediated, the unit manager, shift supervisor or deputy warden/designated staff may conduct mediation with approval of the facility head.

2. Assignment to other general population housing within the same facility may be an option with approval of the facility head.

3. Recommendation of transfer to general population at another facility.

4. Recommendation of transfer to specialized housing for protective custody.

To a certain extent, vulnerable inmates will be protected. But being placed into Protective Custody also comes with a stigma, which is attached to every inmate, who is placed into PC (Protective Custody). This stigma will always be attached to the inmate, who is placed in PC. He will never be able to get rid of it completely. And for the most part, inmates who are assigned to this unit will remain in this unit for the remainder of their sentence. There are of course circumstances which will allow the inmate to return to a General Housing Unit. It is not a very common occurrence, but it can be done. Money owed for instance is one of these things, which can be negotiated over time. A debt in prison doesn't necessarily mean you have to be in PC, if you can't pay back.

Let's say you owe $ 50 because you were desperate at one point in time and couldn't pay it back in the timeframe agreed upon. Before you get killed, you step out of the housing unit, refusing to come back. Now you have a number of Misconduct Reports on your hand, which might or might not extend your time in prison, because your level will be dropped. That is a small price to pay. And if you are already on the lowest level, there is not much you lose to begin with. That stay in PC will buy you sometimes the time you need to collect the money. Now if you want to go back you might have to pay $ 100 instead of the original $ 50, but you can go back.

Or your family stops sending you money to buy commissary food items, because your aunt or your grandmother died. Now that source of income ended. Now you can't pay for your protection any longer. The dominant gang in your housing unit still demands monthly payments for your protection yet your income is gone. The only option might be to flee to PC, provided you don't want to become a paid member of the gang in your housing unit.

However, you look at it, threats, violence and intimidation are all part of prison life. The DOC tries to control it, tries to stop it, tries to negate the outcomes of gang disputes and other uncontrollable events. And it gets less severe, the lower the security level is.

45

It probably is most extreme in a medium security facility, because it provides the most explosive mixture of inmates roaming around relatively undisturbed and an attempt by the facility to "rehabilitate" by providing programs and church services, which gives inmates the opportunity to move around within the prison walls. Every time there is a program, where inmates from different housing units can go, there is an interaction. Information gets exchanged, orders are being submitted and compliance is given. It's a welcome inmate's marketplace. Inmates don't even have to be part of any gang or group. Yet they serve as mules for information, paid or not. Sometimes the inmates don't even have to arrive at the program or the classroom. Sometimes they don't even have to have a physical interaction with another inmate from another housing unit. They pass by a housing unit and exchange signs for instance. They have their hair in a different style. They wear certain types of shoes. The ways inmates interact and exchange vital pieces of information are endless. There are a handful of Corrections Officers, who try to manage a housing unit. There are 300 inmates in a housing unit, or whatever the figures are. The circumstances are always in favor of the inmates no matter the design of the housing unit.

If you have a violent crime or have a second or third conviction for a violent crime, you will end up in a medium security facility, there is just no way around it. And if you do, you will be housed with murderers and gang members of all sorts and kinds. Now don't get me wrong, no matter how large or violent that gang is, they are not interested to draw unwanted attention to themselves either. They will conduct their business in secret. Every attention brought onto them means, less freedom to do whatever they want to do. They will also refrain from violence if they have the option. If a violent incident occurs anywhere on the facility, they will go into lockdown, where nobody can move around. And that again is bad business for the moneymakers inside these walls. They will only resort to open violence if they have to. Sometimes a facility is picked by gang leaders, who are somewhere within the United States prison system, to set an example or to retaliate. Then the freedom to conduct business in that facility is compromised for the sake of the overall purpose of making a statement within the entire, criminal network. It seems random and accidental, but it is not.

A.   Gang units

DOC and prison facilities have so called gang units. They come in different names and in different flavors. Security Threat Unit, Gang Unit and so on. They employ veterans of the DOC who supposedly have an idea of what is going on gang wise and otherwise on this facility. They file reports, they investigate and they qualify and quantify gangs and their members. They make pictures of tattoos and gang related insignia. They run around trying to identify who belongs to whom. And after a violent incident, they try to figure out what happened.

This is DOC's way to try to control prison violence in all forms, because they know, if they don't at least attempt and try to quell violence, they are vulnerable to one lawsuit after another and can't hope to ever stop paying for slain family members. They need to house, take care and separate the most violent offenders and groups, yet they also need to make it in a somewhat secure fashion. It's the classical conundrum. A riddle which never will be solved yet every attempt will be made to do so.

These prison gang units screen the incoming inmates. They have a vital saying, where new inmates are housed, because it is a security issue. Blood gang members go to house 1, Arian Nation members go to house 5 and so on. You want to try to separate these gang members because at any time, whatever these gangs have going on in the real world will make its way into the prison walls. That is the initial idea. But there are also genuine prison gangs, which developed over the years. They are no big issue in the outside world, but have developed their own name within the prison system.

Let's say you have 8 gangs in a medium security prison, all trying to achieve the same goals, make money and increase their influence to make more money. This whole thing works just like any other market place with demand and supply.

A new person comes into a medium security facility. He has no violent history or he has a violent crime. He does five years or he has to do 25. It doesn't matter. What matters are quite different factors.

So, this guy is assigned to House 1. He has no prior gang relations. As far as he is concerned, he wants to do his time, wants to be left alone. His family still supports him to a certain degree, intends to send him some money for telephone and commissary items. He goes to his assigned cell and gets acquainted with his new surroundings.

Since House 1 is mainly controlled by the White-Collar Panthers – let's call them that – he gets a visit by a group of White-Collar Panthers representatives. They lay down the rules. He is to give them 25 % of his earnings, which is any and all monies he receives from any source. He is to only buy dope and tobacco from them. He now has the rank of a White-Collar rookie. If he does what he is told, follows the rules and conducts himself well he will have the chance to move to soldier. But that is a long way and needs to be earned. But if he earns his way, he will eventually be able to tell other newcomers what they are expected to do. For now, he is to lay low, don't cause no problems and generally be invisible. He is not to cause any ruckus or noise. If there is anything going on, it will be initiated by the gang. He is not to complain or talk to anybody except members of the gang. He will go to any meals in the chow hall like everyone else and never miss a meal. Of course, there is a certain hierarchy in the chow hall itself. He has to sit in a certain corner and stand in the chow hall line at a certain place, and always behind the higher ranked people. He cannot play board games with any person of any other race or color. If anybody from the gang, which is higher in rank than himself, approaches him, he is to give him whatever this person asks. If there is a meeting of the gang, he needs to leave his own cell and wait until the meeting is over. The TV program is not his to decide, it depends on what the gang leadership wants to watch. If he is alone however and no demands are presented, he can do what he pleases. And every once in a while, there are collections to be made by the gang to buy more expensive items like cell phones and meth. He needs to participate in these collections. And does this new person have special skills? Can he be used for any special operations? Does he have tattoo experience? Does he know how to work with metals? Can he cut hair? Is he attractive enough to be offered to anybody for money? And so on and so forth.

All of a sudden, this new person is confronted with a world he only heard of. Some other prisoners he met during his jail time told him about certain prisons and what is going on in there, but now it is real. He better does what is expected of him or else. They made it very clear what will happen if he steps out of his boundaries. It is a no option stranglehold. On the good side of that equation is protection against any and all other attempts by other people and gangs to extort him. It is not all that bad. He only has to deal with one gang and doesn't need to concern himself with others. If anybody ever tries to use him for other purposes or even only attempts to extort him, he can go to his gang supervisor and report that individual. They will deal with him accordingly.

Gang units try to negotiate all these activities. They try to somewhat keep all these illegal activities in check. That is their job. And it is a losing proposition. It always was.

B.   Personnel

And the reason, why no gang unit can ever hope to do anything about it is obvious. There are two main reasons. Security Officers run the housing units. They send people to dinner; they send people to their Case Mangers and they count the bodies at each count. Due to the financial restraints in DOC, these Corrections Officers are always outnumbered by a large margin. Three people being responsible for three hundred inmates is not uncommon. Gang Units don't contribute to controlling inmates, the members of a gang unit cannot be used to run chow lines, to escort prisoners to their medical appointments and so on. The first main reason gang units are ineffective is, that they are alone. They are in a prison with 500 to 3500 inmates. They need to interview 50 people on a daily basis to have any inkling of what is going on where. They need to screen and read the history of every new arrival who enters the facility. They need to furthermore monitor all employees and watch camera footage of how these employees interact with certain inmates or inmate groups. Then they need to do 50 cell searches of suspected traffickers or seemingly important gang members of various gangs. Then they need to e- mail other facilities within the continental US to be informed of any potential outburst or development in the world of prison gangs. They can't do all that. But they can pretend in order to serve the facility and its legal needs to show that they tried. Whenever a fight breaks out in any prison or somebody gets harmed or killed, the facility can proudly point to their gang unit which is run by their most experienced and professional security staff and can claim that they did anything and everything within their powers to prevent exactly that. And in most cases, that is good enough, it has to be.

C.   The Wall

The other main reason is what I came to call The Wall. In all these years in Corrections, I always wondered why we as security guards and Corrections Officers never knew, what was going on behind prison walls. In one medium facility I used to work in, there used to be a shift briefing every day. It was intended to inform us what if anything we need to look for when we walk to our housing units. Were there any tensions between gangs? Was there a disruption in the delicate balance of forces? Did we do anything wrong which needed to be corrected? Were there any changes in policies and procedures? These types of things.

And all of a sudden something completely unexpected would happen with no warnings and no signs. Nobody seemingly even had a clue of that incident developing. These events would just happen and the next thing you knew, we were running in circles trying to put the fire out. The whole facility goes into lockdown with no movement, entire groups of people got moved around from one place to another, stricter standards were applied to everything. Certain privileges were suspended and the Segregation Housing Unit filled up with the main instigators. I looked at my supervisors, I looked at the Captains and I looked at the Wardens and wondered, why don't these highly trained and experienced people didn't know anything about what was going on? Why were they taken by surprise? Why didn't at least someone know something about that incident taking place? Weren't we supposed to be in control of the facility and not the other way around? Who was running what for real? And it took me a surprisingly long time to finally realize what was going on.

Every time you talk to an inmate, you talk to a wall. You aren't really talking to the person, you are talking to another entity, which the inmate put up to talk to you. Imagine a ventriloquist with his puppet, except the puppet has prerecorded responses and answers, like one of

51

these plastic dolls for kids you can buy in any store's kids' section. You press one button and you will get a number of responses, depending a little bit of how often you pushed that button. The other buttons give a variety of other responses, but they will always be the same. They might sound that they vary, but they aren't because they are prerecorded.

You walk up to an inmate and start talking to him. As long as it is about the TV program, the food in the chow hall, the availability of the Case managers and the recreation possibilities, you will have a good chance, that you can have a conversation with the person himself. But as soon as you want to talk about anything which might give you a glimpse into that inmate's life and how he is doing, you will have a conversation with his puppet.

You might have the idea that you talk to the person, but you are talking to an electrical circuit. You say "Hey, Mr. Hopps, how are you doing today?" The answer will be "Bla, bla, bla, blub, blub." Or you ask him, if there are any problems or concerns in his housing unit. His response will be, that everything is ok, there are no problems and he is doing his time and that is all that he is interested in. He will tell you, that he has no friends and doesn't bother with anybody. You notice a tiny, little, seemingly fresh tattoo on his left wrist. You asked him about it and he will tell you, that he had this tattoo even before he got here and that it signifies the birth of his daughter, because he is the family man, everybody knows that. There is nothing going on ever, all is just fine. He deserves to be here and you guard guys are doing a fabulous job in keeping him secure. He has done wrong in life and is thankful to redeem himself.

You know, a whole bunch of crap. What is really going on is that not half an hour ago, he needed to give up half of his commissary he just bought with his family's money to pay the prize for his protection. But he can't tell you that. No staff member, security guard, gang unit, Unit Manager has ever had an honest conversation with an inmate. The world inside a prison is a world of its own. To penetrate that wall of silence and secrecy is like climbing Mount Everest in your underwear.

Even when I worked in a Community Corrections Center, which is almost the lowest security level facility an inmate can be there is still this wall. Even when I drove inmates to the bus station on their way out and back into the real world, not one single time was I able to coerce any scrap of viable information out of this inmate. It's quite fascinating. The entire prison system is divided into two worlds.   One of the worlds is of the Officers, Guards, Managers und general staff, who are there to do a job. Guards count the inmates, unit managers assist the inmates with programs, level promotions and the lot, Lieutenants manage a shift, kitchen staff order, receive and prepare food, teachers provide education opportunities, mail personnel go through every outgoing and incoming piece of mail.

And behind that façade of a controlled prison life lies the underworld, which is managed by gangs and shot callers, which is so hidden and obscure, that any attempt to expose the information to the wrong people would result in a cataclysmic meltdown.

Yet that is the world every new inmate faces when he enters this system. Nobody is immune, because as an inmate, you become part of it, with your consent or without. The facility staff have the responsibility to provide protection for any and all inmates and to a certain degree it works.

But if you come into the prison system being a convicted sex offender, that is an entirely different animal again. Especially if your crime involves women and far worse, minors, the only thing we can do for you is, to assign you to Protective Custody and hope for the best, cross our fingers so to speak.

3 Lack of money

If you are interested how the prison population increased over the last few years, I am sure there are plenty of information resources available online and otherwise.

To gain a little understanding and background on this subject, it might be a good idea to go to TED.com and watch Jeff Rosen's video about the American prison system and how the prison population went into a steep incline in the mid-seventies. It sure is interesting to watch the American prison population grow so much larger compared to other western countries or democracies in general.

According to the Bureau of Justice Statistics, the State of Oklahoma had the second highest incarceration rate of male prisoners in the nation as well as the highest women incarceration rate, all for the year of 2016.

Put in numbers, it means that per ODOC website, there are currently 26380 people actually in prison, supervised by about 1803 Correctional Officers. That of course doesn't account for all individuals on supervised Parole or in Half way houses, that number is actually higher and round out the total number of about 62 000 individuals under direct or indirect supervision of the DOC in the State of Oklahoma.

As you can already see, the "lack of money" subject is a pure numbers game. You put so many prisoners in so many prisons and supervise them with so many officers, case managers, maintenance workers, kitchen staff, records personnel and so on. If you keep the amount of money received by DOC steady and don't account for an actual increase in prison population or don't account for building maintenance and repairs as well as for completely new buildings and vehicles, you wind up in the situation the Oklahoma DOC finds itself in. If the prison population increases but the budget doesn't, well, you get problems.

Between 2010 and 2015, the Oklahoma Department of Corrections didn´t get more money to fund their operations, but they got more inmates to take care of.

On the DOC website, the Director of DOC states that in the year 2016, the DOC hit yet another population record and he expects that number to rise even further, which is the exact reason, why he asked for about 1.5 billion in funding. That number is about a Billion dollars above the average budget allocation, since he only got $ 483 Million in 2017, but the man has to do something, doesn't he. He is only trying to do his job; you hardly can fault him for that. He might or might not be a little overenthusiastic in asking for three times the amount of money he would usually get, but there are reasons for that. If you look at his proposed budget for 2019, you begin to gain both an insight and a little bit of an understanding, where he comes from. Below is an excerpt of that budget proposal.

The text continues on page 87 if the DOC budget is of no interest to you.

55

Oklahoma Department of CorrectionsFY-2019 Appropriation Request

A Salary Increases	$ 10,153,457
B Immediate Facility Needs	$ 107,262,871
C Programs	$ 3,021,616
D Information Technology	$ 6,670,432
E Training	$ 1,500,000
F Probation and Parole	$ 2,027,130
G Inmate Health Care	$ 88,496,783
H Fleet Vehicles	$ 5,000,000
I Community Sentencing	$ 995,924
J New Medium Security Prisons	$ 813,294,552
K Increased Food/Clothing Costs	$ 3,200,000
L Classification/Records/Medical Security Units	
	$ 1,880,491
M Audit and Compliance	$ 67,300
Total Requested Appropriation Increase	$ 1,043,570,556
FY-2018 Appropriation	$ 485,011,555

TOTAL REQUESTED APPROPRIATION FOR FY-2019

$ 1,528,582,111

FY-2019 Budget Request Priority A

A. Item Description

Salary Increases for All Staff Salary (5%)

$ 7,907,677

Benefits $ 2,245,780

$10,153,457

C. Justification

An agency salary increase is desperately needed to recruit and retain staff.

FY-2019 Budget Request Priority B

A. Item Description

Facility Maintenance/Repair/Critical Needs

Bill Johnson Correctional Center

Camera Replacement $ 500,000

HVAC Replacement for Units 1, 3 and Administration Building

Intercom System Replacement $ 80,000

Electrical System Upgrades for Units 1,2,3 and Medical Building

Fire Alarm System Upgrade $ 180,000

Washer and Dryer Replacement $ 65,000

4 Fireproof Drawer File Cabinet $ 10,000

300 Stackable Chairs $ 14,100

50 Stand Up Lockers $ 22,400

275 Pan Bed Bunks $ 83,536

Tractor with Mower and Front Loader $ 42,000

Paint and Tile Replacement $ 85,000

Lock Cylinders $ 39,000

Total: $1,303,036

Dick Conner Correctional Center

Two Replacement Water Softeners $ 56,576

Two Replacement Boiler Recycle Pumps $ 28,736

Water Softener Replacement $ 9,713

Hot Water Tank Maintenance $ 160,000

Replace Two Exhaust Fans in Boiler Room $ 65,000

Electronics Upgrade for Stun Fence $ 250,000

Repair Boiler Room Wall Leaks $ 15,500

Main Generator Repair/Replacement $ 45,000

Security and Non-Security Door Replacement $ 1,200,000

Replace Plumbing Chase Panels, Painting and Tile

$ 2,750,000

Replace Light Fixtures with High-Security Tamperproof Fixtures

$ 1,300,000

Replace Numerous Sinks, Fixtures and Toilets $ 350,000

Mechanical Room Repair/Replacement of Valves, Piping, Ventilation

$ 350,000

Replace Roofs – Gym, Medium Security Kitchen/Laundry Room, Medium Security Chow Hall, MSU Dining/Visitation, Front Administration and Education Building $ 903,786

Perimeter Road and Parking Lot Resurfacing $ 183,261

Replace 150 Windows with Glass or Lexan $ 112,000

Upgrade Phone System $ 550,000

Phone Upgrade to "Service Call" Program $ 5,000

Total: $11,334,572

Eddie Warrior Correctional Center

Plumbing Repairs $ 760,000

Emergency Generator Installation/Replacements

$ 75,000

Repair Wall Damage in Programs Building $ 110,000

Auditorium Roof/Wall Replacement $ 650,000

Water Softeners to Meet Boiler Manufacturer's Recommendations

$ 70,000

Gym/Visiting Room Air and Heat Replacement

$ 120,000

Perma Jack Foundation Repair for West Foundation

$ 75,000

Exhaust Fan Repair/Replacement $ 6,000

Parking Lot Resurfacing $ 240,000

Water Tower Repair/Painting $ 165,000

Roof Replacement – Programs Building, Armory, Maintenance Shop, and Gym $ 506,232

Emergency Generator Installations for Supply Dorms and Warehouse

$ 3,000,000

Total: $ 5,777,232

Howard McLeod Correctional Center

Emergency Generator Installations $ 600,000

Jackie Brannon Correctional Center

Emergency Generator Installations for Laundry, Security Control, Lift

Station, Medical, A Unit, C Unit, and Food Warehouse

$ 350,375

Install 5 80 ft. High Mast Lighting Arrays $ 400,000

Perimeter Fencing for Security and Contraband Interdiction

$ 1,350,000

Construction of SHU $ 4,300,000

Freezer Food Warehouse Ceiling Replacement $ 13,364

Wastewater Treatment Plant Improvements to Comply with DEQ

Standards $ 3,800,000

Perimeter Road and Control Parking Area Repair

$ 529,452

Electrical Upgrades for C Unit Housing, Garage and Maintenance

$ 3,726,526

Purchase of 50 Rolls of Razor Wire $ 11,000

C Unit Housing Front Entry Door Repair $ 5,323

Purchase Counter Top Griddle and Tilting Kettle for Kitchen

$ 28,596

Shower and Plumbing Fixture Repair/Ceiling Replacement

$ 1,200,000

Replace Fences $ 500,000

C Unit Sewer Line Collapse Repair/Replacement

$ 1,000,000

Total: $ 17,214,636

James Crabtree Correctional Center

New Pill Line Addition to Medical $ 5,300

Additional Radios $ 10,000

Security Doors and Frames Replacement $ 306,000

Minimum Unit Perimeter Road Repair	$ 200,000
Replacement Sinks, Fixtures, Toilets and Exhaust Fans in Showers/Bathrooms	$ 210,000
Shower Replacement and Repair	$ 85,000
Replace 100 Gallon Steam Pot, 1 Convention Oven, 1 Coffee Pot, & 1 Tilt Skillet	$ 63,000
Replace Key Watcher System	$ 23,000
Roofing Replacement/Repair for Gymnasium, Education, Old Administration, Units 4 and 5	$ 878,000
Upgrade Phone System to VOIP	$ 550,000
Perimeter Fencing Repairs and Updates	$ 500,000
Purchase Air Conditioning	$ 2,600,000
Replace Two Emergency Generators and add Generators to Kitchen, Medical, & Housing Units	$ 465,000
Upgrade to "Service Call" Program	$ 5,000
Replace SHU and MSU Access Control Weatherby Panel	$ 280,000
Total:	$ 6,180,300

Jess Dunn Correctional Center

Chemically Treat 3 Chillers for Protection and Preventive
Maintenance $ 12,000

Replacement of Boiler and Water Softener

For D&E Units $ 72,000

Shower Area Fixture/Faucets/Sinks/Toilets Replacement

                                                 $ 340,000

HVAC Repair for East Wing $ 4,500

Replace All Facility Windows $ 550,000

Upgrade Fire Alarm System to FireLite System $ 260,000

Replace Wetherby Control Panel $ 139,350

Condemned Garage Cleanup $ 65,000

Water Tower Paint $ 99,000

Total: $ 1,541,850

Jim E. Hamilton Correctional Center

Kitchen/Laundry Hot Water Replacement $ 70,938

Entrance and Perimeter Roadway and Parking Lot Repair

                                                 $ 550,000

Purchase Water Softener $ 95,000

Replace 4 HVAC Units $ 14,600

Cell window Repair and Screen Replacement	$ 28,000
Concrete to Cover Exposed Sewer Line	$ 52,000
Shower Facility Maintenance and Repair	$ 85,000
Secure SHU Cells Sheet Rock Ceiling	$ 19,000
Replace Back Dock of Food Service	$ 2,500
Gym Roof Replacement	$ 400,000
Emergency Generator Upgrade	$ 1,048,000
Road Repair/Improvements	$ 750,000
New Phone System	$ 440,000
Replace Roofs – Warden's and Deputy Warden's Houses, Replace Sewer Line	$ 55,000
Upgrade Fire Alarm System to FireLite	$ 225,000
"Service Call" Preventive Maintenance	$ 5,000
Total:	$ 3,840,038

John Lilley Correctional Center

HVAC Replacements and Repairs	$ 240,000
Perimeter Road Upgrade	$ 260,000
Increase Current Influent Flow of Lagoon System to Meet DEQ Demands	$ 250,000

Replace Front Gate Entrance Building	$ 22,500
Door and Frame Replacement/Repair	$ 120,000
Fence Pole Replacements	$ 5,000
Shower/Fixture Replacement/Repair	$ 50,000
42 Bed Restricted Housing Unit	$ 2,426,345
Replace Roofs – Units 1,2,3,4 and Gym	$ 1,815,000
Total:	$,5,188,845

Joseph Harp Correctional Center

Water Tower Refurbish/Repaint	$ 132,000
13 Mechanical Room Door Replacements	$ 21,462
Update Remaining Core Building RA/RB from the Old Simplex to FireLite	$ 230,000
Electrical Service Replacement	$ 330,000
Parking Lot Resurfacing	$ 300,000

Replace Roofs on Units D, E, MHU, J, and MHU Administration

$ 748,000

Domestic Hot Water Line and Valve Replacement

$ 2,400,000

Perimeter and Facility Roads	$ 840,000

Replacement of Housing Unit Control Panels and Doors

$ 4,300,000

Total; $ 9,301,462

Lexington Assessment & Reception Center

Perimeter Fence/Repair/Stabilization	$ 55,000
Cold/Hot Water Lines Replacement	$ 350,000
Perimeter Roads Replacement	$ 1,800,000
4 High Mast Lighting Repair/Replacement	$ 320,000
Water Tower Refurbish/Repaint	$ 99,000
Security Camera Installation/Upgrade	$ 2,500,000
Emergency Generator Replacements	$ 225,000
Total:	$ 5,349,000

Mabel Bassett Correctional Center

HVAC Unit Replacements	$ 160,000
Control Room Door Repair	$ 320,000
Perimeter Light Installation/Upgrades	$ 1,200,000

Repair/Replace Security Door/Logs Access Control Systems

$ 1,227,050

Exterior Block Walls Sealing and Painting $ 36,000

Replace Warehouse Freezer $ 4,800

Roof Replacement – C-1, C-2, C-3, Kitchen, and Administration Bldg.

$ 1,172,500

Upgrade Dukane System $ 180,000

Total: $ 4,300,350

Mack Alford Correctional Center

Roof Replacement –Training, Programs, and Tool Control

$ 54,250

Upgrade Bathrooms and Showers $ 420,000

Resurface South Parking Lot $ 260,000

Central Control Generator Repair $ 18,000

New Water Treatment Plant Contract Fees to CAP

$ 500,000

Roof Replacements – Housing Units A,B, Kitchen, MSU, Minimum,

Warehouse, and Vo-tech $ 3,000,000

Purchase Housing Unit Generators	$ 640,000
Housing Unit Lock and Panel Replacement	$ 3,000,000
Repair Fire Alarm System	$ 43,000
Upgrade to "Service Call" Program	$ 5,000
Total:	$ 7,940,250

Northeast Oklahoma Correctional Center

Repairs/Replacement of Facility Doors, Frames, and Hinges

	$ 1,200,000
Purchase Water Softeners	$ 16,000
2 HVAC Units	$ 21,925
Emergency Generator and Backup for Kitchen	$ 55,000
Repair Concrete Tunnel Under Unit 3 and 4	$ 16,500
Soffit Maintenance	$ 28,000
Delta Quad Transformer Upgrade	$ 28,000
Canteen Floor Repair	$ 8,500

Roof Repairs – Unit 3, Staff Housing and Administration Cottages

	$ 580,000
Update Fencing	$ 65,000

Total: $ 2,018,925

Oklahoma State Penitentiary

Purchase New Equipment to Accommodate Single Mode Fiber for

Cameras $ 400,000

Install New Second Barrier Fence Around H Unit Parking Construction

                                      $ 194,000

Install 80 ft. High Mast Lighting Array $ 480,000

Lighting Upgrade Around Perimeter $ 3,600

Replace Wooden Electric Poles $ 200,000

Remove and Repair Damaged Electrical Panels and Raceways

                                      $ 75,000

Replace Damaged Water and Sewer Line on

City Easement $ 570,000

Demolition of Talawanda Heights Bldg. & East Cell House Hallway

                                      $ 65,000

Replace Chiller Components with Individual Roof Mounted Package
Units $ 2,800,000

Repair of Tilt-Wall Constructed Units to Prevent Moisture Leaks and

Seepage $ 35,000

70

Construction of New Parking Lot	$ 360,000
Replace Food Service Area Concrete Floor and Sub-structure	
	$ 45,000
Replace Sewer, Water and Gas Lines	$ 1,200,000
Electrical Transformer Service Upgrades	$ 1,500,000
Food Service Area Sidewalk, Stairwell, Elevated Walk-way Renovation	
	$ 660,000
Replace Hot Water Tanks and Storage Tanks on	
Units D, E and H	250,000
Replace Main Hot and Cold Water Service Lines	
	$ 2,200,000
Resurfacing of Perimeter Road	$ 1,800,000
Replace Hot Water Tanks and Storage Tanks in Food Service Area	
	$ 140,000
Upgrade Network Infrastructure	$ 150,000
Repair Intercom System on H Unit	$ 510,000
Repair Broken Glass with ½ in Lexan	$ 185,000
Replace Chapel A/C	$ 35,000
20 Ton A/C with Heat for IHCC	$ 52,000
Install Two Mixing Valves for H Unit	$ 12,750

Install Two Hot Water Holding Tanks on D and E Units

$ 14,500

Install Metal Roofing for Towers 1,4,5 and 6 $ 51,500

Install Metal Roofing on 3 Existing Admin. Housing

$ 86,000

Total: $ 14,074,350

William S. Key Correctional Center

Purchase Water Softener	$ 9,500
Kitchen Walk-in Cooler Repair	$ 35,000
Kitchen HVAC Repair	$ 14,500
Upgrade Fire Alarm to FireLite System	$ 207,900
Roofing Repair	$ 2,218,000
Transformer and Electrical Service Upgrade	$ 2,600,000
Boiler/Chiller Replacement	$ 2,400,000
Install New Telephone System	$ 550,000

Implement "Service Call" Preventive Maintenance

$ 5,000

Total: $ 8,039,900

Oklahoma State Reformatory

Mowers/Weed Eaters	$ 52,800
Renovate 2 Bathrooms	$ 25,000
Replace Water Tower	$ 1,100,000
Boiler for Laundry Hot Water	$ 25,000
Reroof Units B & C	$ 429,000
Replace Gas Lines Throughout Facility	$ 187,660
Total:	$ 1,819,460

Clara Waters CCC

Maintenance and Repair	$ 60,000
Repair 83' x 58' Driveway Entrance	$ 16,527
Total:	$ 76,527

Enid CCC

Replace Doors, Door Frames and Locks	$ 6,000

Heater and HVAC Maintenance	$ 4,000
Replace Sinks, Toilets, Ice Machines, Milk Dispensers	
	$ 15,300
Roofs for 6 Buildings	$ 75,000
Rebuild Stairs	$ 1,200
Sidewalk Repair	$ 5,000
Electric Panel Replacement (26)	$ 15,000
HVAC Replacement (9)	$ 7,000
Replace Windows	$ 1,000
Install Door Pulls and Panic Buttons	$ 2,250
Total:	$ 131,700

Kate Barnard CC

Ice Machine	$ 5,000
Generator and Intercom Replacement	$ 131,000
Roofing – Kitchen/Housing	$ 247,500
Electrical Upgrade	$ 220,000
Total:	$ 603,500

Lawton CCC

Commercial Mowers and Weed Eaters	$ 4,600
Heat and Air Unit Replacement	$ 1,800
Replace 4 Exterior Doors	$ 5,200
Inmate Bathroom Remodel	$ 25,000
Total:	$ 36,600

Oklahoma City CCC

Maintenance and Repair	$ 60,000
Pest Control Equipment	$ 5,000
Total:	$ 65,000

Union City CCC

High Mast Lift Rental	$ 17,192
Carpet	$ 25,000
Roof Replacement	$ 483,096
Total:	$ 525,288

Total – Facility Maintenance/Repair/Critical Needs

$ 107,262,871

C. Justification

Aging and deteriorating infrastructure and systems at all facilities continue to intensify and adversely impact security and operations.

FY-2019 Budget Request Priority C

Education	$ 355,432
Substance Abuse Treatment	$ 208,423
Cognitive Behavior Programs Case Manager	$ 331,512
Re-Entry Case Manager	$ 1,420,765
Re-Entry Transition Coordinator	$ 321,865
Substance Abuse Treatment	$ 80,000
Cognitive Behavior Programs	$ 43,400
Re-Entry	$ 78,000
Total – Programs	$ 3,021,616

C. Justification

The additional staffing and resources will teach inmates the skills they will need when released from incarceration.

FY-2019 Budget Request Priority D

A. Item Description

Information Technology Operational Needs

Description Cost

OMS Replacement (1 year costs include application software,

implementation services, operational support and infrastructure costs)

$ 4,841,500

Computer Refresh (825 desktop computers with 2 monitors, 50 laptops/tables with docking stations and monitors replacing 8-10 year old computers)

$ 997,332

45 Multi-Function Copiers $ 75,000

Adobe Pro Software for Lexington Assessment & Reception Center 200

6 New computers and 1 desktop printer for Mabel Bassett

Assessment & Reception Center $ 6,400

Safety and Security Technology Cameras - (Needed to replace

funding that was lost through PREA grants from previous years.)

$ 750,000

Total – Information Technology $ 6,670,432

C. Justification

Additional funding is needed to improve the agency's operational performance.

This includes replacement of offender management system, upgrading of computers across the state and continuing efforts to improve core IT systems and equipment across the agency. The LRCPC has approved for legislative consideration a bond proposal for funding the Offender Management System.

FY-2019 Budget Request Priority E

A. Item Description

Training Positions and Operating Expenses

Training Manager	$ 95,081
Secretary	$ 39,132
Corporal	$ 93,147
Expansion of Correctional Leadership	
Development Program	$ 652,640
Wilson Training Academy	$ 600,000
Tuition Assistance Program	$ 20,000
Total – Training	$ 1,500,000

C. Justification

Increased funding is necessary to equip staff with the proper knowledge and skills to carry out the responsibilities of their assignments in a proficient manner to ensure the safe and effective operation of the agency. This is to provide funding for increased training for leadership development, expansion of training facilities, curriculums, and support staff employee development.

FY-2019 Budget Request Priority F

A. Item Description

Probation and Parole Positions and Operating Expenses

Probation and Parole Officers	$ 1,216,061
Psychological Clinician IV	$ 375,844
Probation and Parole Supervisor	$ 71,352
Administrative Technician	$ 78,086
Psychological Clinician	$ 79,815
Weapons	$ 5,726
Weapon Locker Boxes	$ 246
Cell Phones for Probation Officers	$ 200,000
Total – Probation and Parole	$ 2,027,130

C. Justification

The additional staffing and resources will expand the level of supervision to released inmates, decreasing the likelihood of recidivism.

FY-2019 Budget Request Priority G

A. Item Description

Inmate Health Care – Operating, Staffing and Treatment

B. Cost

Operating Costs for FY-2019

An increase of 3.8% is requested from the current FY-2018 Health Services budget.

This calculation is based upon the actual increase in expenditures from FY-2015 to FY-2017. The Centers for Medicare and Medicaid Services project healthcare spending to grow at an average rate of 5.8% per year from 2015-2025. This requested increase will allow Health Services to operate in an "as is" state for FY-2019 barring any unforeseen or uncontrollable factors. (National Health Expenditure

Projections 2015-2025, CMMS)

FY-2018 Budget $40,999,469 x 3.8% = $1,557,980

Hepatitis C Treatment

Current number of inmates suspected as having Hepatitis C: 2,724

Genotype testing is $300 per inmate

$28,861 (average cost per course of treatment)

Total testing cost	$817,200
Total treatment cost	$78,617,364
Combined cost of treatment	$ 79,434,564

Convalescent Beds/Infirmary Conversion

Currently there are 49 infirmary beds available within the agency. Due to the aging population and the acuity of their medical needs, there will continue to be a need for skilled nursing care beds. To better manage these needs, 30 additional infirmary beds are needed within the system to serve as step-down beds from infirmary care and hospitals.

Additional medical staffing and equipment cost breakdown:

Registered Nurse III	$ 245,854
Licensed Practical Nurse II	$ 232,744
Patient Care Assistant	$ 124,192
Electrical Hospital Beds with Rails 30	$ 33,200
Wheelchair Scale 1	$ 2,000
Vital Signs Machine 2	$ 2,400
Miscellaneous Medical Equipment	$ 2,000
Total:	$ 642,390

Competitive Pay for Medical/Mental Health/Dental Positions

In addition to the challenges associated with finding qualified health care staffing in the general public, ODOC faces the challenges associated with prisons being located in rural areas and the public perception associated with working in a prison setting.

When faced with critical shortages of staff, the ODOC has been forced to contract with temporary staffing agencies to bring in part-time health care providers to ensure that the constitutional level of health care is provided to the inmate population.

Competitive Pay Cost	$ 6,661,849

Dental Surgery Clinic Equipment

Dental surgical hand pieces utilized in the dental surgical clinic are obsolete and will not be supported by the manufacturer after December 2017. This equipment is vital to the dental surgical process.

Equipment Cost	$ 100,000

Medical Services

Upgrading medical polycom equipment to include peripheral instruments. These upgrades will help curb the use of follow up specialty appointments at OUMC.

Telemedicine Cost	$ 100,000
Total – Medical Services	$ 88,496,783

C. Justification

Additional funding is necessary to maintain standards of healthcare while contending with rising medical costs, care of the aging population, and increasing medical and mental health treatment needs.

FY-2019 Budget Request Priority H

A. Item Description

Replacement of Aging Fleet Vehicles

Sedans - 91	$ 2,002,000
Transport Vehicles - 67	$ 2,010,000

Fleet Management and Preventative Maintenance

$ 988,000

Total – Fleet Vehicles $ 5,000,000

C. Justification

The agency has deferred replacing vehicles due to funding deficits. Increased funding is needed to replace vehicles that are averaging 200,000 miles and are not cost-effective to maintain. Increase based on continuing need to expend facilities funds for fleet preventative maintenance needs, along with developing a replacement schedule for vehicles associated with core functions such as inmate transports and emergency response.

Fleet Needs

FY-2019 Budget Request Priority I

A. Item Description

Community Sentencing Expansion

Local Administrator 1	$ 74,714
Administrative Assistant I 3	$ 117,130
Total Payroll	$ 191,844

Expansion of Councils/County Operating Costs

Expansion of Community Sentencing for 10 county/councils
$ 400,000

Statutory change to include offenders with no priors
$ 400,000

Additional Fuel and Vehicle Maintenance Expenses

	$ 2,160
Laptop and Cell Phone	$ 1,920
Total Operating	$ 804,080
Total – Community Sentencing	$ 995,924

C. Justification

The additional staffing and resources will allow expansion of the Community Sentencing program, providing a more successful and cost-effective alternative to incarceration.

FY-2019 Budget Request Priority J

A. Item Description

Two New Medium Security Facilities

Estimated Costs to Build Two - 2,000 Bed Medium

Security Facilities	$ 749,700,000
Yearly Operating Costs	$ 63,594,552
Total:	$ 813,294,552

Notes: This number was inflated 5% per year for two years assuming it would take three years to build a prison from the point an architect is secured and also assumes no land cost. Estimated yearly operating costs were based on actuals for James Crabtree Correctional Center which had the lowest per diem rate of the medium security facilities in FY-2017.

One male facility and one female facility.

C. Justification

Increased funding is needed to manage projected growth through construction of additional prisons providing a true institutional environment.

FY-2019 Budget Request Priority K

A. Item Description

Increased Food and Clothing Costs

Inmate Food Master Menu Changes	$ 2,200,000
Inmate Clothing	$ 1,000,000
Total:	$ 3,200,000

C. Justification

Additional funding is needed for increased clothing costs and to support master menu changes to improve the quality, satisfaction and nutritional balance of meals served to the inmate population.

FY-2019 Budget Request Priority L

A. Item Description

Classification, Consolidated Records Unit and Medical Security Unit

Medical Security Unit - 18 FTE Correctional Officers	$ 705,157
Sentence Administration - 3 FTE - APO II	$ 143,586

Consolidated Records - 10 FTE - Correctional Records Officers

	$ 476,430
Consolidated Records - 3 FTE - APO II	$ 143,586

Mabel Bassett Assessment & Reception Center - 2 Case Managers

	$ 107,688
Evaluation and Analysis – 3 FTE	$ 254,044

C. Justification

The additional staffing and resources will streamline assessment and reception processes and remove burdens, and reduced increased workloads' that are created due to a lack of needed resources.

Operating

Consolidated Records	$ 10,000
Medical Security Unit	$ 30,000
Lexington Assessment & Reception Center	$ 4,000
Lexington Assessment & Reception Center	$ 6,000
Total:	$ 1,880,491

FY-2019 Budget Request Priority M

A. Item Description

Audit and Compliance Operating Cost Needs

Professional Services – ACA Accreditation Costs $ 7,283

Travel Expenses – Travel costs and lodging for ACA

$ 37,315

Miscellaneous Administrative Expenses – Increased postage

$ 487

Supplies and Material Expenses – Fuel costs $ 8,200

General Operating Expenses – Office supplies and software

$ 9,315

Shop Expenses – Maintenance and repairs $ 2,000

Equipment and Library Resources – Information Technology

$ 2,700

Total: $ 67,300

C. Justification

Funding is needed to maintain the operational performance providing audit and compliance standards for the agency.

As in any budget request such as this with so many factors, facilities and personnel involved, you can scrutinize every single item on this list and come up with a more viable or economical solution, if you really try hard enough. That is a given. But what the current Director of DOC really tries to convey is a bunch of factors, which weren't part of the budget for years. The buildings and its component such as heating, sanitation, electric and technology (computers, networks) as well as the expansive fleet of vehicles don't stay in shape by sheer willpower. Heavy usage and the time itself take a toll. You try to keep your house in shape over a time span of 20 years without any money to do it and you will realize that this is impossible without investments.

And in these days, we are paying the toll for the "hard on crime" politics we have embraced for the last 35 years. Prisoners don't get younger and bodies need more attention as they get older. The three strikes system of punishment and mandatory minimum sentencing laws extended prison stays. Not to mention the 85% crime categories, which prevents prisoners with violent crimes to gain any type of credits until they served at least 85% of their time as determined by the judge.

Prisoners get older, stay longer and new people come into the system, which is why the Director sees the need to build two more prisons. It is a simple calculation but is not likely to happen. If the DOC would get the $ 1.5 Billion, they asked for in the 2019 budget, it would mean a year-on-year budget increase of 300 %. Well, that is not going to happen, which means buildings still get patched up before they crumble into the dust, vehicles with 265 000 miles will get their regular oil changes and new tires as seen fit and most likely no salary increases in the foreseeable future. Welcome to the everyday state budget wars of any State.

The State of Oklahoma relies heavily on oil and its various products and as long as the oil price stays or hovers around the current level, the State budget is not going to change.

4.   Training

I included the subject of training as a bad point as far as the inmates are concerned. And there is some truth to it if you look at other countries and how they approach and conduct Corrections Officer training.

In this State, you simply don't get a lot of training, which not only amounts to a negative point for the inmates but for the officers as well. Training is an essential part of any one´s job and it doesn't matter what you do. The amount of training you would have to receive to be able to completely and efficiently clean the interior of a house already requires a good amount of knowledge about cleaning products, the negative effects of certain products on different surfaces and so on. How do you clean windows streak free might be common knowledge for some, but for people who don't clean windows on a regular basis and on a big scale, the art of cleaning a window most effectively is a piece of knowledge all by itself. And it goes on from here. Then you have to account for anything else which comes onto the market of cleaning, both cleaning solutions and cleaning tools. In other words, it is a constant learning process. And similar to car companies which are under constant and permanent pressure to stay ahead or at least even with their competition, you can be outdone by another company which comes up with more advanced and thus efficient means to clean a house. And all of a sudden, prices for house cleaning drop and you are out of business; that is it for your honest attempt to come up in life.

Now as far as comparing the Corrections industry with other fields of business is concerned, I think it is slightly different.

I don't think Corrections has changed significantly over the last 150 years. If you still would do what we did 150 years ago, I don't think we could do much wrong as far as keeping prisoners secure in one spot. The whole idea always has been to put a criminal behind a locked door and provide him with basic necessities to live with. There is no need to have fancy gadgets, there is no need to have the latest and greatest in technological advancements. There is really no need to have anything more than a housing unit with lockable doors and maybe a recreational yard somewhere. Heck, the Recreational yard can even be right next to the cell block. Just open a door and that would be that.

So, I think, in order to understand the Training in Corrections, you have to have an understanding, even if ever so basic, in what we do.

The status of training Correctional Officers and above is basically a homemade solution. Whereas medical professionals are hired already being trained, the DOC provides training for guards and security personnel in general.

How the hiring process in DOC works is pretty simple. As long as you don't have prior, criminal convictions and as long as you can pass a drug screening test, you can get hired as a correctional officer. And even if you are overweight and have problems keeping up in a one mile run down a stretch of a park, it is no deal breaker. Physical fitness is not a big part of the Corrections Officer selection process. It seems as though many employers, including the DOC have come to peace with the fact, that a certain percentage of the general population and thus the hiring pool, is obese; so the idea in hiring obese people is based on the notion, that all you have to accomplish as far as physical fitness is concerned is to do the best you can. As long as someone demonstrates a real effort in getting through the fitness program which is part of the training program, he should be good to go. Also bear in mind that being a Corrections Officer is not a physically demanding task.

So here is in a nutshell, what the DOC is going to do for you as far as training you for the job at hand is concerned. One of the references covering this subject in a more general manner is DOC policy P100100. It reads as follows:

Employee Development Standards

I.Training and Staff Development

The Oklahoma Department of Corrections (ODOC) will provide employees with the opportunity for training and staff development necessary to develop job related expertise, foster professional growth, and encourage the pursuit of career goals. (2-

CO-1C-14)

Qualified staff will plan, coordinate, and supervise the training program. (2-CO-1D01,

4-4073)

A. Orientation

Orientation standards will be developed for the training of new staff. All new employees, part-time and contract staff and volunteers will receive orientation prior to job assignment. (2-CO-1D-05, 4-4088)

B. Job Specific Training

The ODOC will provide job specific training that is oriented toward specific learning objectives designed to prepare new employees to perform their jobs in a professional, safe, and effective manner.

C. In-Service Training

Employees will be provided with mandatory and elective training opportunities that meet statutory requirements and foster continuing professional development.

D. Leadership/Management Training

Section-10 Training P-100100 Page: 2 Effective Date: 03/03/2017

Employees will be provided with the training necessary and required to develop supervisory and managerial capabilities. (2-CO-1C-14)

E. Succession Planning

The ODOC will develop a program to provide a systematic approach to ensure leadership continuity, develop potential successors in ways that best fit their strengths, and identify the best candidates for categories of positions.

F. Professional Seminars and Conferences

Employees will be provided opportunities to attend professionally related seminars and conferences that enhance professionalism and job knowledge.

(2-CO-1D-10, 4-4094) Resources of other public and private agencies may be utilized as available. (2-CO-1D-04, 4-4079, 4-4094)

It is understood, that initial training will be provided. Points A through C are in place, if only rudimentary, depending with what other job fields someone would like to compare the DOC with. How much training does a Corrections Officer need? Per the DOC it consists of about five to six weeks of training. Like a job at McDonalds, you start on your first day and get oriented and are able to perform certain, basic functions of your job assignment. While you get acquainted with the scope of your responsibilities and functions, the HR department along with the training department will schedule your slot in the training academy, which, as I mentioned, currently is designed to take five to six weeks.

The academy will be your point B in the above-mentioned policy. DOC policy OP100101 lists in Attachment A the training requirements for Corrections Officers:

III. Correctional Officers

Correctional officers are all employees included in any correctional officer series from Correctional Officer Cadet to Chief of Security. Correctional officer cadets will attend orientation at the worksite and attend the Correctional Officer Cadet Academy at a designated location.

A. Orientation Courses

40 Hours

Airborne/Bloodborne Pathogens

Anatomy of a Sting

Bullying in the Workplace

Computer Usage

Contraband

Corrections Overview

Criminal Justice Overview

Cultural Diversity/Awareness

"Downing a Duck "

Emergency Plans

Employee Assistance Program

Employee Rights, Responsibilities and Conduct

Facility Tour

Fire Safety

Games Inmates Play

Hazard Communication

HIPAA

Key Control

Inmate Disciplinary Process

Inmate Grievance Process/ Request to Staff

Inmate Rights and Responsibilities

Preventing Sexual Harassment

Prison Rape Elimination Act (PREA)

Report Writing

Sexual Harassment

Use of Force Policy

Video: Avoiding Inmate Setups

Working with Female Inmates

Workplace Safety

B. Correctional Cadet Academy

240 hours

Week 1:

Orientation

Public Image

Wellness

Disciplinary Procedures

Overview of the Criminal Justice System

Sexual Harassment

Workplace Violence

Week 2:

Culture and Communication

Special Needs Inmates

Riot Prevention

Suicide Prevention

Report Writing

Week 3:

Environmental Security Procedures (Sections I-V):

Maintaining a Safe and Secure Environment

Seven Basic Principles of Inmate Management

Inmate/Staff Relationships

Professional Development

Creating Safety in a Correctional Environment

Toxic/Caustic/Flammable/Hazardous Materials

Radio 10 Codes/Radio Communication

Emergency Plans/Escapes/Tornados/Natural Disasters/Fire

Response/Toxic Chemical Spills

Oklahoma Board of Corrections

Agency Policy/Post Orders

Logs

Inspections/Equipment Checks

Environmental Cues for Behavior Predictors

Counts

Key Control

Tool Control

Searches

Crime Scene Preservation

Contraband

Physical Evidence

Segregation

Indigent Inmates

Property

Week 4:

Cardio-Pulmonary Resuscitation (CPR)

First Aid

Use of Force

Inmate Rights, Privileges, and Responsibilities

Firearms Training Simulator (FATS)

Female Inmates

Use of Restraints

Week 5:

Self-Defense

Week 6:

Fixed/Extendable Baton

OC Spray

Graduation

I haven't seen or experienced much of points D through F in the "Employee Development Standards" above, at least not in the places I worked as a Correctional Officer. The lack of any enhanced or advanced training opportunities in places like the DOC can probably be traced back to the lack of funding. As it is, the DOC must try to not only hire Corrections Officers but to keep them as well. Thus, it shouldn't come as a surprise that they must focus on the task at hand which is keeping the facilities running with a decent number of staff.

And that is in the final analysis the reason why I mention the training as a negative point for both inmates and staff. No matter how long you work in the world of the DOC, which in my case is ten years, the initial training as described above is going to be all you will ever get.

During the course of your employment, there are going to be frequent adjustments to policies and that is being dealt with in the form of occasional refresher courses. These consist of an hour to a daylong installment. They are being conducted either on site or in a designated building, which is picked based on how many people are planned to partake and how long of a drive they will have going there.

What does that all mean then as far as the Corrections Officer is concerned? For starters, some might think, that six weeks of training should be plenty. How much do you need to learn in order to accomplish such simple tasks as counting bodies, looking for contraband, telling inmates to go from A to point B, telling inmates to clean this or that? What is so difficult in shackling an inmate, putting him into a van or a bus and driving him from one facility to another? Of course, you also have to conduct visitation, where the outside world meets the confines of a prison. And there are a host of other tasks and responsibilities, which are too numerous to mention.

The basic function of a Corrections Officer is to enforce DOC policy as written by DOC, which is based on State law. These policies are then in part and where appropriate and permissible, slightly adjusted by the Warden of the facility. There is some wiggle room how a Warden feels like a facility should be run.

If the life of a Corrections Officer is so easy, what factors make the training of such people a negative point for inmates and staff alike?

Because if you want to do your job right, you basically need to be a psychology major and have an advanced degree in Criminal Justice. The variety of personalities you are dealing with is too wide to even attempt to make everyone happy, you just can't. The result is that Corrections Officers only can do the basic functions of supervising the inmates. After a while, an Officer will either quit because the inmates or staff wore him down or he finds a way to shield himself from the mad world of prison life. And the latter is mostly accomplished by ignoring the human factor. There is no other way. You cannot have conversations with 300 inmates every day to listen to their problems like a good psychologist would. The inmates are on their own. You can only provide basic security, you can provide food and you have the responsibility to keep them in place, protect the public, protect the employee and protect the inmate, in that order.

And since you are the first place of contact for any inmate, you are not only their keeper, you are their problem solver for anything and everything.

If you don't watch out, it will wear you down pretty quick, which is why in many corrections settings the fail rate is pretty high. Sometimes the inmates even count on that. If you do a good enough job, they want you gone. If you cannot be coerced to bring in contraband for them, they don't care much if you live or die.

So, the moral of training in Correction settings is, that you can never have too much training but only a basic amount of training can be provided because of cost restrains. That is simple enough.

One last word to the subject of training. It is not that the DOC hasn't tried to make things better either. If you poke around in the State statutes a little bit and invest a little time and energy on the subject, you will find, among other things, the "Transformational Justice Act" from around 2007. It's State statute §57-521.2. Unfortunately, it was only designed to last until July 1 2010, so it was a pilot project to see, if things couldn't be made to get better. To not bore you with a barrage of justice mumble, I would like to quote just a few interesting points:

3. Ensure that those who supervise offenders in prison are linked to those that will supervise them after release;

...

9. Establish collaboration among corrections and community corrections, technical schools, community colleges, and the workforce development and employment service sectors to:

a. promote, where appropriate, the employment of people released from prison and jail, through federal efforts such as educating employers about existing financial incentives and facilitate the creation of job opportunities, including transitional jobs, for this population that will benefit communities,

b. connect inmates to employment, including supportive employment and employment services, before their release to the community, and

c.address barriers to employment;

...

D. There is hereby created in the State Treasury a revolving fund for the Department of Corrections to be designated the "Transformational Justice Revolving Fund". The fund shall be a continuing fund, not subject to fiscal year limitations, and shall consist of monies received from appropriated funds to be used for bonuses to corrections officials who demonstrate improvement in recidivism rates of inmates that were previously under the custody of the Department of Corrections. All monies accruing to the credit of the fund are hereby appropriated and may be budgeted and expended by the Department of Corrections. Expenditures from the fund shall be made upon warrants issued by the State Treasurer against claims filed as prescribed by law with the Director of the

Office of Management and Enterprise Services for approval and payment.

...

E. The Department of Corrections shall develop rules and policies which ensure that recidivism rates are included in the performance reviews, promotions and compensation adjustments of correctional officers.

That fits in with what I already mentioned on the training of Corrections Officers. It seems some people had the idea, that Officers should be more involved in the life of an inmate, at least at the stage of an inmate's life, where he can already see the end of the tunnel so to speak. And we were even supposed to benefit from these activities, whatever they were supposed to be.

Imagine a life, where Corrections Officer and Admin personnel of a Community Corrections Center were in part compensated, how an inmate does in life after his release. In practical terms, if you look at point E. above, the DOC would have to keep track of each released inmate for a number of years to determine, if he comes back into the system. If he stays out of prison, let's say for five consecutive years, all people involved in his care when he was incarcerated, would get a bonus.

If you would compare that idea to the world of cars, it would go something like that: Porsche sells you a vehicle. The date of the purchase with some of your personal data is being entered into a nationwide database for safe keeping. After five years, an automated letter is being issued to you to find out, if you are still happy with your vehicle and whether or not you regret any part of the buying experience or if the promises given to you came out all correct. If you answer would be 75% positive, the government would issue a check to the car manufacturer, let's say in the amount of $ 500.

What a noble idea, only it didn't work. And it didn't work, because there is no such system; but an interesting idea nevertheless. As things stand, all we can do as CO's is counting inmates, feeding inmates and telling them what to do and when to do it.

But the pure existence of the "Transformational Act" tells another story as well. At least in the past, people tried to improve the system. There were some undeniable attempts to negotiate the rising costs of Corrections, only it didn't work out just yet.

But you can even undercut the training in State run prisons by looking at privately run facilities. The privately owned prison I worked at provided exactly two weeks of training. Everything a Corrections Officer and Case Manager need to know is furthermore deflated from six weeks to two weeks.

You can learn a lot of things in two weeks, if you talk about a car for instance. You can learn how that darn navigation system works and the controls for the adjustable suspension. And by mistake you will probably find out how to look up the transmission temperature. And at the end of week two you can get a glimpse of how the 360-degree camera view functions. All that is good and great, but since you are in the business of dealing with people, you will learn nothing but the absolute basics of basics. In fact, there is no training for people at all. I guess the idea is that inmates are not people, but let's not get too sarcastic just yet. In two weeks, you will learn what three different types of keys there are, you learn how many housing units there are on this particular facility and you will learn how to deal with bodily fluids. You will learn a few simple things and everything needs to be learned on the job. The one thing you unfortunately will never learn or even hear about in either State or privately provided training is how to be a good Corrections Officer. You have to figure this one out all by yourself.

The DOC of course wants you to be the best Officer you can be by providing some guidance. Just look at DOC policy OP-110215:

I. Establishment of Rules and Code of Conduct

A. Code of Conduct

Employees of the agency will, at all times, conduct themselves in a manner befitting the office or position that the employee holds. Employees will uphold the correctional employee oath, as well as the public's trust, and will reflect the highest ethical standards. Employees will:

1. Devote full time, attention and effort to their duties during assigned hours of duty;

2. Engage in conduct which affords respect, courtesy, and preserves the dignity of others;

3. Refrain from conduct which is corrupt, illegal, serves to denigrate, demean, or disregard the welfare of others;

4. Promote and model exemplary, law abiding behavior; (4-ACRS-3A07)

5. Avoid any conduct, interest, or relationship which is in conflict with, or detrimental to, the proper and effective discharge of official duties; (2-CO-1C-24, 4-4069, 4-APPFS-3C-02)

6. Be efficient and effective managers of public resources;

7. Conduct work in a manner which contributes to and supports a safe and healthful work environment; (4-APPFS-3E-01)

8. Promptly and truthfully report any improper actions which violate agency policies and

9. Refrain from conduct which constitutes violation of the agency's sexual abuse/sexual harassment policy as described in Section IV. B. 2. item a. of this procedure (28 CFR Part 115, Section 115.76 [PREA]).

That looks pretty simple and basic, not much different than you would probably read in many other company's procedures and policies. And in case you wonder, what the correctional employee oath is and what it says as mentioned in point A. above, here it is:

I do hereby solemnly affirm to support the Constitution and the laws of the United States of America and abide by the Constitution and the laws of the State of Oklahoma, as well as the policies and procedures of the Oklahoma Department of Corrections. I will treat all employees and offenders with respect and dignity. I will obey the lawful orders of those appointed over me. I will conduct myself in such a manner to enhance and establish a positive tradition of excellence for the Oklahoma Department of Corrections.

All right now, try to bring this lofty goal in alignment with the current state of affairs and you see where we are at and what lies ahead of us.

5.   Plea bargain

"The plea bargain is any agreement in a criminal case between the prosecutor and defendant whereby the defendant agrees to plead guilty to a particular charge in return for some concession from the prosecutor". (Wikipedia)

"plea-bargaining: an arrangement between the prosecutor and defendant whereby the defendant pleads guilty to a lesser charge in the expectation of leniency" (Oxford Dictionary)

United States Constitution Bill of Rights VI:

In all criminal prosecutions, the accused shall enjoy the right to a speedy and public trial, by an impartial jury of the State and district wherein the crime shall have been committed, which district shall have been previously ascertained by law, and to be informed of the nature and cause of the accusation; to be confronted with the witnesses against him; to have compulsory process for obtaining witnesses in his favor, and to have the Assistance of Counsel for his defense.

And that is almost all there is to say about the subject of Plea Bargaining.

And why is the subject of plea bargaining bad for the inmate? It is bad for the inmate because it is essentially a very bad, but currently obviously necessary procedure. And it is a very bad procedure because it takes justice out of the justice system; that is why it is a very bad idea. The idea that everybody has the right to a speedy, public trial is a noble one and was created in a time, when such a thing was somewhat possible. These days you have the following situation.

In each State there are several thousand inmates incarcerated in jails, which basically functions as a holding tank. These people await their charges. When they are officially charged, they will see some type of attorney. That can already take weeks. The attorney will hopefully be able to tell the accused what charges the prosecution has in store for them. Then the defendant will see the judge for his initial appearance. He can tell the judge whether or not he will plead guilty or not guilty. After the initial appearance and the publication of the charges leveled against the defendant, all cards are on the table. Now the attorney will battle with the prosecution what to do with these charges and where to go from here. I say battle but that is hardly the case. Rightfully or not, a person is in jail. And rightfully or not, he now faces charges. And if the prosecutor is one of these "hard on crime" types, the charge will probably be on the upper end of the punishment scale. I haven't even mentioned the possibility of the person being innocent. That is a completely different subject matter and happens as well. Now a decision needs to be made of whether the attorney should go to a trial because his defendant pleads not guilty or should the attorney/client team find a lesser middle ground with the prosecutor to avoid a trial.

And here it already starts. One of the questions many attorneys and defendants ask themselves, is how long does the defendant want to stay in jail? Because if they decide to go to trial, the Court Clerk is going to tell them to settle in, order some donuts and have no plans for the next two years. Now the person faces charges for arson in the first degree, because he tried to burn down the Post Office. That is the crime he is being charged with. I don't want to go into details how the prosecutor got to this one, but it is not important for the sake of this argument.

Arson in the first degree is a serious crime because in the State of Oklahoma, it fits into the 85% crime category, which is the violent crime category. That prevents inmates from gaining certain privileges in prison, which I explained earlier in this book. Since the prosecutor has leveled that charge, the defendant faces 10 years in prison, if they go to trial. Now the trick is, to prevent a trial to save everybody time and money. So, the defendant pleads guilty to destruction of public property and gets 2 years incarceration instead, one year in prison and one year on supervised probation.

It is not an optimum solution, but if the person has done what the prosecution says he did, then it might be considered a good deal. But it is still not justice, because he didn't get a trial, speedy or otherwise.

But how many trials can one jurisdiction perform in the course of a year? Not many if you don't want to be accused of a mock trial either. You have 4000 people in jail awaiting sentencing and if everybody wants a trial, that would take twenty years. That is of course a very subjective number, which I just made up, but you get the idea. And who

106

in the world would benefit from all that? People would sit in jails for years for offenses that, if convicted, would have them out in six months. Then imagine the public outcry which that would cause. All the jails we have to pay for, all the people we have to feed and take care of, hundreds of court clerks, dozens of judges, thousands of jury members. It would amount to absolutely mind-blowing numbers. The country of the United States of America just managed to maneuver itself into a situation, where a fair trial as envisioned by its founding fathers is not an option any longer.

The current justice system is a system of handshakes between the prosecution and the public or paid defender. And I say paid defender very loosely, because the same justice system also makes it financially unfavorable to spend a lot of time with one defendant. There is much more money to be made in other branches like product liability, personal injuries and the lot.

In almost all cases, whatever you see on TV about any court room proceedings, it is for show only. It is a myth.

The facts of guilt or innocence are no longer the deciding factors in the fate of somebody in jail. It is certainly still a factor, you cannot and shall not discount that. After all, that person ended up behind walls for a reason, I would like to assume in most cases. However, more important are the plea bargains. How do you as a defendant get out of that situation? With two million dollars, that is how.

If you can throw enough well dressed and well known and well-respected people at the prosecutor for an enough amount of time, then you might have a chance of getting out. If you can succeed to question anything and everything the prosecutor thinks he knows about that case, then you might have a chance. But it has to be done immediately. The seeds of doubt need to be planted in the judges' head before he knows enough about that case to form an opinion.

107

With enough money you can annoy the heck out of that prosecutor. With enough money you can make him so uncomfortable, that he rather drops the case than to answer all the questions by the Major of why he wants to prosecute somebody who just donated $ 450 000 to construct a gymnasium for the local school. That is how you get out of jail.

Of course, nobody has two million dollars, so what is the solution?

Well, I am glad you asked, because I asked that question myself. And I also asked that question dozens of my co-workers in the course of 10 years. And the answer is simple and is always the same: Don't come to prison.

Well, isn't that fantastic. What a fabulous solution to the overcrowding dilemma of the American prison system. Why in the world did nobody come up with that answer before? It is as simple as it is true. At the same time, that answer unfortunately didn't solve nothing for nobody, ever. The prison population still rises, the costs still rise, the judges still cannot give anybody a fair trial and the plea bargain still causes innocent people to end up behind bars.

I compare that answer to the health care system.

Why do you come to the hospital? Because I hurt myself. Well, don't hurt yourself then.

Why do you come to the dentist? Because I have a hole in my tooth. Well, why do you have a hole in your tooth? Because I eat. Well then, don't eat.

My point here is that "Don't come to prison" didn't work. It is as simple as that. And for anything to function as a solution or as a part or a beginning of a solution, it has to work. That too, is both simple and true.

The plea bargain at first glance seems to be a good idea. The assumption is that we cannot give all people a trial, fair or otherwise. Both the prosecutor and the trial judge face a problem. There is a higher number of people coming into the prison system and sitting in jails awaiting their trial then they can process. I don't know what the numbers are in particular, but it probably is a very high discrepancy. And let's not forget the idea, that this type of arrangement can also benefit the defendant, the accused. Instead of taking a risk of being convicted by a jury with an uncertain outcome, he takes the golden middle and accepts a term of imprisonment or probation or whatever the judgment holds for him, which in most cases is far less than the punishment allowed and permitted by law.

It is still not justice, let's not forget about that.

But it sounds like a good way out of a judicial, financial and organizational dilemma.

And let's not forget, that judges already have a substantial amount of freedom as far as how sharp, bitter or light the judgment shall be put onto the offender.

Let's look at §21-27:

Mitigation of punishment.

Where it is made to appear at the time of passing sentence upon a person convicted, that such person has already paid a fine or suffered an imprisonment for the act which he stands convicted, under an order adjudging it a contempt, the court authorized to pass sentence may mitigate the punishment to be imposed, in its discretion.

That is saying a lot. And if I learned anything from sitting in courtrooms and following the arraignments of dozens of people, I must come to the realization that this short paragraph in the law is already being used to a good extent. It is a tool already being used in courtrooms. The judge knows that, the attorneys know that and the defendant knows it. Only because you committed a crime, which by law calls for a certain amount of time behind bars or under supervision of the Pardon & Parole division of the DOC, is not a guarantee that the full extent of that judgment is being handed down to you. There are numerous factors which can work in favor of a guilty person. The time you spent in jail is one of them. Your personal situation can be another, the appearance of your family in court, your social environment, your own, personal history, etc.

There also exist the "Departure from minimum sentencing Act". If a person is eligible, his punishment can be mitigated.

§22-985.1. Departure from mandatory minimum sentencing – Requirements - Exceptions.

A. When sentencing a person convicted of a criminal offense for which there is a mandatory minimum sentence of imprisonment, the court may depart from the applicable sentence if the court finds substantial and compelling reasons on the record, after giving due regard to the nature of the crime, history, and character of the defendant and his or her chances of successful rehabilitation, that:

1. The mandatory minimum sentence of imprisonment is not necessary for the protection of the public and imposition of the mandatory minimum sentence of imprisonment would result in substantial injustice to the defendant; or

2. The mandatory minimum sentence of imprisonment is not necessary for the protection of the public and the defendant, based on a risk and needs assessment, is eligible for an alternative court, a diversion program or community sentencing, without regard to exclusions because of previous convictions, and has been accepted to the same, pending sentencing.

B. The court shall not have the discretion to depart from the applicable mandatory minimum sentence of imprisonment on convictions for criminal offenses under the following circumstances:

1. The offense for which the defendant was convicted is among those crimes listed in Section 571 of Title 57 of the Oklahoma Statutes as excepted from the definition of "nonviolent offense";

2. The offense for which the defendant was convicted was a sex offense and will require the defendant to register as a sex offender pursuant to the provisions of the Sex Offenders Registration Act;

3. The offense for which the defendant was convicted involved the use of a firearm;

4. The offense for which the defendant was convicted is a crime listed in Section 13.1 of Title 21 of the Oklahoma Statutes requiring the defendant to serve not less than eighty-five percent (85%) of any sentence of imprisonment imposed by the judicial system prior to becoming eligible for consideration for parole;

5. The offense for which the defendant was convicted is a violation of the Trafficking in Illegal Drugs Act as provided in Sections 2-414 through 2-420 of Title 63 of the Oklahoma Statutes;

6. The defendant was the leader, manager or supervisor of others in a continuing criminal enterprise; or

7. The offense for which the defendant was convicted is a violation of the Oklahoma Antiterrorism Act as provided in Sections 1268 through 1268.8 of Title 21 of the Oklahoma Statutes.

Added by Laws 2015, c. 243, § 2, eff. Nov. 1, 2015.

Many mitigation procedures in the State of Oklahoma and other States hinge on the classification of a certain crime as mentioned earlier in this book and in the text above. So even though a judge has the authority to lessen the punishment of a crime, he only can do so for a range of convicted criminals, which does not include offenses which are violent in nature and belong to the 85 % crime category.

I included this text to demonstrate the range of Plea Bargain possibilities a prosecutor and the attorney have in making recommendations to the judge for sentencing. For instance, point number 6 above can mean a lot of things and it is not likely that a prosecutor can prove this point in an undeniable manner and beyond reasonable doubt without investing a lot of time and money in the case. It is not going to happen. In a similar matter, point 5 can be discussed endlessly. Depending of course on the particulars of the case, an argument can be opened, in which way the defendant engaged in trafficking illegal drugs. Is it merely an observation the arresting Police Officer made or do photographs of scales exist, which show the amount of drugs? And if the scales show the amount of drugs detected, were these scales the permissible type of scales as authorized by the department or other types?

The Plea-Bargaining subject in other words is a tool for endless opportunities. Of course, sometimes a case is as clear cut as the edge of a broken piece of glass. In some cases, there is no such a thing as plea bargaining. And sometimes, as probably in more cases than not, the defendant will benefit from this form of sentence administration, if he/she committed the crime.

So, the question can be brought up, whether or not the Plea Bargain is good or bad for the Justice system. I brought it up as being a bad thing for the justice system but we also can observe all the good points, which can come from that, which are undeniable. Just ask any defendant who ever benefitted from a plea bargain. I guarantee it, he will sing a song about it and praise the heck out of it, because as far as he is concerned and as far as his own, personal case goes, he benefitted greatly from it. He not only got away with a far lesser sentence than the law allows, he is also happy about the other 25 times, where he didn't get caught doing the same crime for which he is in jail now.

112

So, it decreases the workload on courts considerably and makes the entire justice train move that much faster. In all honesty however, it can't be called justice, especially if we look at the United States Constitution. We can lament endlessly about how beneficial it can be to most. And in that regard, it can probably even be considered a success. But for a minority, it is not justice, because they don't get a trial. Yes, they can ask for a trial and they will get a trial. But they won't get the time back they lose sitting in jail if they eventually will get one, at least not if it turns out they are innocent before the law.

The question then is should we turn a blind eye on the wrongfully accused or even the innocent for the benefit of most? I don't know about you; I can't speak for you. If I would be in a situation where somebody accuses me of a crime and I know, I didn't commit it, I would hate to be in jail for a year only to be acquitted at the end of a trial with a proper jury. Is my record going to be expunged if found innocent so I can move on with my life, doing anything and everything I used to do before with the same clean sheet of paper as before? No, it won't be.

6.   "Expungement" of Records

I love it when some inmates would come up to me and proudly announce how they are going to pay some obscure company $ 5000 or whatever the figure is to have their criminal history expunged or the record of any conviction deleted so that they will be able to move on with their lives.

It is a dream; that is the only thing that is. In my opinion, there is no such a thing as the deletion of your criminal record. Let's see, what expunge means in the dictionary:

"Obliterate or remove completely"

This is what the Oxford dictionary says about the word "expunge".

Let me make this clear to everyone and anybody, who thinks that there is such a thing: It does not exist. You can't delete your criminal record and it doesn't matter if you pay $ 5000 or $ 5 Million to anybody. From the time you have been booked into a jail, there is going to be a trail of your name, your date of birth and possibly your social security number, if applicable, not to mention your age, height and weight. From the moment you enter the criminal justice system, your information becomes public property. Your information will show up in arrest papers. These things are fairly common where I live. It is a newspaper type of publication listing all persons who have been arrested in various counties and municipalities, complete with your picture and the reason for the booking. And that is only the beginning. Your photograph has been taken by a jail official. It is now public property. It now goes around the world. Any person looking for your picture can now see with his/her own eyes that you are a criminal. And there is absolutely nothing you can do about it, not a single thing. And now you can go through court records of your jurisdiction and find your name and your information on official, publicly available court documents. And that is now public property as well. You might not have done anything; you might have been mixed up with another person or another person used your information to commit a crime. Whatever the circumstances might be, if you go to jail, you are branded for life. The only real question you have to ask yourself is how many people you come in contact with who care? And how many people believe, that you were wrongfully booked?

We read about misbehaving celebrities here and there. They got booked for drunk driving, some altercations at their home and what have you. But they don't apply for jobs. I mean, they do, but they are in the public's eye, because they already made some stuff, which caused us to recognize them. Otherwise, they wouldn't be celebrities, would they?

114

If we are talking about film stars, a film studio can now open a database with actors, who were aver booked in jails. And if the public outcry would be great and consistent enough to shun such behavior, they probably would. But the truth is we don't much care for drunken actors, because it is not a big issue and we know that. We all have been drunk at one point in our lives and it didn't amount to much but a big headache. So we sympathize with them.

But the general employer is not that forgiving, or your potential future mother-in-law. A quick search will reveal your past and if you didn't mention it already, they will automatically assume that you are a bad person because you weren't straight forward. Your idea of this whole subject of course is that you don't have to mention anything, because you weren't convicted, you were either innocent to begin with or whatever the circumstance might have been. There was just no reason to make people concerned about your past. That time is behind you so you think.

But in every job application I have ever filled out in this country, the question comes up of whether or not you have ever been convicted of a crime. And some employers are even compelled to add a little side note to the whole subject by trying to tell you that even if there is anything in your past, it doesn't mean that it would be counted as a negative point for you.

The law tells us the following on this subject and I am sorry that this one is a little lengthy, but I wanted to give you the whole picture.

§22-18. Expungement of records - Persons authorized.

A.   Persons authorized to file a motion for expungement, as provided herein, must be within one of the following categories:

1.   The person has been acquitted;

2.   The conviction was reversed with instructions to dismiss by an appellate court of competent jurisdiction, or an appellate court of competent jurisdiction reversed the conviction and the prosecuting agency subsequently dismissed the charge;

3.   The factual innocence of the person was established by the use of deoxyribonucleic acid (DNA) evidence subsequent to conviction, including a person who has been released from prison at the time innocence was established;

4.   The person has received a full pardon on the basis of a written finding by the Governor of actual innocence for the crime for which the claimant was sentenced;

5.   The person was arrested and no charges of any type, including charges for an offense different than that for which the person was originally arrested, are filed and the statute of limitations has expired or the prosecuting agency has declined to file charges

6. The person was under eighteen (18) years of age at the time the offense was committed and the person has received a full pardon for the offense;

7. The person was charged with one or more misdemeanor or felony crimes, all charges have been dismissed, the person has never been convicted of a felony, no misdemeanor or felony charges are pending against the person, and the statute of limitations for re-filing the charge or charges has expired or the prosecuting agency confirms that the charge or charges will not be re-filed; provided, however, this category shall not apply to charges that have been dismissed following the completion of a deferred judgment or delayed sentence;

8. The person was charged with a misdemeanor, the charge was dismissed following the successful completion of a deferred judgment or delayed sentence, the person has never been convicted of a felony, no misdemeanor or felony charges are pending against the person, and at least one (1) year has passed since the charge was dismissed;

9. The person was charged with a nonviolent felony offense, not listed in Section 571 of Title 57 of the Oklahoma Statutes, the charge was dismissed following the successful completion of a deferred judgment or delayed sentence, the person has never been convicted of a felony, no misdemeanor or felony charges are pending against the person, and at least five (5) years have passed since the charge was dismissed;

10. The person was convicted of a misdemeanor offense, the person was sentenced to a fine of less than Five Hundred One Dollars ($501.00) without a term of imprisonment or a suspended sentence, the fine has been paid or satisfied by time served in lieu of the fine, the person has not been convicted of a felony, and no felony or misdemeanor charges are pending against the person;

11. The person was convicted of a misdemeanor offense, the person was sentenced to a term of imprisonment, a suspended sentence or a fine in an amount greater than Five Hundred Dollars ($500.00), the person has not been convicted of a felony, no felony or misdemeanor charges are pending against the person, and at least five (5) years have passed since the end of the last misdemeanor sentence;

12. The person was convicted of a nonviolent felony offense, not listed in Section 571 of Title 57 of the Oklahoma Statutes, the person has received a full pardon for the offense, the person has not been convicted of any other felony, the person has not been convicted of a separate misdemeanor in the last fifteen (15) years, no felony or misdemeanor charges are pending against the person, and at least ten (10) years have passed since the felony conviction;

13. The person was convicted of not more than two nonviolent felony offenses, not listed in Section 571 of Title 57 of the Oklahoma Statutes, the person has received a full pardon for both of the nonviolent felony offenses, no felony or misdemeanor charges are pending against the person, and at least twenty (20) years have passed since the last misdemeanor or felony conviction; or

14. The person has been charged or arrested or is the subject of an arrest warrant for a crime that was committed by another person who has appropriated or used the person's name or other identification without the person's consent or authorization.

B. For purposes of this act, "expungement" shall mean the sealing of criminal records, as well as any public civil record, involving actions brought by and against the State of Oklahoma arising from the same arrest, transaction or occurrence.

C. For purposes of seeking an expungement under the provisions of paragraph 10, 11, 12 or 13 of subsection A of this section, offenses arising out of the same transaction or occurrence shall be treated as one conviction and offense.

D. Records expunged pursuant to paragraphs 8, 9, 10, 11, 12, 13 and 14 of subsection A of this section shall be sealed to the public but not to law enforcement agencies for law enforcement purposes. Records expunged pursuant to paragraphs 8, 9, 10, 11, 12 and 13 of subsection A of this section shall be admissible in any subsequent criminal prosecution to prove the existence of a prior conviction or prior deferred judgment without the necessity of a court order requesting the unsealing of the records. Records expunged pursuant to paragraph 4, 6, 12 or 13 of subsection A of this section may also include the sealing of Pardon and Parole Board records related to an application for a pardon. Such records shall be sealed to the public but not to the Pardon and Parole Board.

118

This whole idea of deleting your criminal record might have worked 25 years ago. This whole thing might have even worked before 9/11; but not today my friend. The creation of an electronic document in a database cannot be deleted easily. What can work for a prosecutor who is trying to recover deleted computer files in a child pornography case to his and our benefit also works the other way. The moment you click "Send" or "Publish" or "Enter" or any such commands into a computer network with computer servers, you made that information available to the world. Now I invite you to spend the next 50 years and an Army of people to hunt down anybody who might have downloaded that information which was entered a second ago. This is the modern age of information technology. And who knows what information federal agencies get? What crime categories for what people do they track? In other words, if you think part of your records or your entire record is ever going to be deleted, innocent or not, I am here to tell you that this is not going to happen, ever.

To go the plain legal way alone is an undertaking. And read it in 14 B, C and D above. Not many people have the legal right to file for expungement of records, but not many records are being deleted at all. In fact, the legal definition of expungement only means "sealing" of criminal records as you can read in 14B above. Nobody even uses the word "delete" or "destroy" for that matter. And if all these agencies can file to access your records as defined in 14D, it is easy to see, that your entire history is being kept, no matter what. Because in all honesty, who can tell what is going to happen in the future? Who can tell what crimes or misdemeanors are going to be re-classified? A few years down the road, a certain misdemeanor will be classified as a felony and vis versa. There just is no telling what is going to happen, which is why the courts rather keep your records. And as we see in their definition of the word expungement, they don't have to destroy or delete them to begin with.

And so your criminal record will follow you no matter where you go and what you do. It might not matter to most or it does matter to most but the matter of fact remains that it doesn't matter if you did your time for the crime. Your conviction will be permanent and some people take offense to people with former convictions, that is all there is to it. Some people prefer to hire someone with no criminal history of whatever kind. They just feel safer and assume their customers will feel safer as well.

7.   No voting rights

This point always struck me as odd in the United States.

Prisoners cannot vote, why is this so?

The person in question committed a crime; he needs to serve a specific amount of time in prison. It is clear, that person is restricted in his movements, what he can eat, where he can go, what TV channels he can watch. He normally cannot just leave the prison walls and conduct his normal life; he cannot work in the places he wants to work and a whole number of other opportunities and tasks reserved for the people who are not incarcerated. He needs to serve his punishment, which is the entire idea of punishment by imprisonment. So far, so good.

The question then is what would happen, if prisoners could vote? I am contemplating this subject for a while now and could not come up with a decent answer. You are still part of society and live within the framework of that society. The decisions lawmakers, politicians and panels make are still viable to you. Each new or changed law, which will be passed is still going to affect you after you served your time. You are not permanently deported to another planet or to another universe. When you leave prison, you walk right into the circumstances of the changes which took effect without your saying or input while you were gone.

§26-4-120.4. Convicted felons - Cancellation of registration - Liability.

A. The Secretary of the State Election Board shall accept written notice from the United States Attorney of persons convicted of felonies in a district court of the United States. The Secretary of the State Election Board shall cause the voter registrations of persons listed in the written notice to be cancelled in the county of the person's residence and shall notify the secretary of the appropriate county election board of the cancellation.

B. The court clerk in each county shall prepare a list monthly of all persons convicted in the county of a felony and shall transmit the list to the secretary of the county election board. The list shall include information necessary to identify a person on the list as a registered voter prescribed by the Secretary of the State Election Board. The secretary shall cancel the registration of registered voters in the county included on the list. The secretary of the county election board shall forward the names of any persons on the list who are not residents of the county to the Secretary of the State Election Board. The Secretary of the State Election Board shall cause the voter registrations of persons from a list who are forwarded to the Secretary to be cancelled in the county of the person's residence.

C. The Secretary of the State Election Board, secretaries of county election boards, and their agents and employees shall not be held civilly liable for any action taken based upon information concerning felony convictions received from a United States Attorney or a county court clerk pursuant to subsections A and B of this section if a reasonable effort was made to make an accurate match of the information provided with voter registration records before canceling any voter's registration.

Added by Laws 1981, c. 45, § 5, emerg. eff. April 8, 1981. Amended by Laws 1990, c. 331, § 10, eff. July 1, 1990; Laws 1994, c. 260, § 22, eff. Jan. 1, 1995; Laws 1995, c. 290, § 7, eff. Nov. 1, 1995; Laws 2002, c. 447, § 7, eff. July 1, 2003.

The above is a quote from the State of Oklahoma statute and refers to people who were convicted of a felony within the State.

If there are about 2 million people currently incarcerated in the United States that means that maybe about 1 million people cannot vote. This is a rough draft of course, because we have to deduct from the total number of 2 million the number of persons not convicted of a felony, since this law only applies to people with a felony conviction. I mean, where is the problem? I think it is added nonsense to further punish people who are incarcerated. It can be put up for discussion, if and what kind of an impact the deletion of that law could or would mean. What would happen to the political landscape if prisoners could vote? That is of course hard to say since it currently is purely hypothetical.

There is one or two more things worth mentioning on this subject. The length of time you cannot vote is not equal with the amount of time you spend in prison. The amount of time you cannot vote is equal to the amount of time written on a person's Judgment and Sentence. That is the document which is given to you by the judge. As mentioned in the "Good for inmates" section above, the level system allows a prisoner to shorten his sentence considerably. That does not account for his voting rights. 10 years of incarceration as ordered by the judge means ten years no voting rights.

ODOC policy OP-060901 puts it in simple terms on page 5:

I. Case managers will be responsible for informing and providing releasing inmates a copy of Attachment C entitled "Voter Rights for Convicted Felons" (attached) in accordance with 26 O.S. § 4-120.4.

1. **Inmates may vote once the period of time equal to the time prescribed in the judgment and sentence has been completed; for example, a person convicted on August 1, 2002 to a five year sentence cannot vote until August 1, 2007, regardless of the release date from prison.**

And in case you wonder what Attachment C is and what it says, wonder no longer, here it is:

Attachment C

OP-060901(R 6/17)

Voter Rights for Convicted Felons

26 O.S. §4-120.4

TO: Releasing Inmate

RE: Voter Registration Information

You are eligible to register to vote if you are a United States citizen, a resident of Oklahoma and at least 18 years of age. However, as a person who has been convicted of a felony, you may not register to vote or renew your voter registration until after the period of time it takes for your original judgment and sentence to expire. This means that although you may have been released from custody, you still must wait until your sentence expires before you can register to vote.

To register to vote you must fill out a voter registration application form. Voter applications are available at your county election board, post offices, tag agencies, libraries and many other public locations. You will be offered a voter registration application when you get your driver's license and when you apply for assistance atsome government agencies.

You may also download an application form from www.ok.gov/-elections/ or send a request to receive a form by U.S. mail. The application form asks for: your name and address; your political affiliation; your birth date; your driver's license number; and the last four digits for your Social Security number (required if no driver's license). You must sign and date the oath printed on the form. When you sign the voter registration application form, you swear that you are eligible to vote.

If you are incarcerated in the US, you are not only stripped off your freedom, which is fair and which is the whole point of being punished for your crime, you are also stripped off your voting rights. Why that is eludes my understanding and comprehension. It wouldn't be so hard to do either. It wouldn't be hard at all. For the most part, prisoners are incarcerated in their county of conviction. If you committed a crime in the county of Comanche for instance, you likely will be incarcerated in the county of Comanche. Of course, the DOC can move you around the State as they see fit. But even if they do, you still could be a legal resident of the county you had your last residential address. And thus, you could send in your voting documents as all military members can do who are located outside of the United States. I don't know why no prisoner tried to bring to a court a lawsuit related to that subject. I guess it is not so important to a convict. I must assume there are many other, more important factors in his life than caring for the subject matter of voting rights.

I reckon it probably is not very important to any prisoner. In fact, in my years within the DOC, that subject hardly ever came up, which is another indication of its relevancy. And if you look at how many people go to the polls and vote at all, it shouldn't come as a surprise. The percentage of people voting in the general public is probably reflected in the prison population.

And that is all fine and dandy, but if I look at this entire subject with the eyes of an outsider, I still need to wonder why no inmate can vote. It is really not so much a question of curiosity or popularity; I think it is a simple question of arbitrary administration. It would be interesting to see, what would happen if prisoners can vote. Because after all, I as a voter would look at the candidates and would look at their respective

124

programs and so on and would make my decision based on what I read, experienced in the past and hear from each candidate. And a prisoner is not going to stay in prison forever either, at least not in most cases. He will eventually get out and once again be a citizen.

So maybe in the future, prisoners will be able to vote again. I can't see why not. And if that happens, some parties and candidates will have some interesting points on their program.

I list this whole voting subject as a negative point for prisoners not because voting is very popular in prisons, but because to me and for my understanding, it just seems so arbitrary.

In practical terms this means the inmate is out of prison, gets a job, is again part of the working society, pays his taxes and so on and so forth, but he cannot influence the political structure of his environment. So even though he is for all goals and purposes no different than any other working member of the society, he is deprived of his voting rights. You might think that doing the time for your crime is the end of the story but it is not.

8.   Employment limitations

A lot of employers in the United States put this sentence into their job application sites: Have you ever been convicted of a crime?

It is a voluntary addition. It is not required by law. It is there because many corporations want it to be there. And even though it is not part of a law, it is also not against any law. The managers and personnel departments of many firms and businesses just want to know, if you have ever been convicted of a crime. Is this a fair undertaking? How is this a negative point for an inmate?

Well, actually and to be precise, it is not a negative point for an inmate. An inmate is somebody, who is still in prison and obviously we can't escort a whole bunch of inmates from the prison to a store and watch over them as they work which is, what would be required by law since we are responsible for the security and safety of all citizens. So that is out of the question. And even though many inmates can work as long as they are able to make it to a Community Corrections Center or to a Half Way house, roughly 95 % of all inmates cannot work. I want to make that distinction because for the purpose of this chapter, we are not exactly looking at inmates, but at released inmates.

Once again, you have done your time for the crime and are now ready to re-enter the working-class society. If you know somebody who could give you a hand, you are in luck. If you know a person who has known you all your working live and is more than willing to give you another chance, you are in luck. This is especially the case, if you have family members who own businesses. For them it makes sense to give you another chance because they have worked with you before and generally speaking, they don't expect for you to have completely changed your personality while incarcerated. And last but not least they probably have a certain amount of compassion, after all the inmate is still family. I have heard this many times before from inmates. After they discharge their sentence, they would go back to where they came from and work for their brother, cousin or for somebody in their family. This is a good outcome for an ex -felon.

If the person is not in that position, he has to look for a job on his own, just like anybody else on the job market and this is where certain limitations take effect. For some HR departments it is all about making the right decision. This is especially true for large companies. They make a simple calculation in their headquarters. Should we go through the potential troublesome trial in hiring a former inmate or should we avoid that obstacle altogether? And if you have a large pool of qualified candidates to choose from that decision is made pretty easy. If you hire someone with no criminal past and that employee messes up in one way or the other, than it was just a bad decision on the part of the HR department. If you hire a former inmate and he messes up, the

126

perception is that the hiring official should have known better in the first place.

Why do HR departments deem it a greater risk hiring former inmates? This is not very clear to me, never was. Yet to the outsider, this seems to be exactly what is going on, otherwise they could delete that sentence altogether, couldn't they? You could even make the case in favor of the inmate. You could even assume that the motivation of a former inmate to do his best on the job is slightly greater than in someone, who hasn't gone to prison. But this is not what is happening. What is happening is the opposite. There is obviously a perception in the job market that to hire a former inmate is not a good thing. Let me give you a real-life example.

When I worked in a Community Corrections Center, certain inmates are qualified to go out on the streets and look for jobs, while they are still incarcerated. This system has its limitations and doesn't apply to everyone in such institutions. One example would be the nature of your crime. If your crime doesn't fit into the violent crime category however, there is a good possibility that you can roam the streets of the neighborhood looking for a job. Simply put, we would drop inmates off at a certain point and a few hours later we would pick them up at a certain point. They will get an itinerary of where these points are. Now you have two points, one drop-off point and one pick up point and during the course of a few hours he or she can move between these two points, knock on doors and try to get a job. This whole procedure is by the way covered in DOC policy OP-090110.

I. Eligibility

A. Criteria

Inmates will meet the following criteria prior to assignment to work release:

127

1. Male inmates will have no more than 2,000 days remaining prior to placement on work release.

Female inmates will have no more than 2,500 days remaining prior to placement on work release.

2.   Inmates with a community/work release stipulation as approved or imposed by the Governor or recommended by the Pardon and Parole Board.

3.   Inmates who receive no earned credits due to a controlling, concurrent, or consecutive offense for drug trafficking or have prior Section-09 Programs OP-090110 Page: 3 Effective Date: 07/17/2017convictions for drug trafficking (57 O.S. § 510.1), are not eligible for work release until they have no more than 330 days remaining to serve.

4.   An active class "B" misconduct will not be sufficient grounds to deny work release/halfway house placement.

5.   Inmates are not required to spend 30 days at a community facility prior to work release/halfway house placement.

6.   Has no current sentence for any disqualifying "Crimes Against Children" as listed in OP-060104, Attachment A

7.   Inmates who have a controlling, concurrent or consecutive offense for Distribution of a Controlled Dangerous Substance Within 2,000Feet of a School, or Possession/ Purchase of a Controlled Dangerous Substance Within 1,000 Feet of a School are not eligible for work release until they have no more than 330 days remaining to serve.

8.   Inmates who have offenses in the highest crime category, active parole and suspended sentences excluded, (in accordance with OP-060102 (Male) (Female), DOC 060102A (M) (F) entitled "Initial

Custody Assessment/Facility Assignment Form") must have no more than 330 days remaining prior to placement on work release.

9.   Inmates must be assigned to earned credit level 3 or 4, to include enhanced level 3 and 4. Inmates assigned to level 2 should be submitted if they are level 2 due to being incarcerated for less than three months.

10. Inmates must be medically approved by the sending facility prior to assignment to work release status.

This is as far as the qualifications go. In other words, there are quite some limitations of who is qualified to be on Work Release. You can't have a violent crime unless you don't have more than 330 days left on your entire sentence. You have to be on a certain earned credit level, which is an indication that you can adhere to simple rules and regulations, which is covered in point 9 above. Work Release is not for everyone.

To get back to the example I mentioned earlier. Our inmates are not allowed in certain areas. Certain companies don't want the inmates to even come inside their facility, for no reason. The local Mall in our little town is completely off limits. Walmart is off limits. Hobby Lobby is off limits and many other stores which I don't bother to mention in their entirety. All these stores chose not to employ inmates. Now I can't tell you whether or not they would employ former inmates, this all depends on their corporate policy. But as far as current inmates are concerned and the often-mentioned reintegration into society, it certainly is a struggle because the current inmate already has all these limitations in just looking for a minimum wage job. You wouldn't think that minimum wage jobs are such an exclusive commodity, but for many companies, they apparently are.

More understandable are other limitations. For obvious reason, inmates cannot work in stores which deal mainly with guns or ammunition. They are excluded to work in day cares, hospitals and even churches, even though I really don't understand that church limitation. Why wouldn't inmates be able to work in churches, what is the story on this one? I don't know. But anyway, take it directly from the horses' mouth. In the same policy on page 6, the DOC gives you a rundown of all the employment limitations.

VII. Guidelines for Acceptable Employment

A. Employment Guidelines

The facility will be responsible to ensure inmates are approved for jobs that are located in areas that do not cause unnecessary risk to public safety.

1. Inmates must work for at least minimum wage and must be paid by payroll check, cashier's check, debit cards or money order. If payment is by cashier's check or money order, supporting documentation from the employer must be attached which indicates, at a minimum, actual hours worked and deductions. Inmates who are paid by debit card must provide a check stub for each pay period. Inmates cannot accept employment which pays by cash. For inmates receiving tips, cash received is required to be turned in after each shift when they return to the facility. The money will be counted in front of the inmate and facility staff, and both inmate and staff will sign documenting the amount. The inmate will receive a receipt for the amount the money will be placed in a Section-09 Programs OP-090110 Page: 7 Effective Date: 07/17/2017 sealed envelope, be placed in a safe and turned into the business office the following business day. The money will be deposited as outlined in OP-120230 entitled "Offender Banking System."

2. Inmates may not be self-employed or work for, or with, family members without the approval of the facility head.

3. Inmates may not work for commission only.

4. Inmates may not accept end-of-contract payment, defined as payment upon completion of a job. Inmates may not work as day laborers with payment at the end of the day by companies or individuals. Temporary employment agencies may be used for employment; however, this excludes employment by individuals. Payment must be weekly or bi-weekly. Employers will provide workers compensation insurance coverage to all employed inmates.

5. Inmates may not work where the primary business is the sale of alcoholic beverages or weapons.

6. Inmates may not work in day-care facilities, hospitals, nursing homes or churches.

7. Inmates may not accept employment more than 30 miles from the contract facility, unless approved by the facility head. Executive Review inmates may have additional requirements.

8. Employment must be full time, preferably no less than 30 hours per week.

a. Secondary employment may be approved.

b. Full time employment may be acquired through a temporary agency.

c. An exception may be approved for inmates who receive Veterans' Administration (VA) disability.

(1) Inmates who receive VA disability may have 100% of their benefits reinstated when placed on work release status as referenced in OP-120230 entitled "Offender Banking System" and will have all disbursement checks mailed to the host facility.

(2) These inmates will not be required to work outside the facility if their disability precludes them from employment.

9. Effective January 1, 2016, inmates will be awarded achievement credits for reentry programs available in specified facilities and

programs as references in OP-060211 entitled "Sentence Administration."

Not all is bad for the inmate as far as employment goes in other words. The DOC tries to give eligible inmates an opportunity for meaningful employment and re-integration. But this whole "former conviction" moniker is not really a DOC problem to begin with. It is more like a society problem and how this one wants to deal with former inmates. The EEO laws provide protection for certain categories of people. To remind you what it is, here is a quote from their website:

The U.S. Equal Employment Opportunity Commission (EEOC) is responsible for enforcing federal laws that make it illegal to discriminate against a job applicant or an employee because of the person's race, color, religion, sex (including pregnancy, gender identity, and sexual orientation), national origin, age (40 or older), disability or genetic information. It is also illegal to discriminate against a person because the person complained about discrimination, filed a charge of discrimination, or participated in an employment discrimination investigation or lawsuit.

It doesn't protect against the real or perceived negative effects of hiring a former criminal. This whole subject of equal employment opportunities is obviously a little bit elusive. We don't have to kid each other by assuming or claiming that it can be anything more than a guideline for employment. If you as the head of HR or the manager of a branch responsible for hiring look at all your candidates at hand, you will choose the one, which you think is right for the job. You normally would put all the good and the bad in a can and come up with what you believe is the best candidate. Does that include your own, personal opinion and perceptions? Of course it does, you are a human, not a robot. That is part of life as a hiring and firing official and we don't have to pretend that personal factors are not involved.

So back to the inmate and his chances for employment. As long as corporate policy doesn't exclusively state not to hire former inmates, there are no problems or official restrictions in hiring formerly incarcerated persons. We should simply look at these restrictions as what they are: Fear. Every hiring official needs to be able to justify his or her decision. And to exclude former inmates is just one factor in their decision-making process, which could potentially bite them.

I don't intent to make a case for former inmates other than putting them on the same level as everybody else after they served their time. I think it is only fair. You have done your time, now move on with your life and welcome back to society. This however is not how it seems to work.

9.   Enhancing crime categories

The enhancing of punishments for the same type of crime is a new idea, which probably developed out of sheer frustration. A lot of stupid people would do a lot of stupid things and when they served time for the stupid things they did, they would come right back and do it again. And along with that behavior, you apparently also had more people doing stupid things. So, somebody in the federal government or wherever had this idea to lengthen the times an inmate will spend behind bars for certain crime categories, if he committed that same type of crime more than one time. It was meant as both a deterrent and as a punishment. One of the assumptions was, that people would think twice about committing certain types of crimes again since now they could be locked up for the same type of crime three times longer. Only nobody seemed to care too much. The net result was that more people ended up behind bars and for longer periods of time.

Now to list this as a negative point for criminals is debatable. One might think that they sure deserve what they got coming by being so stupid to commit the same crime again, and again. And people who follow that line of logic can't be too wrong, because on the surface it makes sense, so far so good. After all, this whole subject of enhancing crime categories was not accomplished by some lunatic, crazy person in a closet, but by learned and professional law makers in a somewhat open session in some courtroom or big hall with wood paneling and comfortable chairs. It was done by the people we voted into office. And for better or for worse, we trusted these people in doing the right thing. And where did we arrive at after all these years? The highest incarceration rate of any modern democracy. At first glance I have to admit, that doesn't mean a lot. Who should care that we have the highest incarceration rate of all modern or western democracies. After all, if people break the law and break the law repeatedly, we will lock them up, this is how the system works. Does that mean that people tend to be more criminal in the United States than in other countries? If you look at the number of citizens in prisons you would not be mistaken to make that assumption. It is a simple calculation after all.

If you think that the percentage of people who are willing to commit crimes and who do commit crimes in this country is that much higher here than in other countries, you don't even have to read this chapter, because then this all makes sense. The overcrowding of prisons make sense, the enhancing of crime categories make sense whereby you will be locked up for the same crime that much longer, the whole subject of Plea Bargains makes sense since nobody has time to provide anybody with a fair and speedy trial anymore and the fortified, gated communities make sense, where nobody can even come close to a compound without having the proper access card.

As for me, I still try to make things better because I realize that the number of prisoners might be high, but the number of people who are really evil or bad and don't want to do anything good for themselves or anybody is quite low. I think most people will respond to treatment and respect. When you are thrown into a pack of vicious and hungry hyenas, you yourself need to become alike to survive. Unfortunately, the system doesn't make that distinction. For the justice system, one

134

prisoner equals the other prisoner equals the next prisoner. Triple murderers and rapist walk among people who got caught one too many times with a little amount of dope. Or people who struggle with a drinking problem are faced with a prison gang, which gives him no option but to join them or die.

To make a case for inmates is not an easy thing in this country, this is especially true when you work in Corrections since there is no room to make distinctions between inmates. Thus, this chapter applies to the majority of inmates, who are willing to pay for their crime and get on with their lives. Right now, this is not an easy thing to do. But I personally believe that we developed a habit of distance. We seem to have developed this notion to distance ourselves from everything and anything which is prison. Only until one of our own family members is doing time behind bars do we sometimes realize how quickly the tides can turn. All of a sudden prison comes to one of us to remind everybody, that we all have done wrong in life to a bigger or lesser degree and we are so quick to judge.

I think the enhancement of crime categories has been taken too far. But what are we talking about to begin with? This is how it works:

§21-51.1. Second and subsequent offenses after conviction of offense punishable by imprisonment in the State Penitentiary.

A. Except as otherwise provided in the Elderly and Incapacitated Victim's Protection Program and Section 3 of this act, every person who, having been convicted of any offense punishable by imprisonment in the State Penitentiary, commits any crime after such conviction, within ten (10) years of the date following the completion of the execution of the sentence, and against whom the District Attorney seeks to enhance punishment pursuant to this section of law, is punishable therefor as follows:

1. If the offense for which the person is subsequently convicted is an offense enumerated in Section 571 of Title 57 of the Oklahoma Statutes and the offense is punishable by imprisonment in the State Penitentiary for a term exceeding five (5) years, such person is punishable by imprisonment in the State Penitentiary for a term in the range of ten (10) years to life imprisonment.

2. If the offense of which such person is subsequently convicted is such that upon a first conviction an offender would be punishable by imprisonment in the State Penitentiary for any term exceeding five (5) years, such person is punishable by imprisonment in the State Penitentiary for a term in the range of twice the minimum term for a first time offender to life imprisonment. If the subsequent felony offense does not carry a minimum sentence as a first time offender, such person is punishable by imprisonment in the State Penitentiary for a term in the range of two (2) years to life imprisonment.

3. If such subsequent offense is such that upon a first conviction the offender would be punishable by imprisonment in the State Penitentiary for five (5) years, or any less term, then the person convicted of such subsequent offense is punishable by imprisonment in the State Penitentiary for a term not exceeding ten (10) years.

4. If such subsequent conviction is for petit larceny, the person convicted of such subsequent offense is punishable by imprisonment in the State Penitentiary for a term not exceeding five (5) years.

B. Every person who, having been twice convicted of felony offenses, commits a subsequent felony offense which is an offense enumerated in Section 571 of Title 57 of the Oklahoma Statutes, within ten (10) years of the date following the completion of the execution of the sentence, and against whom the District Attorney seeks to enhance punishment pursuant to this section of law, is punishable by imprisonment in the State Penitentiary for a term in the range of twenty (20) years to life imprisonment. Felony offenses relied upon shall not have arisen out of the same transaction or occurrence or series of events closely related in time and location.

Nothing in this section shall abrogate or affect the punishment by death in all crimes now or hereafter made punishable by death.

C. Every person who, having been twice convicted of felony offenses, commits a subsequent felony offense within ten (10) years of the date following the completion of the execution of the sentence, and against whom the District Attorney seeks to enhance punishment pursuant to this section of law, is punishable by imprisonment in the State Penitentiary for a term in the range of three times the minimum term for a first time offender to life imprisonment. If the subsequent felony offense does not carry a minimum sentence as a first time offender, the person is punishable by imprisonment in the State Penitentiary for a term in the range of four (4) years to life imprisonment. Felony offenses relied upon shall not have arisen out of the same transaction or occurrence or series of events closely related in time and location. Nothing in this section shall abrogate or affect the punishment by death in all crimes now or hereafter made punishable by death.

Added by Laws 1999, 1st Ex.Sess., c. 5, § 434, eff. July 1, 1999. Amended by Laws 2001, c. 437, § 3, eff. July 1, 2001; Laws 2002, c. 455, § 1, emerg. eff. June 5, 2002.

§21-51.1a. Second offense of rape in the first degree, forcible sodomy, lewd molestation or sexual abuse of a child.

Any person convicted of rape in the first degree, forcible sodomy, lewd molestation or sexual abuse of a child after having been convicted of either rape in the first degree, forcible sodomy, lewd molestation or sexual abuse of a child shall be sentenced to life without parole.

Added by Laws 2002, c. 455, § 3, emerg. eff. June 5, 2002.

§21-51.2. Second and subsequent offenses 10 years after completion of sentence.

Except as provided in Section 3 of this act, no person shall be sentenced as a second and subsequent offender under Section 51.1 of this title, or any other section of the Oklahoma Statutes, when a period of ten (10) years has elapsed since the completion of the sentence imposed on the former conviction; provided, said person has not, in the meantime, been convicted of a misdemeanor involving moral turpitude or a felony. Nothing in this section shall prohibit the use of a prior conviction for physical or sexually related child abuse as a prior conviction for second and subsequent offender purposes if the person is presently charged with a felony crime involving physical or sexually related child abuse.

Added by Laws 1999, 1st Ex.Sess., c. 5, § 435, eff. July 1, 1999. Amended by Laws 2000, c. 245, § 2, eff. Nov. 1, 2000; Laws 2002, c. 455, § 2, emerg. eff. June 5, 2002.

In case of 4B above, an initial term of up to 10 years in prison can turn into life upon a second conviction. To look at these terms realistically, ten years in prison would normally amount to roughly three to four years since you can earn credits for good behavior and after that, there is always the possibility of parole. As far as a 20 years long sentence goes, that can lead up to 10 years in prison even with credits for good behavior. And if the prosecutor convinces the judge successfully that you not only committed a felony crime for the second time but you are also prone to ignore the law due to having several outstanding parking or speeding tickets, these ten years can turn into quite a lengthy sentence.

Even point 2 above is remarkable. It basically says the same as in 4B, except it says, that even if the felony conviction does not carry a minimum term, you still can be receiving a term of 2 years to life in prison. This chapter basically says that no matter what you did and what you are charged with, if you commit a felony offense for the second time, all cards are on the table. Your life is in the prosecutor's hand; and of course, in the hand of your attorney. You really don't want to put yourself in that situation and I think that is exactly the point, the law makers were trying to make when these laws were put into effect. They wanted to make it extraordinary repulsive to commit felony crimes. They wanted to clearly make that statement: Don't commit crimes, don't come to prison, because if you do, there is nothing good waiting for you. Now we also understand the Plea Bargain a little better and why they came to be so popular. The prosecutor threatens you with life, you accept 10 years, case closed, next one. And in case you wonder what type of crimes we are talking about. Section 571 of Oklahoma Title 57 is mentioned several times, because it lists all types of crimes, which fall into that category. Whenever anybody talks about a felony crime, then you can take that list and find out, what they are talking about. For reference I listed it below:

2. "Violent crime" means any of the following felony offenses and any attempts to commit or conspiracy or solicitation to commit the following crimes:

a.   assault, battery, or assault and battery with a dangerous or deadly weapon;

b.   shooting with intent to kill, assault, battery, or assault and battery with a deadly weapon or by other means likely to produce death or great bodily harm, as provided for in Section 652 of the Oklahoma Statutes;

c.   aggravated assault and battery on a police officer, sheriff, highway patrolman, or any other officer of the law;

d.   poisoning with intent to kill;

e.   shooting with intent to kill;

f.   assault with intent to kill;

g.   assault with intent to commit a felony;

h.   assaults while masked or disguised;

i. murder in the first degree;

j. murder in the second degree;

k. manslaughter in the first degree;

l. manslaughter in the second degree;

m. kidnapping;

n. burglary in the first degree;

o. burglary with explosives;

p. kidnapping for extortion;

q. maiming;

r. robbery;

s. robbery in the first degree;

t. robbery in the second degree;

u. armed robbery;

v. robbery by two (2) or more persons;

w. robbery with dangerous weapon or imitation firearm;

x. child abuse;

y. wiring any equipment, vehicle or structure with explosives;

z. forcible sodomy;

aa. rape in the first degree;

bb. rape in the second degree;

cc.   rape by instrumentation;

dd.   lewd or indecent proposition or lewd or indecent act with a child;

ee.   use of a firearm or offensive weapon to commit or attempt to commit a felony;

ff.   pointing firearms;

gg.   rioting;

hh.   inciting to riot;

ii.   arson in the first degree;

jj.   injuring or burning public buildings;

kk.   sabotage;

ll.   criminal syndicalism;

mm.   extortion;

nn.   obtaining signature by extortion;

oo.   seizure of a bus, discharging firearm or hurling missile at bus;

pp.   mistreatment of a mental patient;

qq.   using a vehicle to facilitate the discharge of a weapon pursuant to Section 652 of Title 21 of the Oklahoma Statutes;

rr.   bombing offenses as defined in Section 1767.1 of Title 21 of the Oklahoma Statutes;

ss.   child pornography or aggravated child pornography as
        defined in Section 1021.2, 1021.3, 1024.1 or 1040.12a of
        Title 21 of the Oklahoma Statutes;

tt.   child prostitution as defined in Section 1030 of Title 21 of
        the Oklahoma Statutes;

uu.   abuse of a vulnerable adult as defined in Section 10-103 of
        Title 43A of the Oklahoma Statutes who is a resident of a
        nursing facility;

vv.   aggravated trafficking as provided for in subsection C of
        Section 2-415 of Title 63 of the Oklahoma Statutes;

ww.   aggravated assault and battery upon any person defending
        another person from assault and battery;

xx.   human trafficking as provided for in Section 748 of Title 21
        of the Oklahoma Statutes; or

yy.   terrorism crimes as provided in Sections 1268 et seq. of
        Title 21 of the Oklahoma Statutes.

If you really want to get into it, some of these crime categories
are just listed but to fully understand them, you would have to look them
up in the sections mentioned. For instance, "yy" Is terrorism, which has
specific definitions, which they don't include in Section 571. Most of
these crimes are pretty self-explanatory, there are however several,
which can have a wide spread of definitions and circumstances. Every
case is different and if you look at "ee", there is probably a wide range of
possible ways, your case could turn. What is an offensive weapon? What
does "attempt to commit a felony" even mean? Let's look at one made
up example. You heard or observed that one of your next-door neighbors
is out of town. You visited him once or twice picking up something,
borrowing a cup of sugar or what have you and thus you know, that
there is no alarm system or cameras. So, you set out at night to go over
to his house to rob the place. For good measure, you have a multi tool in

142

your pocket, to prey open a door or unscrew a metal mesh or whatever. Halfway to your neighbor's house, you get a phone call and for one or the other reason, you abandon your original plan. You turn around and let it be. Per definition, this however could be already a felony. Or does attempting to commit a felony start with you entering his house?

This of course is the playing field of lawyers and prosecutors, going into the nitty, gritty details of things to either enhance a point for the prosecutor or to disprove one for the lawyer.

The point of enhancement of punishment for the same crime or for felony crimes in general is a rather noble idea. I guess it is supposed to be part of this whole "hard on crime" subject matter which came into being after the drug wars in the seventies. The lawmakers, who are our elected officials, wanted to send a loud and clear message to everybody who thought about robbing anybody, dealing in drugs and other crimes. They wanted to put an end to these types of crimes. And every normal person couldn't help but applaud this notion. What is wrong with punishing somebody harder a second time around, after he/she commits a felony crime for the second time? Who in the world could possibly see a problem with that? After all, that is what we used to do with our children. And that is what our parents used to do to us, when we were their children. If you do something wrong, you get the waving finger. If you do it a second time, your weekly allowance might get cut and so on. It was not a totally unfamiliar procedure and most people could relate to it which is probably why it was so easily passed.

And as is the case with kids, it might work and it might not work in the field of criminal justice. You tell your kids that smoking is bad yet you can clearly smell the cigarette in her breath one day when she came back one evening from a friend's house. She had to try it no matter what you told her. And it goes on from there. You can do only so much. You can basically show your kids the doors to a healthy, crime-free life but in the end, it will be up to them to choose the correct path.

143

As far as the criminal justice system is concerned and the subject matter of enhanced crime categories, when something works, it should be kept in place. If the United States of America has so many more criminals than other, modern democracies, than the system works. If the US has 10 times the criminals than other countries, than our justice system is good because then it would be just and fair. Ten times the number of criminals equals ten times the amount of inmate's, it would be a simple calculation.

If it turns out there are other factors involved in the criminal justice system and the United States doesn't have ten times more criminals per 100 000 citizens, than we need to do something about it.

I think the truth demands more than one simple answer. I think it is a combination of things. But I do know, that enhancing crime categories hasn't worked out as good as we thought it would, I think it is safe to make that claim which is why this system is really not only a negative point for inmates, but for me as well as the person who pays for it.

10.   Private Prisons

If a person commits a crime, he/she is sentenced to the custody of the Department of Corrections, which is a State owned and State run facility. The inmate was prosecuted by the "people" of the State. If he was given a trial, he was sentenced by a selection of his peers as the justice system calls it and as the constitution calls it. Since the State makes, approves, adopts and puts into effect the laws of the State, it is only fair and just that the State is responsible for not only the prosecution of people who break the law, but also for their incarceration. And people get booked by the Police, also a State run and State-owned operation.

Somewhere along this line, I'd say about 1986, a person had a seemingly bright idea. That idea was to privatize prisons. As in any other privately owned and privately ran corporation, the purpose of a firm is to make a profit at one point in time. Depending on the nature of the business, this might take a while because you have to earn enough money first to pay for your investments. Building prisons is not a cheap undertaking. But as history can tell us and as the stock market can tell us, businesses involved in private prisons are doing ok, none has gone under yet, sold maybe, but not gone under.

Title 57 Section 502 defines private prisons:

8. "Private prison contractor" means:

a. a nongovernmental entity or public trust which, pursuant to a contract with the Department of Corrections, operates an institution within the Department other than a halfway house or intermediate sanctions facility, or provides for the housing, care, and control of inmates and performs other functions related to these responsibilities within a minimum, medium, or maximum security level facility not owned by the Department but operated by the contractor, or

b.a nongovernmental entity or public trust which, pursuant to a contract with the United States or another state, provides for the housing, care, and control of minimum or medium security inmates in the custody of the United States or another state, and performs other functions related to these responsibilities other than a halfway house or intermediate sanctions facility within a facility owned or operated by the contractor.

Some lawmakers decided in other words, that there is one section in the criminal justice system, which doesn't have to be State owned or State run. This subject matter is open for discussion I suppose. Where do we start to replace State functions with private contractors and where do we stop? We now know the answer to the first part of the question. Of course, it is not the first private institution, which is trusted to do the State's job. This honor goes to the private war contractors, who get enlisted to provide protection for State officials in enemy territories.

It is the State's responsibility to protect their citizens. Maybe that is the reason, why they didn't privatize part of the police force yet, because why stop at prisons? Because the public outrage would be enormous, if the police force or parts of the government would be privatized. Can you imagine a for profit police force? How often do you already hear the complaints about how the police always tries to catch you speeding in a section of a street, where you just come off a 75 miles per hour rush and you slow down, because it's 40 now. Any statement of the obvious is not going to help you, the trooper still wants his $ 40 or whatever the amount is. The people probably would not be in favor of privatizing any part of the police force.

How about judges and prosecutors, they don't have monetary motives. A judge gets about $ 120 000 a year and there is not much a judge can do to enhance his income in one way or the other. He could get some chickens and sell eggs, buy storage lockers and sell their content online, things of that nature. The real question is, can you privatize the duties of a judge? Even if you have a private judge, that judge would need to be monitored by another judge to make sure that State laws are followed.

That is not so much the case in a prison setting. Yes, private prison contractors need to follow the same rules, laws and policies as State prisons, but if 2500 inmates are locked up in one private prison, then you also have 2500 people who will cry murder if that prison contractor does anything wrong and I think the State counts on that as well. The private prison contractor I think is under heavy scrutiny as far as following the rules and regulations of prisons are concerned, because if anything is found to be wrong and the contractor can be held responsible for it, a heavy fine will be accessed, which is not something the contractor wants, because he will lose money.

146

The State of Oklahoma provides in Title 57 Section 561.1 the following for proposals to become a contractor:

C. A contractor proposing to enter a contract with the Department of Corrections for construction or operation, or both, of a correctional facility pursuant to this section must demonstrate:

1. The qualifications and the operations and management experience to carry out the terms of the contract; and

2. The ability to comply with the standards of the American Correctional Association and with specific court orders.

D. In addition to meeting the requirements specified in the requests for proposals, a proposal for the construction and operation of a correctional facility must:

1. Provide for regular, on-site monitoring by the Department of Corrections;

2. Acknowledge that payment by the state is subject to the availability of appropriations;

3. Provide for payment of a maximum amount per fiscal year;

4. Demonstrate a cost benefit to the State of Oklahoma when compared to the level and quality of programs provided by state-operated facilities that have similar types of inmates at an operational cost not more than the cost of housing inmates in similar facilities and providing similar programs to those types of inmates in state-operated facilities. The Department of Corrections shall be responsible for determining the cost/benefit of the proposal;

5. Permit the state to terminate the contract for cause;

6. Contain a proposed per diem operational cost per inmate for the initial year and subsequent years of operations;

7. Subject to appropriations, provide that cost adjustments may be made only once each fiscal year, to take effect at the beginning of the next fiscal year using as the maximum percentage increase, if any, an increase not to exceed the previous year's Consumer Price Index for All Urban Consumers (CPI-U) as prepared by the United States Bureau of Labor Statistics, except as otherwise provided by subsection K of this section;

8. Have an initial contract term of not more than one (1) year, with an option to renew for additional periods not to exceed twenty (20) years;

9. If the proposal includes construction of a facility, contain a performance bond approved by the Department that is adequate and appropriate for the proposed contract;

10. Provide for assumption of liability by the private vendor for all claims arising from the services performed under the contract by the private vendor;

11. Provide for an adequate plan of insurance for the private vendor and its officers, employees, and agents against all claims, including claims based on violations of civil rights arising from the services performed under the contract by the private vendor;

12. Provide for an adequate plan of insurance to protect the state against all claims arising from the services performed under the contract by the private vendor and to protect the state from actions by a third party against the private vendor, its officers, employees, and agents as a result of the contract;

13. Provide plans for the purchase and assumption of operations by the state in the event of the bankruptcy of the private vendor; and

14. Contain comprehensive standards for conditions of confinement.

That doesn't sound too bad, doesn't it, sounds like anybody could do that who can come up with the initial cost of constructing a

148

prison facility in the first place. I read the contract the State of Oklahoma has with one private prison contractor, which is available in the Law Library or at least used to be. I am just not up to date on that subject. But why did I mention Private Prisons as a bad thing for inmates to begin with? What is wrong with the fact that the State wants to save some money? Well, because as the saying goes, there is more than one way to skin a cow.

The subject of saving money is probably one of the things, which the private prison contractors and the law makers will tell you as the main reason, why private prisons are necessary, after all it is point number four in the text mentioned above. It says demonstrate a cost benefit to the State. As you can read if you do a little research on this subject, this point is highly debatable. But before I get into the trials and tribulations of being housed in a privately run prison facility, I need to mention one more thing, which is not commonly known.

As you can see in point 2 above, the private prisons must be able to adhere to the standards of something which calls itself the American Correctional Association. And by the way, State owned prisons must accomplish the same thing. Who is this ACA? No, it's not the affordable care act. But you can go to aca.org and find out everything about them. It is basically a private, non-profit organization which develops rules and policies for corrections institutions. It sets forth standards for prisons. And if you read their declaration of principles, which you find in the section "About Us" on their website, you can get a sense of what the public mind in this country looked like in 1870 as far as prisoners are concerned. It is really a journey back in time. But the ACA also mentioned that even though these principles might sound a little outdated as far as the language is concerned, they are nevertheless still true today. And I for one must concur, because it is so human and respectful. If you work in corrections for a while and you come across these written principles, you can't help but take a step back in awe and wonder. And you must think for yourself: What ever happened to this country? What ever happened to the corrections system in America? I

149

am not going to bore you to death with the manuscript of the ACA and the endless little and big points each corrections institution must follow to gain ACA accreditation. And the other reason I am not going to do that, because you have to pay for it. But I will quote some of the principles of the ACA because it is just too good not to include it.

VII. Special training, as well as high qualities of head and heart, is required to make a good prison or reformatory officer. Then only will the administration of public punishment become scientific, uniform and successful, when it is raised to the dignity of a profession, and men are specially trained for it, as they are for other pursuits.

VIII. Peremptory sentences ought to be replaced by those of indeterminate length.

Sentences limited only by satisfactory proof of reformation should be substituted for those measured by mere lapse of time.

XII. A system of prison discipline, to be truly reformatory, must gain the will of the convict. He is to be amended; but how is this possible with his mind in a state of hostility? No system can hope to succeed, which does not secure this harmony of wills, so that the prisoner shall choose for himself what his officer chooses for him. But, to this end, the officer must really choose the good of the prisoner, and the prisoner must remain in his choice long enough for virtue to become a habit. This consent of wills is an essential condition of reformation.

XIV. The prisoner's self-respect should be cultivated to the utmost, and every effort made to give back to him his manhood. There is no greater mistake in the whole compass of penal discipline, than its studied imposition of degradation as a part of punishment. Such imposition destroys every better impulse and aspiration. It crushes the weak, irritates the strong, and indisposes all to submission and reform. It is trampling where we ought to raise, and is therefore as unchristian in principle as it is unwise in policy.

XIX. Prisons, as well as prisoners, should be classified or graded so that there shall be prisons for the untried, for the incorrigible and for other degrees of depraved character, as well as separate establishments for women, and for criminals of the younger class.

XXXII. As a general rule, the maintenance of penal institutions, above the county jail, should be from the earnings of their inmates, and without cost to the state; nevertheless, the true standard of merit in their management is the rapidity and thoroughness of reformatory effect accomplished thereby.

XXXV. It is our conviction that one of the most effective agencies in the repression of crime would be the enactment of laws by which the education of all the children of the state should be made obligatory. Better to force education upon the people than to force them into prison to suffer for crimes, of which the neglect of education and consequent ignorance have been the occasion, if not the cause.

It is quite a document. You should read it in its entirety, it makes for some surprising realizations of how our forefathers looked at the whole subject of prisons. It can also serve as a humble reminder of what could have been would we as a Nation adhere more to these principles. I already mentioned in "Exposure to violence" how inmates of all types are being locked up together. This is covered as a negative point in XIX above and for good reasons. Another interesting fact is that in 1870 they deemed it completely sustainable and logical to make inmates pay for their own stay. And I quote once more: **"As a general rule, the maintenance of penal institutions, above the county jail, should be from the earnings of their inmates, and without cost to the state."** Now isn't that rather interesting.

These days, hardly any of these principles are left or are even looked at in a serious manner it seems. The principle of letting the inmate work for his stay would accomplish so much. Give some meaning to the inmate and save us all some money. That sounds almost too good to be true. And these days it probably is. Certain entities were very successful with their endeavor to create this public opinion that all inmates are bad people and basically possessed by the devil. All inmates should be locked up forever and completely separated from society. That is more or less the attitude which you find today. And talk to some people among your family and friends, not to mention corrections officials on various levels, and you will find pretty much the same mental image. Yet the original idea in corrections was to separate the "incorrigible" and other "depraved characters" so that others who are incarcerated can be provided with work and education possibilities. That distinction is not part of corrections anymore. Even though inmates with non-violent crimes and such have the possibility to move to lower-level security facilities and such, that number is relatively low compared to the total number of inmates. Just count the number of inmates in Half Way houses and Community Corrections facilities and compare that to the total number of people incarcerated.

It's time than to come to the essence of this point, which is Private Prisons. As I already pointed out, prisons are the only arm of the government which saw privatization. There is no private army of police officers, there is no private army of judges or prosecutors. There are some private institutions which work with the Department of Human Services and such, but this Department in itself is not a private place of work either. I am not really sure what event spiked this interest in private prisons, or maybe it was a series of events, a culmination of desperate attempts to curb the rising prison costs. When the incarceration rates spiked in the mid-seventies, some people probably put their heads together to look for solutions. Along came somebody who made a convincing proposal to the law makers. Realizing that the government is a pretty slow-moving mass of molasses and that it takes decades to really affect long lasting changes, he opened up a simple calculation. "Look" he said, "right now you are spending $ 50 on one inmate per day in any of your current prisons, give more or less. You have a whole bunch of corrections officers working in each prison, the inmate/corrections officer ratio is pretty high. Just look at Timbuktu. Their system works on a ratio of 1 to 300. Now, I am not saying that this can work here as well, but I will say that you can save a lot of money by bending this ratio a little bit better in favor of your overall cost of operation You also have a whole bunch of long term employees who get a lot of money for the same job as completely new officers and who also will get a whole lot of money for doing nothing when they retire. Look at your retirement accounts, it's already at 15% your wages budget. Where is this going to be in another 20 years? You are asking for disaster here. You have to do something about it especially with the current, exploding rate of incarcerations, otherwise it's not going to be pretty. You have to get these costs down. The incarceration rate already climbed 12% from here to there. Give it another 10 years and you are going to be completely overwhelmed financially and the people are not going to like it. Get ready for some pretty angry customers. But you can be the one who can be remembered for having found a solution. This is where we come in. We will get you a prison which will house 1500 of your medium security inmates for $ 38 per inmate per day".

That sounds fantastic, doesn't it. If a private facility can house an inmate for $ 38 instead of the current $ 50, that not only a saves $ 12 per inmate per day, it is $ 18 000 a day for 1500 inmates. That is unheard of, who would not like that. And there are no extra costs for medical, there are no extra costs for retirement accounts, there are no extra costs anywhere. Who would not just love that idea? It is an absolute no-brainer, that is what that is, so it seems.

Of course, over the years, State prison administrators learned a thing or two from the same people they rewarded these contracts to, that you can save costs if you do incarceration a little bit more cost efficient and they did. So much so that over the years, these costs leveled each other out because two things happened. One thing was that the private contractor raised the cost per inmate over the years so that after the first ten years of that facility in operation, the cost per inmate was not $ 38 anymore, but $ 48. And for two, State administrators themselves looked and learned from private companies so that their costs were now on the same level as the private prisons, if not lower.

But by that time, dozens of private prisons were already built, the State's laws were already changed to allow for private prisons to begin with. The whole money machine in other words was rolling like a steam train and if there was anybody who seriously would doubt or even think about putting a stop to this, well, there was now enough money to go around.

That accounts for the State. But why is the private prison bad for the inmate or for me?

Morally it is the State's responsibility to take care of inmates. That has been the case for 250 years on this continent alone and was the case for a good reason. The State provides the laws which puts an inmate behind bars, the State provides the prosecutor and the judge as well as the jury if necessary to convict the inmate.

The idea of private prisons is the same idea of paying a prosecutor per person he successfully prosecutes. In other words, the fuller the prison is, the more money is to be made. It is the same idea than paying a juror per person he/she puts behind bars. The State as part of their contract with the private contractor has the obligation to send a certain number of inmates to that facility or otherwise pay a fine in one way or the other. The State also has the option to pay out the contractor and take over the complete facility at certain points. If the State can no longer fill that particular facility, they can buy the prison for a price. Well, good luck with that. It's a catch 22. If the State succeeds in lowering the amount of people they put behind bars, they are now faced with the need to buy a prison no one needs anymore. Either way, the State loses. They pay a premium for the incarceration of people at a price they no longer can afford and if they don't need that private facility anymore, they have to buy it. Then they will have a 1500 inmates housing unit sitting in their municipality they just had to buy for $ 200 000 000 and no use for it.

The reason why a private prison is bad for the inmate is the same why it is bad for me. Just like any other company, private prisons have the purpose of making money. If a company sells T-shirts and they can't increase their T-shirt sales over the years, they eventually will falter, because the costs for producing T-shirts is not going to go down, they will go up. To keep good employees, they need to pay out bonuses or slowly but surely raise the pay. Electrical companies will raise their prices for power supply to that T-shirt business, fuel costs and prices for raw materials will rise.

A private prison doesn't want to lose inmates. They want more inmates, the more the better. If it would be up to them, they will build two more prisons in the same State. It is a very simple business calculation, there is no magic to it, there is no hidden agenda to it. The agenda is on the table.

And even though a private prison company needs to adhere to the same policies and procedures than a State run facility, there is always ways to keep your bottom line even. All you have to do is keep the environment unstable.

For instance, a private prison needs to provide classes to qualifying inmates. They need to provide classes and education. They need to provide church services and libraries. They need to provide personal to run visitation on the weekend and on holidays. In other words, they need to provide the same services a facility offers, which is operated by the State.

But if there is a fight in the prison population every other day, security concerns spring into place and everything is cancelled. No need

155

for additional personnel or overtime. Another simple calculation. Of course, you might argue that the discrepancy between fights in private and State run facilities is due to the fact that the State tries to transfer the most difficult inmates to the private prison since they have to pay the same amount per inmate. And there might or might not be some truth to it as well.

No matter how you look at this whole subject, there always will be a slightly bitter taste to the subject. The State could privatize prisons because we managed to label an inmate a non-person. If you are in prison, you are out of sight, out of mind for the general public. The idea of what an inmate is in America is quite demeaning it seems. If you are not the mother or girlfriend/wife of an inmate, you basically could care less of what is going on in prisons because after all, you didn't put the inmate there, he himself has done so. The inmate is not a neighbor anymore, past or in the future. He is a criminal and you don't want to see him anymore. Yet he will become your neighbor again and I think we better realize that because to break the endless cycle of crime/incarceration/release, crime/incarceration/release we have to do something about it even if it only consists of the simple notion to treat the maybe 75% of inmates who respond to treatment like human beings.

I have seen some pretty, discouraging behavioral patterns in a private prison both from corrections officers as well as their supervisors. It is probably safe to say, that the life of an inmate in private prisons is slightly different than in State run facilities. The private prison operates on even less personal than any State prison because of the cost factors involved. To employ and pay a Corrections Officer cost a certain amount of money. To train one for a private prison is an expense which doesn't immediately provide a return to the contractor. In addition to the initial hiring costs, there are the expenses connected to the annual one-week-block training each officer need to go through. That is not all that different to State run facilities, but always remember, the contractor needs to make money and lots of it. Wherever there is the possibility to save money, he will go that route. It is a game of with how little you get

156

away with. Where are the areas within your private prison where you can allow yourself to make shortcuts without anybody taking offense to it? Where can you cut costs without sacrificing your mission and if you do sacrifice your mission parameters, is it tolerable or even dangerous?

There is very little room for error because three factors in private prisons narrow down that margin so much, that the private prison needs to be extremely tough and tightly run in order to operate without too many major incidents.

a.   The amount of personnel is calculated extremely tight. Every person must accomplish his duties in the most effective manner.

b.   There is very little interaction with inmates. All the corrections officers time goes into the basic functions of his job description. Feed the inmate, give the inmate his mail, count the population.

c.   Every mistake by any person employed can ruin the bottom line of the company, because the DOC will access a substantial fine to the contractor for breach of contract or any part of that contract.

In essence however the question if private prisons are necessary or a viable option for the State is less a legal one than it is one of costs and philosophy. The punishment of offenders by locking them up for a certain amount of time or even for the rest of their lives has always been with the government. This was the case for thousands of years and is still the case in almost all countries and democracies. The subject of private prisons was a shimmer of hope 30 years ago to find ways to save costs. It was heralded by lawmakers who went out and announced that they are going to save thousands of dollars per week for the sake of the taxpayers. They waved numerous calculations around and proved that these companies found a way to keep inmates for less. I guess it was an easier approach than to reform the system of incarceration itself. Nobody wanted to appear weak or inmate friendly.

157

Nobody wanted to take the heat for the few inmates per year who escape due to less restrictive measures of incarceration.

But why stop with prisons? Because inmates are out of sight, they are locked up. The life of an inmate is no longer a subject matter to the voting public. If a State were to privatize the police force or even part of the police force, there probably would be a public outcry and all government positions would be terminated at the next election and no lawmaker or public officer wants that. But in all honesty, it is no big difference as far as the law is concerned. It could be accomplished fairly easily, just like the text of law was adopted to make private prisons a thing of the real world. Police officers enjoy the same benefits as State employed corrections officers, for the most part. There is also a wide range of cost saving opportunities. Police officers also get enhanced benefits compared to a private company, they get retirement benefits and good insurance, including a substantial life insurance policy paid by the State. I can see it already. I get pulled over by one of these private police officers and he gives me a ticket, because his position depends on how well he performs for the company and the company gets fifty percent of each ticket issued, the rest goes to the State. And even though it probably would be morally wrong to also include the police officer in the ticket revenue, there nevertheless would be a certain level of motivation to do good for your company. The more money you generate for your employer, the better the chances of enhancements and promotions. And who could argue against it in all honesty? As a citizen, you just have to obey the laws which you are supposed to do in the first place.

But it doesn't stop with traffic laws. How about making arrests for possession? How about arrests for domestic assaults? How about fines for illegally carrying a firearm? And it goes on from there.

It is just another idea of privatization which might or might not work. If the privatization of prisons worked out as many claimed it has,

158

then we need to be honest with ourselves and must be willing to go into the next face of government privatization. It is only logical.

The only problem with that idea is, that inmates can't vote, so they don't have a voice for or against private prisons. That is the difference and I think is one of the bigger plus points, an advantageous entrepreneur saw in forming the idea of private prison companies. He only had to convince a handful of people in the government of the need for his company. He didn't have to deal with neither inmates nor their relatives. The only thing he needed to do is to provide a convincing table of numbers and calculations which would have shown how the government can sell cost savings to the public. I dare anyone to challenge the government for the installation of privately owned and ran police forces and other branches of the government.

Let's see how this works out, because in legal terms, the government has theoretically opened the door to a playing field which could very quickly spin out of control. In fact, I shall formulate a contract for a private traffic ticketing organization in my municipality and submit it to the local authorities, with cost saving calculations and all. Who would be able to argue against it? I am going to get my wife to sew me together some sort of uniform which looks official and imposing, get me a used Crown Vic, get me a mobile credit card machine and on I will go, stopping vehicles, issuing traffic violation tickets, making a million or two.

11.   Property

Property is both food and clothing items as well as all permissible electronics such as TV, radio, headphones, alarm clock and what have you.

159

It is obvious that once incarcerated, you can't have a lot of stuff. Your place of living is a fairly confined space, which you have to share with other people as well. The place where you are incarcerated also determines how much space you will have available to store and keep your personal items. The management of space is mainly determined by the Warden of the facility and by DOC policy. The Warden of the facility can determine to give you all the space you will ever need, which you won't be able to appreciate, because the DOC has limitations of what you can have. So even if you would have a lot of space, which you won't, you can't fill it up because DOC is fairly restrictive on the whole subject. They are restrictive on this because they have to use the facility with the least amount of space per inmate as a reference point. They move people around quite a lot, they have to. For one reason or the other, there is a constant movement of inmates. If they steal or rat somebody out on one facility, inmates have to move to another facility for the sake of their own security. If you are a gang member you can't be anywhere, you have to be in an environment, which can to some degree assure your survival.

The other factor are security points. The more security points you have, the higher your security level will be, which will restrict you to certain medium or even maximum-security level prisons. If you lose your points over the years due to decent conduct and behavior, you will move to a lower security level facility. I mentioned the level system earlier and security points go hand in hand with your assigned level.

The last factor is your medical condition. For cost reasons, not every facility can provide proper medical care if you are diabetic or have other health conditions which would require monitoring on a constant basis. There are only a few prisons which have a proper medically trained unit attached to it with nurses available and a doctor either on call or even on the facility during normal business hours. There are a lot of factors which could determine your assignment to a certain prison. And these factors can also change over the years of incarceration, which means you will get moved frequently and thus the need to restrict the amount of property you can have.

With these factors known, why would it be a negative point for an inmate? It is after all simply a necessity. Even if you are not in prison and rent a place, there is no unlimited amount of property you can have. You will only be able to afford a certain place with a limited number of rooms in it and so on. In other words, it is nothing new that you only can have a defined amount of space. If you want more space, you would have to pay more, a simple calculation, isn't it.

The following is from OP 030120 "Inmate Property" Attachment C:

Maximum Allowable Male Clothing

Item	number allowed	comments
Athletic shoes	1	
Athletic supporters	2	
Baseball cap/stocking cap	2	no graphics, gray or Orange
Belt	1	
Boxer short/briefs	7	Gray or white only
BDU's	3	Orange, Bill Johnson Correctional Center only

Item	Qty	Notes
Coats	1	
Gloves	1	
Gym/Walking shorts	2	
Insulated coveralls	1	
Insulated Underwear	2	
Jumpsuit	1	
Personal Jeans	5	
Personal shirt	5	Not to exceed total of 5
Shower shoes	1	
Socks	7	
Sweat suits	2	Grey only, no logos or graphics
T-shirt	7	
Scrub pants	¾	
Scrub shirts	¾	
Work boots	1	No cowboy boots, Black, brown or tan only

That is pretty much the extend of what you as a DOC inmate can have as far as clothing items are concerned. It is worth mentioning that you basically can have a total of two pair of shoes, one athletic pair and one pair of work shoes. That is pretty basic I would say, but then again, the space you are being provided is very limited. I didn't make the distinction between medium facilities and lower security facilities, which differs slightly. It is not a big difference, but for instance if you are assigned to a Community Corrections Center and if you managed to acquire a job, you will of course be able to keep your work cloth in your locker. And depending on where you work, these work cloths can also be in colors, which would normally be not permissible on the facility. If you are interested in going through the entire document you can go to the Oklahoma Department of Corrections website, click on the square link named "Policies and Procedures" and it will take you to the above-mentioned policy.

As far as clothing is concerned, you easily can see that all these items should fit into two Walmart sized plastic bags and that is the whole idea, because if you are being transferred from one facility to the other, all the stuff you have at this point need to be able to fit into one military style Duffel bag and one cardboard box. It is also covered in the same reference, it reads:

1. Upon transfer, the amount of allowable inmate personal property will not exceed the volume that can be transported in a military style duffel bag issued by the sending facility. An inmate's television will be transported in a 16" x 16" x 16" cardboard box or a box of similar size. Other electrical appliances, allowed legal, religious, and arts/crafts materials will be transported in a 24" x 18" x 16" cardboard box or in the duffel bag. The duffel bag and cardboard boxes will weigh no more than 50 pounds per bag or box. Any additional items must be disposed of at the inmate's expense in accordance with this procedure.

All of their property needs to fit into a Duffel bag and a box. If your TV doesn't fit in the box as well, you can also have a small box for your TV, but that is it. What about other items you can have? Well, there is all the electronics, hygiene items and what have you and that also needs to fit into either the bag or the box, all of it. If you just happened to have purchased a bunch of canteen items from the money of your family and if you happened to get scheduled for transport, you are out of luck. If it doesn't fit, it doesn't ship. Rules for other property items which you can have are covered in the next attachment, which comes from the same policy. It is attachment B of OP-030120:

Maximum Allowable Property

Item	Amount	Comments
Bath Towel	3	white or yellow only
Bowl with lid	1	
Clock	1	
Comb/Brush/Pick	1	
Combination padlock	2	
Denture cup	2	
Disposable razor	5	
Earrings	2	female only
Electric Razor or Beard Trimmer	1	
Electrical power bar	1	
Electronic games	1	
Emery board	2	female only
Fan	1	

Fingernail clippers	1	
Hairbands	5	
Hair clip	1	female only
Hair iron/curling iron	1	female only
Hair dryer	1	
Hair rollers	20	female only
Hot pot	1	
Ice bucket	1	no larger than six bottle Container
Inmate ID	1	
Laundry bag	1	
Linens	1	pillow case, two flat sheets
Make up	1	female only
Mattress	1	retained by facility upon transfer
Mattress air	1	clear plastic only
Mattress with integrated pillow	1	Does not transfer with inmate
MP 3 player	1	
Necklace	1	
Nicotine patches	1	one complete series
Photo album	1	

Picture frame	1	no glass
Pillow	1	
Plastic coffee cup	1	
Plastic drinking cup	1	
Playing cards	1	
Postage stamps	20	except Community Corrections
Property bags	2	clear plastic only
Radio or Clock radio	1	
Reading light	1	
Ring	1	no gemstone, wedding band only
Sewing kit	1	
Soap dish	1	
Spoon	1	
Television set	1	up to 15"
Toothbrush	1	
Toothbrush cap	1	
Tweezers	1	female only
Wallet	1	
Washcloth	3	
Watch	1	

That gives you a rough estimate of what inmates can have. Some of the items are restricted to facilities with certain security levels. For instance, there are no hair dryers in medium facilities, period. As a woman for instance, you would have to move to a minimum first in order to be able to possess one. It does look a lot at first glance, but if you look closer, it really shrinks down to another two Walmart bags, if you exclude the TV, which you can have a separate box for anyway if you want, because most of the items are small stuff, like postage stamps, toothbrush, wash cloth, soap dish and plastic cups. There is not a lot to go around. And some Wardens are lenient with inmates and so are some Chiefs of Security or even Corrections Officers. And by lenient, I mean that we don't get a heart attack if you have two tooth brushes or if you have two plastic bowls to cook your Ramen noodle soup in.

Another factor is the color of property. Apparently, the color red and blue can be an issue. For instance, as far as athletic shoes are concerned, they only can be white, black or grey in color or any combination thereof. The Department of Corrections doesn't like red or blue because apparently that stands for certain gang colors and they won't have it. Electrical devices like TV or radios have to have clear housings in medium facilities. They can't have a solid color like white or black. That is prohibited. The reason for that is pretty obvious for a Corrections Officer. Inmates in medium security prisons have nothing but time on their hand. They cannot go anywhere, they hardly can do anything but go to the recreation yard if weather permits, read a book or watch TV. They have weeks and month to figure out where they possibly can hide their drugs, tobacco or telephones. The ingenuity of some of these chaps is pretty amazing and if you work in medium security for a while, you will come across all sorts and kinds of hiding spots.

If you do cell searches, which is part of any Corrections Officer's job description you want to see what, if anything is hidden inside that TV. And if that TV doesn't have a clear plastic housing, you

167

would have to take it apart every time you do a search and that is a time-consuming activity, and we don't have that time, thus all devices in medium prisons and above need to have clear housings.

Sometimes it is just amazing to witness what hiding spots inmates will come up with. Take a broom for instance. An inmate pushes his broom through the hallways of his housing unit on a daily basis. When he starts his job, he asks the officers for his broom and they will give it to him and go on with their business and activities. While we pass out the daily mail, that inmate moves around the corner and into a specific spot he knows is not covered by cameras. And what do you know, he removed a section of the bristles of the broom, which was attached to a piece of wood like any other broom. But in this case, the entire wooden section of the broom is carved out and was hiding a cell phone.

This guy spent the better part of his job not cleaning, but carving out a section out of the broom just big enough to hold his cell phone. It probably took him quite some time to do that, but we as officers had no idea of that little hiding spot, even though it was right under our nose the whole time since he gave the broom back to us every time he was finished with his job. That is what you can come up with if you have nothing but time. Sure enough, somebody must have brought that cell phone into the facility to begin with, but bringing contraband into a prison is not the main problem. The main problem consists of keeping that contraband hidden and secure as long as they can, because after all, that telephone cost him a lot of money.

So, the property issue is a bad thing for the inmate and always will be because prisons don't have an unlimited amount of space available. If I could change anything on that subject of property, it would be for minimum security inmates or lower, which is Community Corrections. If you have shown over the years, that you don't have a problem following rules and regulations and if you managed to stay out of trouble for several years and if the Case Management and the Security staff can attest to this fact and are willing to provide an inmate with an outstanding work and behavior evaluation, he should have the opportunity to be rewarded for his actions by allowing him to have a wider variety of property.

12.   Perception of inmates

This is one of these things, which cannot be easily quantified or qualified. It is, as the heading already says, a perception people have or don't have. I have thought about this subject matter for a while even before I started this chapter. It is not covered in State law or in any DOC policy, yet it is what you come across if you talk to anybody in your circle of family, friends or co-workers, at least here in the United States of America. It apparently comes down to the following difference. There are these people who have made their acquaintance with prison life and there are those who had no contact with anything prison. The first group looks at inmates in quite a different way than the latter. The first group realizes that this inmate is not just another inmate, it is a son, a father, a cousin or mother, it is a close relative in one way or the other and they have a connection with that person. And that blood bond is not going to go away and these years they spend with that person in close, personal contact is not all of a sudden going to go away. The memories they share in good or in bad will not be erased only because that person is incarcerated. It is not the case that they approve of what that person has done, that is not the case. They themselves in most cases are just as law abiding citizens as anybody else who managed to stay out of jail or prison. And some relatives might have disconnected to that individual completely a long time ago already. But if you have a relative in prison, you know that this person has not done bad all his life and he or she is not the devil himself. A few inmates might be, but not all of them by a long shot and those that are reside in the most restrictive maximum-

169

security facilities anyway, because they were convicted of the most heinous and evil crimes.

But for most inmates, it is drugs and all that comes along with it. They had a life before prison and they will have one after prison. The one thing they need to worry about is to find a way not to continue to do the things which got them locked up in the first place. That is their main struggle and their chances are the better, the better the support will be by their family and friends when they leave the confines of concrete walls and steel gates.

In my own case, I have eight relatives and friends, who have a history of incarceration to a smaller or bigger degree or simply were behind bars at one point in their lives. Out of the eight, two are currently still behind bars. The other six left prison behind and never looked back. The moral of this particular story is quite simply to illustrate the fact that prison is part of a lot of people's lives. That might not be a good thing and it is not as you can imagine and I don't try to make it sound good at all. I don't try to make this a story about good or bad, I try to bring the point across that most people do their time and should be able to move on after that.

Do I try to make this a chapter about redemption and second chances? I am not so sure myself. I guess all I really try to say is that an inmate is being punished for his crime by being behind bars. He is locked up for a certain time for something he or she did which was against the law of this State.

I think the best way to explain this chapter is this: The State with its combination of police, detectives, prosecutors, judges and the Department of Corrections already worked successfully together to apply the law to this person. They found a crime, made a connection to a person who committed this crime and followed their call of duty to remedy the situation. After all, their duties include to protect the public and the laws of the State are designed to accomplish exactly that.

Beyond that clearly defined undertaking and beyond the punishment a person receives for committing a violation of the law, my opinion is, that a former inmate should be treated as any other person in this society.

As I laid out in points 6, 7 and 8 above, that is not the case.

If an inmate is on Parole or on supervised release or has to wear an ankle monitor before he can discharge the crime completely, he is not really a free person yet, he has not fully discharged his punishment as provided by the DOC. Thus it is logical that this person is still under restrictions. The good part of this procedure is however, that he is out of prison, which is always a good thing. He is not totally out of the woods yet, but at least his chances and possibilities increased dramatically.

But how about someone who had no strings attached? And this is what I am talking about. I just have this idea that a citizen should be free of harassment, limitations and discrimination after he or she has done his or her time. I occasionally hear my co-workers, some family members and friends talk about former inmates and it is in these moments when I realize that the struggles of someone, who used to be an inmate is not going to get easier when he gets out. There seemed to be a very negative opinion on former inmates. And it doesn't have anything to do with what he does at that moment. You rarely hear something like "Well, he is out of prison, he has done his time. Now he got a decent job for starters, he can take care of his children again and what do you know, he actually seems to be doing all right, kudos to him". What I hear more often is something like "If this guy was to walk up to the front of my house, I just have to shoot him. I have a wife and kids I have to think about." Or some less violent reactions would be "If I meet him on the street and he wants to start talking to me, I just ignore him and walk the other way, I got nothing to say to this guy."

If you look into the psychology of a former inmate and compare him to a general public individual, there might be one thing which could turn out being a positive attribute.

Compared to the person, who has never seen a prison or jail from the inside, the former inmate has been caught already. And here is the simple theory behind this assumption. If I look around my family and friends and their access to drugs and illegal substances, I must assume that no drug dealer or no person has ever been caught trying to sell or deal in drugs, because they still have access to any drug or illegal substance they want to purchase. It is as though that there is an unlimited supply of people who are willing to pick up the slack, to pick up the void which was created when your neighborhood drug dealer got locked up. In other words, there has to be a number of people out there, who are still doing the same thing, which the guy did, who supplied you or someone you knew, so far so good.

Now, the former inmate has a chance of redemption to do better in life. He has seen prison life and if he has any sense of pride, humanity, willingness to life, joy to see his kids grow up, etc. left in him, he will not only try to avoid the activity which got him locked up, but he will simply put try to do better in life. I don't know to how many former inmates this character trade will apply to, but even if it is slim and low in percentage, it is still there. And I think that notion is a good conviction. I think if this is his general frame of mind, he should be supported by anyone in this society, because his intentions are good or at least they get him going in the right direction. The person who was never caught on the other hand, goes on with his criminal behavior until he too, will get caught.

I think there is a compelling incentive to look at former inmates in a little bit more neutral way. Even though the record of a former conviction cannot be ever fully erased or deleted, we as a society should stop the obsession to penalize someone for the rest of his life after he discharged the punishment for a crime.

172

Remedies

A.   Legalize Drugs?

The drug problem is an interesting one, especially if you look at it in the United States. In recent years in particular you read a lot about the so called "Opioid Crisis" which supposedly crippled entire work forces within the country. It is a bleak picture, which is being painted across the country. You only have to dive into this subject for a short amount of time and if you don't happen to subscribe to any particular newspaper, the Internet provides you with thousands of articles, studies, statistical data and the lot. To find any kind of information about it is an easy task, but if you must know or want to know, where to look, the CDC apparently has plenty of information. That probably would be a good start.

In an attempt to quell the drug consumption or just the illegal manufacturing and use of drugs, the lawmakers have come up with quite an astonishing array of deterrents, in this State mainly locking everybody up who has been caught with anything which resembles any type of drugs, period. If you are in possession of any drug, you will get locked up, no ifs or buts about it.

Maybe we should start by answering the question what drugs are in the first place, because I don't know if everyone is aware of the vast array of definitions for drugs. It is actually quite interesting and in my opinion, you need to have at least a little understanding what it is that we are talking about if we are talking about drugs. This State as I assume many other States in the United States, came up with a level system to define drugs and the legality of drugs. It is a system which is split into Schedules, whereby Schedule I are simply illegal drugs. And if you work yourself down the line, you will arrive at Schedule V, which includes basically simple painkillers and other, over the counter

174

medication. Each Schedule includes a list of drugs, which fit into that specific Schedule.

The determination of what drug fits into what schedule is made by the Board of Pharmacy. They follow a procedure if they want to add drugs to a specific schedule or want to change drugs around schedules. This procedure is covered in § 63-2-201:

§63-2-201. Authority to control - Recommendations.

A. The Director shall administer the provisions of this act except as otherwise provided.

B. The Board of Pharmacy by rule may classify new products determined to have a potential for abuse as controlled dangerous substances after notice and hearing; provided that such rule shall be submitted to the next regular session of the Legislature, and such rule shall remain in force and effect unless a concurrent resolution of disapproval is passed. Hearings shall be conducted by the Board of Pharmacy or such officers, agents or employees as the Board of Pharmacy may designate for the purpose. The Board of Pharmacy shall give appropriate notice of the proposed classification and of the time and place for a hearing. The rule so promulgated shall become effective on a date fixed by the Board of Pharmacy. Such rule may be amended or repealed in the same manner as provided for its adoption. Proceedings pursuant to this subsection shall be governed by the Administrative Procedures Act. A new substance controlled pursuant to this subsection shall be subject to the same regulatory provisions of this act applicable to the Schedule of substances to which it is classified.

C. The Director may recommend to the Legislature the addition, deletion or rescheduling of a substance.

D. In considering whether to make a recommendation or issue an order under this section, the Director or the Board of Pharmacy, as the case may be, shall consider the following:

1. Its actual or relative potential for abuse;

2. Scientific evidence of its pharmacological effect, if known;

3. State of current scientific knowledge regarding the substance;

4. Its history and current pattern of abuse;

5. The scope, duration, and significance of abuse;

6. What, if any, risk there is to the public health;

7. Its psychic or physiological dependence liability; and

8. Whether the substance is an immediate precursor or principal compound of a substance already controlled under this article.

E. Substances which are precursors of a controlled precursor shall not be subject to control solely because they are precursors of the controlled precursor.

F. In addition to the filing requirements of the Administrative Procedures Act, copies of orders issued under this section shall, during the time the Legislature is not in session, be filed with the Chair and Vice Chair of the State Legislative Council's Judiciary Committee.

G. The Board of Pharmacy shall exclude any nonnarcotic substance from a schedule if such substance may, under the Federal Food, Drug and Cosmetic Act and the law of this state, be lawfully sold over the counter without a prescription.

Added by Laws 1971, c. 119, § 2-201. Amended by Laws 2008, c. 359, § 6, emerg. eff. June 3, 2008.

The above looks like a fairly simple text and I am grateful for that. However, as a citizen uneducated in chemistry, I can't help but

176

wonder how points 1 through 8 would pan out in real life. Like point 6 "What, if any, risk there is to the public health". The Board of Pharmacy thus approaches the Director of the Oklahoma State Bureau of Narcotics and Dangerous Drugs or any designee and tries to make its case to re-classify a drug, add a drug to any of the Schedules and so on and so forth. And all this must not be in violation of any Federal Drug Schedule either, because then you have the problem that the State police and the State courts are not going to prosecute somebody who didn't violate State law, but Federal Offices still will, because under Federal law it would be a crime.

So other than simply adopting Federal drug schedules, there is probably not much the Board of Pharmacy or the Director of the Oklahoma State Bureau of Narcotics and Dangerous Drugs can do to implement big changes to the drug schedules. They certainly have the power to do so, but they must tread carefully in so doing, because if they make a change and this change is not watertight, there will be potential for abuse.

How would that even work you asked? Well, let's say, I am a criminal. Not any criminal, but a drug dealer and I want to sell a new kind of drug. Now I am going to pay a chemistry major from my local college to look through the drug schedules and find a hole in it. The purpose would be, how to create a drug with a high potential for addiction made out of substances which are all part of Schedule V or Schedule IV, since these are obviously the least restrictive schedules. If the Board of Pharmacy slipped and didn't fully research and investigate the proposed changes, it might lead to a new drug epidemic in the State of Oklahoma, because all of a sudden there would be a completely new drug being sold in the streets with no legal remedies. You have to be extra careful in these proceedings. Thus, I don't think a lot of changes are going on in that regard, because State employees are not necessarily known for taking risks, not that I know anyway.

If that is good enough for you and you don't see the need to look at a list of 1500 drugs, you can safely skip the next few pages of drug schedules, up to page 205. I added them here to illustrate the sheer amount of materiel somebody has to go through before a new drug can be put onto the market.

What is really interesting is the definitions of each schedule.

§63-2-204. Schedule I.

The controlled substances listed in this section are included in Schedule I.

A. Any of the following opiates, including their isomers, esters, ethers, salts, and salts of isomers, esters, and ethers, unless specifically excepted, when the existence of these isomers, esters, ethers, and salts is possible within the specific chemical designation:

1. Acetylmethadol;

2. Allylprodine;

3. Alphacetylmethadol;

4. Alphameprodine;

5. Alphamethadol;

6. Benzethidine;

7. Betacetylmethadol;

8. Betameprodine;

9. Betamethadol;

10. Betaprodine;

178

11. Clonitazene;

12. Dextromoramide;

13. Dextrorphan (except its methyl ether);

14. Diampromide;

15. Diethylthiambutene;

16. Dimenoxadol;

17. Dimepheptanol;

18. Dimethylthiambutene;

19. Dioxaphetyl butyrate;

20. Dipipanone;

21. Ethylmethylthiambutene;

22. Etonitazene;

23. Etoxeridine;

24. Furethidine;

25. Hydroxypethidine;

26. Ketobemidone;

27. Levomoramide;

28. Levophenacylmorphan;

29. Morpheridine;

30. Noracymethadol;

31. Norlevorphanol;

32. Normethadone;

33. Norpipanone;

34. Phenadoxone;

35. Phenampromide;

36. Phenomorphan;

37. Phenoperidine;

38. Piritramide;

39. Proheptazine;

40. Properidine;

41. Racemoramide; or

42. Trimeperidine.

B. Any of the following opium derivatives, their salts, isomers, and salts of isomers, unless specifically excepted, when the existence of these salts, isomers, and salts of isomers is possible within the specific chemical designation:

1. Acetorphine;

2. Acetyldihydrocodeine;

3. Benzylmorphine;

4. Codeine methylbromide;

5. Codeine-N-Oxide;

6. Cyprenorphine;

7. Desomorphine;

8. Dihydromorphine;

9. Etorphine;

10. Heroin;

11. Hydromorphinol;

12. Methyldesorphine;

13. Methylhydromorphine;

14. Morphine methylbromide;

15. Morphine methylsulfonate;

16. Morphine-N-Oxide;

17. Myrophine;

18. Nicocodeine;

19. Nicomorphine;

20. Normorphine;

21. Phoclodine; or

22. Thebacon.

C. Any material, compound, mixture, or preparation which contains any quantity of the following hallucinogenic substances, their salts, isomers, and salts of isomers, unless specifically excepted, when the existence of these salts, isomers, and salts of isomers is possible within the specific chemical designation:

1. Methcathinone;

2. 3, 4-methylenedioxy amphetamine;

3. 3, 4-methylenedioxy methamphetamine;

4. 5-methoxy-3, 4-methylenedioxy amphetamine;

5. 3, 4, 5-trimethoxy amphetamine;

6. Bufotenine;

7. Diethyltryptamine;

8. Dimethyltryptamine;

9. 4-methyl-2, 5-dimethoxyamphetamine;

10. Ibogaine;

11. Lysergic acid diethylamide;

12. Marihuana;

13. Mescaline;

14. N-benzylpiperazine;

15. N-ethyl-3-piperidyl benzilate;

16. N-methyl-3-piperidyl benzilate;

17. Psilocybin;

18. Psilocyn;

19. 2, 5 dimethoxyamphetamine;

20. 4 Bromo-2, 5-dimethoxyamphetamine;

21. 4 methoxyamphetamine;

22. Cyclohexamine;

23. Salvia Divinorum;

24. Salvinorin A;

25. Thiophene Analog of Phencyclidine. Also known as: 1-(1-(2-thienyl) cyclohexyl) piperidine; 2-Thienyl Analog of Phencyclidine; TPCP, TCP;

26. Phencyclidine (PCP);

27. Pyrrolidine Analog for Phencyclidine. Also known as 1-(1-Phenylcyclohexyl) - Pyrrolidine, PCPy, PHP;

28. 1-(3-trifluoromethylphenyl) piperazine;

29. Flunitrazepam;

30. B-hydroxy-amphetamine;

31. B-ketoamphetamine;

32. 2,5-dimethoxy-4-nitroamphetamine;

33. 2,5-dimethoxy-4-bromophenethylamine;

34. 2,5-dimethoxy-4-chlorophenethylamine;

35. 2,5-dimethoxy-4-iodoamphetamine;

36. 2,5-dimethoxy-4-iodophenethylamine;

37. 2,5-dimethoxy-4-methylphenethylamine;

38. 2,5-dimethoxy-4-ethylphenethylamine;

39. 2,5-dimethoxy-4-fluorophenethylamine;

40. 2,5-dimethoxy-4-nitrophenethylamine;

41. 2,5-dimethoxy-4-ethylthio-phenethylamine;

42. 2,5-dimethoxy-4-isopropylthio-phenethylamine;

43. 2,5-dimethoxy-4-propylthio-phenethylamine;

44. 2,5-dimethoxy-4-cyclopropylmethylthio-phenethylamine;

45. 2,5-dimethoxy-4-tert-butylthio-phenethylamine;

46. 2,5-dimethoxy-4-(2-fluoroethylthio)-phenethylamine;

47. 5-methoxy-N, N-dimethyltryptamine;

48. N-methyltryptamine;

49. A-ethyltryptamine;

50. A-methyltryptamine;

51. N, N-diethyltryptamine;

52. N, N-diisopropyltryptamine;

53. N, N-dipropyltryptamine;

54. 5-methoxy-a-methyltryptamine;

55. 4-hydroxy-N, N-diethyltryptamine;

56. 4-hydroxy-N, N-diisopropyltryptamine;

57. 5-methoxy-N, N-diisopropyltryptamine;

58. 4-hydroxy-N-isopropyl-N-methyltryptamine;

59. 3,4-Methylenedioxymethcathinone (Methylone);

60. 3,4-Methylenedioxypyrovalerone (MDPV);

61. 4-Methylmethcathinone (Mephedrone);

62. 4-methoxymethcathinone;

63. 4-Fluoromethcathinone;

64. 3-Fluoromethcathinone;

65. 1-(8-bromobenzo 1,2-b;4,5-b' difuran-4-yl)-2-aminopropane;

66. 2,5-Dimethoxy-4-chloroamphetamine;

67. 4-Methylethcathinone;

68. Pyrovalerone;

69. N,N-diallyl-5-methoxytryptamine;

70. 3,4-Methylenedioxy-N-ethylcathinone (Ethylone);

71. B-keto-N-Methylbenzodioxolylbutanamine (Butylone);

72. B-keto-Methylbenzodioxolylpentanamine (Pentylone);

73. Alpha-Pyrrolidinopentiophenone;

74. 4-Fluoroamphetamine;

75. Pentredone;

76. 4'-Methyl-a-pyrrolidinohexaphenone;

77. 2,5-dimethoxy-4-(n)-propylphenethylamine;

78. 2,5-dimethoxyphenethylamine;

79. 1,4-Dibenzylpiperazine;

80. N,N-Dimethylamphetamine;

81. 4-Fluoromethamphetamine;

82. 4-Chloro-2,5-dimethoxy-N-(2-methoxybenzyl)phenethylamine (25C-NBOMe);

83. 4-Iodo-2,5-dimethoxy-N-(2-methoxybenzyl)phenethylamine (25I-NBOMe);

84. 4-Bromo-2,5-dimethoxy-N-(2-methoxybenzy)phenethylamine (25B-NBOMe);

85. 1-(4-Fluorophenyl)piperazine; or

86. Methoxetamine.

D. Unless specifically excepted or unless listed in a different schedule, any material, compound, mixture, or preparation which contains any quantity of the following substances having stimulant or depressant effect on the central nervous system:

1. Fenethylline;

2. Mecloqualone;

3. N-ethylamphetamine;

4. Methaqualone;

5. Gamma-Hydroxybutyric Acid, also known as GHB, gamma-hydroxybutyrate, 4-hydroxybutyrate, 4-hydroxybutanoic acid, sodium oxybate, and sodium oxybutyrate;

6. Gamma-Butyrolactone (GBL) as packaged, marketed, manufactured or promoted for human consumption, with the exception of legitimate food additive and manufacturing purposes;

7. Gamma Hydroxyvalerate (GHV) as packaged, marketed, or manufactured for human consumption, with the exception of legitimate food additive and manufacturing purposes;

186

8. Gamma Valerolactone (GVL) as packaged, marketed, or manufactured for human consumption, with the exception of legitimate food additive and manufacturing purposes; or

9. 1,4 Butanediol (1,4 BD or BDO) as packaged, marketed, manufactured, or promoted for human consumption with the exception of legitimate manufacturing purposes.

E. 1. The following industrial uses of Gamma-Butyrolactone, Gamma Hydroxyvalerate, Gamma Valerolactone, or 1,4 Butanediol are excluded from all schedules of controlled substances under this title:

a.   pesticides,

b.   photochemical etching,

c.   electrolytes of small batteries or capacitors,

d.   viscosity modifiers in polyurethane,

e.   surface etching of metal coated plastics,

f.   organic paint disbursements for water soluble inks,

g.   pH regulators in the dyeing of wool and polyamide fibers,

h.   foundry chemistry as a catalyst during curing,

i.   curing agents in many coating systems based on urethanes and amides,

j.   additives and flavoring agents in food, confectionary, and beverage products,

k.   synthetic fiber and clothing production,

l.   tetrahydrofuran production,

m.   gamma butyrolactone production,

187

n.   polybutylene terephthalate resin production,

o.   polyester raw materials for polyurethane elastomers and foams,

p.   coating resin raw material, and

q.   as an intermediate in the manufacture of other chemicals and pharmaceuticals.

2. At the request of any person, the Director may exempt any other product containing Gamma-Butyrolactone, Gamma Hydroxyvalerate, Gamma Valerolactone, or 1,4 Butanediol from being included as a Schedule I controlled substance if such product is labeled, marketed, manufactured and distributed for legitimate industrial use in a manner that reduces or eliminates the likelihood of abuse.

3. In making a determination regarding an industrial product, the Director, after notice and hearing, shall consider the following:

a.   the history and current pattern of abuse,

b.   the name and labeling of the product,

c.   the intended manner of distribution, advertising and promotion of the product, and

d.   other factors as may be relevant to and consistent with the public health and safety.

4. The hearing shall be held in accordance with the procedures of the Administrative Procedures Act.

F. Any material, compound, mixture, or preparation, whether produced directly or indirectly from a substance of vegetable origin or independently by means of chemical synthesis, or by a combination of extraction and chemical synthesis, that contains any quantity of the following substances, or that contains any of their salts, isomers,

188

and salts of isomers when the existence of these salts, isomers, and salts of isomers is possible within the specific chemical designation:

1. JWH-004;

2. JWH-007;

3. JWH-009;

4. JWH-015;

5. JWH-016;

6. JWH-018;

7. JWH-019;

8. JWH-020;

9. JWH-030;

10. JWH-046;

11. JWH-047;

12. JWH-048;

13. JWH-049;

14. JWH-050;

15. JWH-070;

16. JWH-071;

17. JWH-072;

18. JWH-073;

19. JWH-076;

20. JWH-079;

21. JWH-080;

22. JWH-081;

23. JWH-082;

24. JWH-094;

25. JWH-096;

26. JWH-098;

27. JWH-116;

28. JWH-120;

29. JWH-122;

30. JWH-145;

31. JWH-146;

32. JWH-147;

33. JWH-148;

34. JWH-149;

35. JWH-150;

36. JWH-156;

37. JWH-167;

38. JWH-175;

39. JWH-180;

40. JWH-181;

41. JWH-182;

42. JWH-184;

43. JWH-185;

44. JWH-189;

45. JWH-192;

46. JWH-193;

47. JWH-194;

48. JWH-195;

49. JWH-196;

50. JWH-197;

51. JWH-198;

52. JWH-199;

53. JWH-200;

54. JWH-201;

55. JWH-202;

56. JWH-203;

57. JWH-204;

58. JWH-205;

59. JWH-206;

60. JWH-207;

61. JWH-208;

62. JWH-209;

63. JWH-210;

64. JWH-211;

65. JWH-212;

66. JWH-213;

67. JWH-234;

68. JWH-235;

69. JWH-236;

70. JWH-237;

71. JWH-239;

72. JWH-240;

73. JWH-241;

74. JWH-242;

75. JWH-243;

76. JWH-244;

77. JWH-245;

78. JWH-246;

79. JWH-248;

80. JWH-249;

81. JWH-250;

82. JWH-251;

83. JWH-252;

84. JWH-253;

85. JWH-262;

86. JWH-292;

87. JWH-293;

88. JWH-302;

89. JWH-303;

90. JWH-304;

91. JWH-305;

92. JWH-306;

93. JWH-307;

94. JWH-308;

95. JWH-311;

96. JWH-312;

97. JWH-313;

98. JWH-314;

99. JWH-315;

100. JWH-316;

101. JWH-346;

102. JWH-348;

103. JWH-363;

104. JWH-364;

105. JWH-365;

106. JWH-367;

107. JWH-368;

108. JWH-369;

109. JWH-370;

110. JWH-371;

111. JWH-373;

112. JWH-386;

113. JWH-387;

114. JWH-392;

115. JWH-394;

116. JWH-395;

117. JWH-397;

118. JWH-398;

119. JWH-399;

120. JWH-400;

121. JWH-412;

122. JWH-413;

123. JWH-414;

124. JWH-415;

125. CP-55, 940;

126. CP-47, 497;

127. HU-210;

128. HU-211;

129. WIN-55, 212-2;

130. AM-2201;

131. AM-2233;

132. JWH-018 adamantyl-carboxamide;

133. AKB48;

134. JWH-122 N-(4-pentenyl)analog;

135. MAM2201;

136. URB597;

137. URB602;

138. URB754;

139. UR144;

140. XLR11;

141. A-796,260;

142. STS-135;

143. AB-FUBINACA;

144. AB-PINACA;

145. PB-22;

146. AKB48 N-5-Fluorpentyl;

147. AM1248;

148. FUB-PB-22;

149. ADB-FUBINACA;

150. BB-22;

151. 5-Fluoro PB-22; or

152. 5-Fluoro AKB-48.

G. In addition to those substances listed in subsection F of this section, unless specifically excepted or unless listed in another schedule, any material, compound, mixture, or preparation which contains any quantity of a synthetic cannabinoid found to be in any of the following chemical groups:

1. Naphthoylindoles: any compound containing a 3-(1-naphthoyl)indole structure with or without substitution at the nitrogen atom of the indole ring by an alkyl, haloalkyl, cyanoalkyl, alkenyl, cycloalkylmethyl, cycloalkylethyl, benzyl, halobenzyl, 1-(N-methyl-2-piperidinyl)methyl, 2-(4-morpholinyl)ethyl, 1-(N-methyl-2-pyrrolidinyl)methyl, 1-(N-methyl-3- morpholinyl)methyl, (tetrahydropyran-4-yl)methyl, 1-methylazepanyl, phenyl, or halophenyl

196

group, whether or not further substituted on the indole ring to any extent, and whether or not substituted on the naphthyl ring to any extent. Naphthoylindoles include, but are not limited to:

a.   1-[2-(4-morpholinyl)ethyl]-3-(1-naphthoyl)indole (JWH-200),

b.   1-(5-fluoropentyl)-3-(1-naphthoyl)indole (AM2201),

c.   1-pentyl-3-(1-naphthoyl)indole (JWH-018),

d.   1-butyl-3-(1-naphthoyl)indole (JWH-073),

e.   1-pentyl-3-(4-methoxy-1-naphthoyl)indole (JWH-081),

f.   1-propyl-2-methyl-3-(1-naphthoyl)indole (JWH-015),

g.   1-hexyl-3-(1-naphthoyl)indole (JWH-019),

h.   1-pentyl-3-(4-methyl-1-naphthoyl)indole (JWH-122),

i.   1-pentyl-3-(4-ethyl-1-naphthoyl)indole (JWH-210),

j.   1-pentyl-3-(4-chloro-1-naphthoyl)indole (JWH-398),

k.   1-pentyl-2-methyl-3-(1-naphthoyl)indole (JWH-007),

l.   1-pentyl-3-(7-methoxy-1-naphthoyl)indole (JWH-164),

m.   1-pentyl-2-methyl-3-(4-methoxy-1-naphthoyl)indole (JWH-098),

n.   1-pentyl-3-(4-fluoro-1-naphthoyl)indole (JWH-412),

o.   1-[1-(N-methyl-2-piperidinyl)methyl]-3-(1-naphthoyl)indole (AM-1220),

p.   1-(5-fluoropentyl)-3-(4-methyl-1-naphthoyl)indole (MAM-2201), or

q.   1-(4-cyanobutyl)-3-(1-naphthoyl)indole (AM-2232);

2. Naphthylmethylindoles: any compound containing a 1H-indol-3-yl-(1-naphthyl)methane structure with or without substitution at the nitrogen atom of the indole ring by an alkyl, haloalkyl, cyanoalkyl, alkenyl, cycloalkylmethyl, cycloalkylethyl, benzyl, halobenzyl, 1-(N-methyl-2-piperidinyl)methyl, 2-(4-morpholinyl)ethyl, 1-(N-methyl-2-pyrrolidinyl)methyl, 1-(N-methyl-3- morpholinyl)methyl, (tetrahydropyran-4-yl)methyl, 1-methylazepanyl, phenyl, or halophenyl group, whether or not further substituted on the indole ring to any extent, and whether or not substituted on the naphthyl ring to any extent. Naphthylmethylindoles include, but are not limited to, (1-pentylindol-3-yl)(1-naphthyl)methane (JWH-175);

3. Naphthoylpyrroles: any compound containing a 3-(1-naphthoyl)pyrrole structure with or without substitution at the nitrogen atom of the pyrrole ring by an alkyl, haloalkyl, cyanoalkyl, alkenyl, cycloalkylmethyl, cycloalkylethyl, benzyl, halobenzyl, 1-(N-methyl-2-piperidinyl)methyl, 2-(4-morpholinyl)ethyl, 1-(N-methyl-2-pyrrolidinyl)methyl, 1-(N-methyl-3-morpholinyl)methyl, (tetrahydropyran-4-yl)methyl, 1-methylazepanyl, phenyl, or halophenyl group, whether or not further substituted on the pyrrole ring to any extent, and whether or not substituted on the naphthyl group to any extent. Naphthoylpyrroles include, but are not limited to:

a.   1-hexyl-2-phenyl-4-(1-naphthoyl)pyrrole (JWH-147),

b.   1-pentyl-5-(2-methylphenyl)-3-(1-naphthoyl)pyrrole (JWH-370),

c.   1-pentyl-3-(1-naphthoyl)pyrrole (JWH-030), or

d.   1-hexyl-5-phenyl-3-(1-naphthoyl)pyrrole (JWH-147);

4. Naphthylideneindenes: any compound containing a 1-(1-naphthylmethylene)indene structure with or without substitution at the 3-position of the indene ring by an alkyl, haloalkyl, cyanoalkyl, alkenyl, cycloalkylmethyl, cycloalkylethyl, benzyl, halobenzyl, 1-(N-methyl-2-piperidinyl)methyl, 2-(4-morpholinyl)ethyl, 1-(N-methyl-2-pyrrolidinyl)methyl, 1-(N-methyl-3-morpholinyl)methyl,

(tetrahydropyran-4-yl)methyl, 1-methylazepanyl, phenyl, or halophenyl group, whether or not further substituted on the indene group to any extent, and whether or not substituted on the naphthyl group to any extent. Naphthylmethylindenes include, but are not limited to, (1-[(3-pentyl)-1H-inden-1-ylidene)methyl]naphthalene (JWH-176);

5. Phenylacetylindoles: any compound containing a 3-phenylacetylindole structure with or without substitution at the nitrogen atom of the indole ring by alkyl, haloalkyl, cyanoalkyl, alkenyl, cycloalkylmethyl, cycloalkylethyl, benzyl, halobenzyl, 1-(N-methyl-2-piperidinyl)methyl, 2-(4-morpholinyl)ethyl, 1-(N-methyl-2-pyrrolidinyl)methyl, 1-(N-methyl-3- morpholinyl)methyl, (tetrahydropyran-4-yl)methyl, 1-methylazepanyl, phenyl, or halophenyl group, whether or not further substituted on the indole ring to any extent, and whether or not substituted on the phenyl ring to any extent. Phenylacetylindoles include, but are not limited to:

a.   1-pentyl-3-(2-methoxyphenylacetyl)indole (JWH-250),

b.   1-(2-cyclohexylethyl)-3-(2-methoxyphenylacetyl)indole (RCS-8),

c.   1-pentyl-3-(2-chlorophenylacetyl)indole (JWH-203),

d.   1-pentyl-3-(2-methylphenylacetyl)indole (JWH-251),

e.   1-pentyl-3-(4-methoxyphenylacetyl)indole (JWH-201), or

f.   1-pentyl-3-(3-methoxyphenylacetyl)indole (JWH-302);

6. Cyclohexylphenols: any compound containing a 2-(3-hydroxycyclohexyl)phenol structure with or without substitution at the 5-position of the phenolic ring by an alkyl, haloalkyl, cyanoalkyl, alkenyl, cycloalkylmethyl, cycloalkylethyl, benzyl, halobenzyl, 1-(N-methyl-2-piperidinyl)methyl, 2-(4-morpholinyl)ethyl, 1-(N-methyl-2-pyrrolidinyl)methyl, 1-(N-methyl-3- morpholinyl)methyl, (tetrahydropyran-4-yl)methyl, 1-methylazepanyl, phenyl, or halophenyl

group, and whether or not further substituted on the cyclohexyl ring to any extent. Cyclohexylphenols include, but are not limited to:

a.   5-(1,1-dimethylheptyl)-2-[(1R,3S)-3-hydroxycyclohexyl]-phenol (CP-47,497),

b.   5-(1,1-dimethyloctyl)-2-[(1R,3S)-3-hydroxycyclohexyl]-phenol (cannabicyclohexanol; CP-47,497 C8 homologue), or

c.   5-(1,1-dimethylheptyl)-2-[(1R,2R)-5-hydroxy-2-(3-hydroxypropyl)cyclohexyl]-phenol (CP 55, 940);

7. Benzoylindoles: any compound containing a 3-(benzoyl)indole structure with or without substitution at the nitrogen atom of the indole ring by an alkyl, haloalkyl, cyanoalkyl, alkenyl, cycloalkylmethyl, cycloalkylethyl, benzyl, halobenzyl, 1-(N-methyl-2-piperidinyl)methyl, 2-(4-morpholinyl)ethyl, 1-(N-methyl-2-pyrrolidinyl)methyl, 1-(N-methyl-3- morpholinyl)methyl, (tetrahydropyran-4-yl)methyl, 1-methylazepanyl, phenyl, or halophenyl group, whether or not further substituted on the indole ring to any extent, and whether or not substituted on the phenyl group to any extent. Benzoylindoles include, but are not limited to:

a.   1-pentyl-3-(4-methoxybenzoyl)indole (RCS-4),

b.   1-[2-(4-morpholinyl)ethyl]-2-methyl-3-(4-methoxybenzoyl)indole (Pravadoline or WIN 48, 098),

c.   1-(5-fluoropentyl)-3-(2-iodobenzoyl)indole (AM-694),

d.   1-pentyl-3-(2-iodobenzoyl)indole (AM-679), or

e.   1-[1-(N-methyl-2-piperidinyl)methyl]-3-(2-iodobenzoyl)indole (AM-2233);

8. Cyclopropoylindoles: Any compound containing a 3-(cyclopropoyl)indole structure with substitution at the nitrogen atom of the indole ring by an alkyl, haloalkyl, cyanoalkyl, alkenyl, cycloalkylmethyl, cycloalkylethyl, benzyl, halobenzyl, 1-(N-methyl-2-

200

piperidinyl)methyl, 2-(4-morpholinyl)ethyl, 1-(N-methyl-2-pyrrolidinyl)methyl, 1-(N-methyl-3- morpholinyl)methyl, (tetrahydropyran-4-yl)methyl, 1-methylazepanyl, phenyl, or halophenyl group, whether or not further substituted in the indole ring to any extent and whether or not substituted in the cyclopropoyl ring to any extent. Cyclopropoylindoles include, but are not limited to:

a.   1-pentyl-3-(2,2,3,3-tetramethylcyclopropoyl)indole (UR-144),

b.   1-(5-chloropentyl)-3-(2,2,3,3-tetramethylcyclopropoyl)indole (5Cl-UR-144), or

c.   1-(5-fluoropentyl)-3-(2,2,3,3-tetramethylcyclopropoyl)indole (XLR11);

9. Indole Amides: Any compound containing a 1H-Indole-3-carboxamide structure with or without substitution at the nitrogen atom of the indole ring by an alkyl, haloalkyl, cyanoalkyl, alkenyl, cycloalkylmethyl, cycloalkylethyl, benzyl, halobenzyl, 1-(N-methyl-2-piperidinyl)methyl, 2-(4-morpholinyl)ethyl, 1-(N-methyl-2-pyrrolidinyl)methyl, 1-(N-methyl-3- morpholinyl)methyl, (tetrahydropyran-4-yl)methyl, 1-methylazepanyl, phenyl, or halophenyl group, whether or not substituted at the carboxamide group by an adamantyl, naphthyl, phenyl, benzyl, quinolinyl, cycloalkyl, 1-amino-3-methyl-1-oxobutan-2-yl, 1-amino-3,3-dimethyl-1-oxobutan-2-yl, 1-methoxy-3-methyl-1-oxobutan-2-yl, 1-methoxy-3,3-dimethyl-1-oxobutan-2-yl or pyrrole group, and whether or not further substituted in the indole, adamantyl, naphthyl, phenyl, pyrrole, quninolinyl, or cycloalkyl rings to any extent. Indole Amides include, but are not limited to:

a.   N-(1-adamantyl)-1-pentyl-1H-indole-3-carboxamide (2NE1),

b.   N-(1-adamantyl)-1-(5-fluoropentyl-1H-indole-3-carboxamide (STS-135),

c.   N-(1-amino-3,3-dimethyl-1-oxobutan-2-yl)-1-pentyl-1H-indole-3-carboxamide (ADBICA),

d.   N-(1-amino-3,3-dimethyl-1-oxobutan-2-yl)-1-(5-fluoropentyl)-
          1H-indole-3-carboxamide (5F-ADBICA),

e.   N-(naphthalen-1-yl)-1-pentyl-1H-indole-3-carboxamide
          (NNE1),

f.   1-(5-fluoropentyl)-N-(naphthalene-1-yl)-1H-indole-3-
          carboxamide (5F-NNE1),

g.   N-benzyl-1-pentyl-1H-indole-3-carboxamide (SDB-006), or

h.   N-benzyl-1-(5-fluoropentyl)-1H-indole-3-carboxamide (5F-
          SDB-006);

10. Indole Esters: Any compound containing a 1H-Indole-3-
carboxylate structure with or without substitution at the nitrogen
atom of the indole ring by an alkyl, haloalkyl, cyanoalkyl, alkenyl,
cycloalkylmethyl, cycloalkylethyl, benzyl, halobenzyl, 1-(N-methyl-2-
piperidinyl)methyl, 2-(4-morpholinyl)ethyl, 1-(N-methyl-2-
pyrrolidinyl)methyl, 1-(N-methyl-3-morpholinyl)methyl,
(tetrahydropyran-4-yl)methyl, 1-methylazepanyl, phenyl, or halophenyl
group, whether or not substituted at the carboxylate group by an
adamantyl, naphthyl, phenyl, benzyl, quinolinyl, cycloalkyl,1-amino-3-
methyl-1-oxobutan-2-yl, 1-amino-3,3-dimethyl-1-oxobutan-2-yl, 1-
methoxy-3-methyl-1-oxobutan-2-yl, 1-methoxy-3,3-dimethyl-1-
oxobutan-2-yl or pyrrole group, and whether or not further substituted
in the indole, adamantyl, naphthyl, phenyl, pyrrole, quinolinyl, or
cycloalkyl rings to any extent. Indole Esters include, but are not
limited to:

a.   quinolin-8-yl 1-pentyl-1H-indole-3-carboxylate (PB-22),

b.   quinolin-8-yl 1-(5-fluoropentyl)-1H-indole-3-carboxylate (5F-
          PB-22),

c.   quinolin-8-yl 1-(cyclohexylmethyl)-1H-indole-3-carboxylate
          (BB-22),

d.   naphthalen-1-yl 1-(4-fluorobenzyl)-1H-indole-3-carboxylate (FDU-PB-22), or

e.   naphthalen-1-yl 1-(5-fluoropentyl)-1H-indole-3-carboxylate (NM2201);

11. Adamantanoylindoles: Any compound containing an adamantanyl-(1H-indol-3-yl)methanone structure with or without substitution at the nitrogen atom of the indole ring by an alkyl, haloalkyl, cyanoalkyl, alkenyl, cycloalkylmethyl, cycloalkylethyl, benzyl, halobenzyl, 1-(N-methyl-2-piperidinyl)methyl, 2-(4-morpholinyl)ethyl, 1-(N-methyl-2-pyrrolidinyl)methyl, 1-(N-methyl-3-morpholinyl)methyl, (tetrahydropyran-4-yl)methyl, 1-methylazepanyl, phenyl, or halophenyl group, whether or not further substituted in the indole ring to any extent and whether or not substituted in the adamantyl ring to any extent. Adamantanoylindoles include, but are not limited to:

a.   adamantan-1-yl[1-[(1-methyl-2-piperidinyl)methyl]-1H-indol-3-yl]methanone (AM1248), or

b.   adamantan-1-yl-(1-pentyl-1H-indol-3-yl)methanone (AB-001);

12. Carbazole Ketone: Any compound containing (9H-carbazole-3-yl) methanone structure with or without substitution at the nitrogen atom of the carbazole ring by an alkyl, haloalkyl, cyanoalkyl, alkenyl, cycloalkylmethyl, cycloalkylethyl, benzyl, halobenzyl, 1-(N-methyl-2-piperidinyl)methyl, 2-(4-morpholinyl)ethyl, 1-(N-methyl-2-pyrrolidinyl)methyl, 1-(N-methyl-3-morpholinyl)methyl, (tetrahydropyran-4-yl)methyl, 1-methylazepanyl, phenyl, or halophenyl group, with substitution at the carbon of the methanone group by an adamantyl, naphthyl, phenyl, benzyl, quinolinyl, cycloalkyl, 1-amino-3-methyl-1-oxobutan-2-yl, 1-amino-3,3-dimethyl-1-oxobutan-2-yl, 1-methoxy-3-methyl-1-oxobutan-2-yl, 1-methoxy-3,3-dimethyl-1-oxobutan-2-yl or pyrrole group, and whether or not further substituted at the carbazole, adamantyl, naphthyl, phenyl, pyrrole, quinolinyl, or cycloalkyl rings to any extent. Carbazole Ketones include, but are not

limited to, naphthalen-1-yl(9-pentyl-9H-carbazol-3-yl)methanone (EG-018);

13. Benzimidazole Ketone: Any compound containing (benzimidazole-2-yl) methanone structure with or without substitution at either nitrogen atom of the benzimidazole ring by an alkyl, haloalkyl, cyanoalkyl, alkenyl, cycloalkylmethyl, cycloalkylethyl, benzyl, halobenzyl, 1-(N-methyl-2-piperidinyl)methyl, 2-(4-morpholinyl)ethyl, 1-(N-methyl-2-pyrrolidinyl)methyl, 1-(N-methyl-3-morpholinyl)methyl, (tetrahydropyran-4-yl)methyl, 1-methylazepanyl, phenyl, or halophenyl group, with substitution at the carbon of the methanone group by an adamantyl, naphthyl, phenyl, benzyl, quinolinyl, cycloalkyl, 1-amino-3-methyl-1-oxobutan-2-yl, 1-amino-3,3-dimethyl-1-oxobutan-2-yl, 1-methoxy-3-methyl-1-oxobutan-2-yl, 1-methoxy-3,3-dimethyl-1-oxobutan-2-yl or pyrrole group, and whether or not further substituted in the benzimidazole, adamantyl, naphthyl, phenyl, pyrrole, quinolinyl, or cycloalkyl rings to any extent. Benzimidazole Ketones include, but are not limited to:

a.   naphthalen-1-yl(1-pentyl-1H-benzo[d]imidazol-2-l)methanone (JWH-018 benzimidazole analog), or

b.   (1-(5-fluoropentyl)-1H-benzo[d]imidazol-2-yl)(naphthalen-1-yl)methanone (FUBIMINA); and

14. Modified by Replacement: any compound defined in this subsection that is modified by replacement of a carbon with nitrogen in the indole, naphthyl, indene, benzimidazole, or carbazole ring.

Added by Laws 1971, c. 119, § 2-204, operative Sept. 1, 1971. Amended by Laws 1976, c. 291, § 1, emerg. eff. June 17, 1976; Laws 1978, c. 194, § 3, emerg. eff. April 14, 1978; Laws 1984, c. 127, § 1, eff. Nov. 1, 1984; Laws 1987, c. 138, § 3, emerg. eff. June 19, 1987; Laws 1994, c. 140, § 1, eff. Sept. 1, 1994; Laws 1995, c. 54, § 2, eff. July 1, 1995; Laws 1998, c. 100, § 1, emerg. eff. April 13, 1998; Laws 2000, c. 16, § 1, emerg. eff. April 3, 2000; Laws 2001, c. 99, § 2, eff. July 1, 2001; Laws 2001, c. 373, § 2, eff. July 1, 2001; Laws 2005, c. 283, § 1, eff. Nov. 1, 2005; Laws 2008, c. 332,

§ 1, eff. Nov. 1, 2008; Laws 2010, c. 182, § 1, eff. Nov. 1, 2010; Laws 2011, c. 239, § 2, eff. Nov. 1, 2011; Laws 2012, c. 80, § 2, eff. Nov. 1, 2012; Laws 2013, c. 181, § 1, eff. Nov. 1, 2013; Laws 2014, c. 154, § 2, eff. Nov. 1, 2014; Laws 2015, c. 305, § 3.

As you can easily see, the above is a complete nightmare for anybody who doesn't have at least a basic understanding of chemistry or even the basic elements of chemistry. It is nothing an average person should dive into intellectually, nor could he. I don't know what any of the above means. I have absolutely no idea. It doesn't even register. It is a mumble jumble of nonsense. Except it is no nonsense. It is the law. And I am quite sure, when this schedule was adopted in this State from some federal registry, nobody else had any idea what they are signing into law. I only can imagine, they were told that this is what some Federal agency determined is now the reference for drugs and that is all, there is to it. And they have to adopt it or otherwise fall behind or something to that effect.

It is quite overwhelming, isn't it and maybe that was the whole point. Adopt this schedule and let us worry about the rest, we, the Federal agency know, what we are doing. All your State has to do is fall in line so we all can be on the same page. I guess, that was the whole idea.

What is more interesting is the definition of Schedule I.

§63-2-203. Schedule I characteristics.

Schedule I includes substances with the following characteristics:

1. High potential for abuse;

2. No accepted medical use in the United States or lacks accepted safety for use in treatment under medical supervision.

Added by Laws 1971, c. 119, § 2-203.

On the other side of this highly restrictive schedule are the characteristics of Schedule V, which reads:

§63-2-211. Schedule V characteristics.

Schedule V includes substances with the following characteristics:

1. Low potential for abuse relative to the controlled substances listed in Schedule IV;

2. Currently accepted medical use in treatment in the United States; and

3. Limited physical dependence or psychological dependence liability relative to the controlled substances listed in Schedule IV.

Added by Laws 1971, c. 119, § 2-211.

Schedule I thus are basically all illegal drugs, because no good medical use was found or could be determined. And Schedule V are OTC medications and other readily available and prescribed substances. The Schedule I drugs also include a wide array of industrial use chemicals. It must be understood that industrial applications call upon a wide variety of highly poisonous substances which are not meant for consumption.

It probably took a lot of work and a lot of years to put together all these distinctions in drugs and work out the classifications, exceptions and procedures for hundreds of types and classes of drugs. As I said, I only really added the information about the drug Schedules to illustrate the rather complex nature of drugs. It is not a static, never changing picture. Drugs evolve, change, get enhanced, mixed, re-manufactured, re-designed and re-packaged in various forms and variations and it can be hard for any administration to keep up with it and protect the public. To change any formula in the current drug schedule is not so hard if you deal with it in a controlled environment like a submission by a drug manufacturer who wants to introduce a newly developed medicine. To follow up on new street drugs and what they might be and can be is probably much harder. A new illegal drug has to be detected first. And after a few busts and tests on obviously intoxicated persons at a traffic stop or such things, someone might come to the conclusion, that something new is being sold and handed out on the street, because no commonly used test will detect that new player. And somewhere along the line, the Board of Pharmacy will conclude that a new type of street drug has hit the market and will propose to put it on the Schedule I roster, giving law enforcement the tools to do something about it.

The knowledge of the drug schedules gives someone also an understanding of how law enforcement uses these in real life, because they are the basic of drug related arrests.

The drug Schedules are basically the bread and butter of all drug related offenses and define what is legal and what is not. They furthermore define a lot of other things as well. They define who can manufacture and sell any type of drugs legally and under what circumstances. They define who can buy certain drugs and under what circumstances. They define how much of a certain drug someone can buy. They define how certain type of drugs are to be stored. The obvious goal of all these names and rules and definitions is to control the circulation of drugs, legal or illegal.

If I list the drug subject as one of the things by which we will remedy the incarceration rate in the United States, what am I talking about then?

The law in this State provides for some draconian penalties as far as drugs are concerned. The list of punishments and sentences provided is long and multifaceted. If you take §63-2-328 and go down the list, there are already numerous examples of how serious the misuse of drugs is taken in this country. §63-2-332 provides for a penalty of not more than $ 10 000 if you find yourself in the possession of more than 7.2 grams of substances with which you can produce methamphetamine, unless you are a licensed manufacturer or dealer of this substance. It is classified as a misdemeanor. But not long after that, §63-2-333 makes it a felony, punishable by not more than 10 years in prison, if you knowingly sell these types of products to people who aren't supposed to have them. In other words, it can be a very fine line, if you as a prosecutor want to make a case against a maker or dealer of substances, which produce sub-products for certain street or simply illegal drugs, which is why hardly any case is brought to courts on that subject. What District Attorney wants to spend month and countless man hours on trying to find out – beyond a reasonable doubt that is – if a manufacturer of a substance, which serves as a basis to produce a certain, illegal drug, knew exactly about the credentials of a buyer for his drugs. In other words, did he know, that the credentials of this person or company were forged? Is or was it his duty to check any and all paperwork of any and all potential buyers of any State within the jurisdiction of the United States of America? I would say hardly so, which is why there are bigger holes in these paragraphs than you can imagine. They certainly read fairly competent and legally perfect, but if you look at it more closely, you will see that the State tried, which is all the State can really do. You cannot criminalize a dozen of drug manufacturers if they happen to accidentally fail to fully verify a company's credentials or even the real name of a Sales Rep. That is certainly not their job, that is more or less the job of the District Attorney or the police force or whoever. The producer of chemicals wants to sell his chemicals and he does so in the belief, that these chemicals are used for its intended purposes and not for the production of illegal street drugs. That is the reason, why you won't find manufacturers of chemicals behind bars. Only because you produce deadly weapons and sell them, doesn't mean, you tell your customers to use them accordingly. The production of chemicals is necessary and vital for the treatment of crops and people, if criminals use these same chemicals for illegal activities, that can't be their problem. It is not their job to oversee every customer and whether or not he uses the product per its intended use.

That leaves the individual, the end user.

I am not going to bore the reader with how many people are incarcerated because of drug offenses. There are already numerous data collecting sites online on that subject. The more interesting approach is, what the prosecutor will throw at somebody, who commits a felony or misdemeanor in the world of drugs, because it is very interesting. There is an abundance of laws in effect, which provides for an endless number of charges which can be brought against someone, who either deals in drugs or uses drugs. The majority of these offenses are covered in §63. To give you just a little idea of what we are dealing with, I would like to quote §63-2-401:

§63-2-401. Prohibited acts A - Penalties.

A.   Except as authorized by the Uniform Controlled Dangerous Substances Act, it shall be unlawful for any person:

1.   To distribute, dispense, transport with intent to distribute or dispense, possess with intent to manufacture, distribute, or dispense, a controlled dangerous substance or to solicit the use of or use the services of a person less than eighteen (18) years of age to cultivate, distribute or dispense a controlled dangerous substance;

2.	To create, distribute, transport with intent to distribute or dispense, or possess with intent to distribute, a counterfeit controlled dangerous substance; or

3.	To distribute any imitation controlled substance as defined by Section 2-101 of this title, except when authorized by the Food and Drug Administration of the United States Department of Health and Human Services.

B. Any person who violates the provisions of this section with respect to:

1. A substance classified in Schedule I or II which is a narcotic drug, lysergic acid diethylamide (LSD), gamma butyrolactone, gamma hydroxyvalerate, gamma valerolactone, 1,4 butanediol, or gamma-hydroxybutyric acid as defined in Sections 2-204 and 2-208 of this title, upon conviction, shall be guilty of a felony and shall be sentenced to a term of imprisonment for not less than five (5) years nor more than life and a fine of not more than One Hundred Thousand Dollars ($100,000.00), which shall be in addition to other punishment provided by law and shall not be imposed in lieu of other punishment. Any sentence to the custody of the Department of Corrections shall not be subject to statutory provisions for suspended sentences, deferred sentences, or probation except when the conviction is for a first offense;

2. Any other controlled dangerous substance classified in Schedule I, II, III, or IV, upon conviction, shall be guilty of a felony and shall be sentenced to a term of imprisonment for not less than two (2) years nor more than life and a fine of not more than Twenty Thousand Dollars ($20,000.00), which shall be in addition to other punishment provided by law and shall not be imposed in lieu of other punishment. Any sentence to the custody of the Department of Corrections shall not be subject to statutory provisions for suspended sentences, deferred sentences, or probation except when the conviction is for a first offense;

3. A substance classified in Schedule V, upon conviction, shall be guilty of a felony and shall be sentenced to a term of imprisonment for not more than five (5) years and a fine of not more than One Thousand Dollars ($1,000.00), which shall be in addition to other punishment provided by law and shall not be imposed in lieu of other punishment; or

4. An imitation controlled substance as defined by Section 2-101 of this title, upon conviction, shall be guilty of a misdemeanor and shall be sentenced to a term of imprisonment in the county jail for a period of not more than one (1) year and a fine of not more than One Thousand Dollars ($1,000.00). A person convicted of a second violation of the provisions of this paragraph shall be guilty of a felony and shall be sentenced to a term of imprisonment for not more than five (5) years and a fine of not more than Five Thousand Dollars ($5,000.00), which shall be in addition to other punishment provided by law and shall not be imposed in lieu of other punishment.

C. 1. Except when authorized by the Food and Drug Administration of the United States Department of Health and Human Services, it shall be unlawful for any person to manufacture, cultivate, distribute, or possess with intent to distribute a synthetic controlled substance.

2. Any person convicted of violating the provisions of this paragraph is guilty of a felony and shall be punished by imprisonment for a term not to exceed life and a fine of not more than Twenty-five Thousand Dollars ($25,000.00), which shall be in addition to other punishment provided by law and shall not be imposed in lieu of other punishment.

3. A second or subsequent conviction for the violation of the provisions of this paragraph is a felony punishable as a habitual offender pursuant to Section 51.1 of Title 21 of the Oklahoma Statutes.

4. In addition, the violator shall be fined an amount not more than One Hundred Thousand Dollars ($100,000.00), which shall be in addition to other punishment provided by law and shall not be imposed in lieu of other punishment.

D. 1. Any person convicted of a second or subsequent felony violation of the provisions of this section, except for paragraph 4 of subsection B of this section, shall be punished as a habitual offender pursuant to Section 51.1 of Title 21 of the Oklahoma Statutes.

2. In addition, the violator shall be fined twice the fine otherwise authorized, which shall be in addition to other punishment provided by law and shall not be imposed in lieu of other punishment.

3. Convictions for second or subsequent violations of the provisions of this section shall not be subject to statutory provisions for suspended sentences, deferred sentences, or probation.

E. Any person who is at least eighteen (18) years of age and who violates the provisions of this section by using or soliciting the use of services of a person less than eighteen (18) years of age to distribute, dispense, transport with intent to distribute or dispense or cultivate a controlled dangerous substance or by distributing a controlled dangerous substance to a person under eighteen (18) years of age, is punishable by twice the fine and by twice the imprisonment otherwise authorized.

F. Any person who violates any provision of this section by transporting with intent to distribute or dispense, distributing or possessing with intent to distribute a controlled dangerous substance to a person, or violation of subsection G of this section, in or on, or within two thousand (2,000) feet of the real property comprising a public or private elementary or secondary school, public vocational school, public or private college or university, or other institution of higher education, recreation center or public park, including state parks and recreation areas, public housing project, or child care facility as defined by Section 402 of Title 10 of the Oklahoma Statutes, shall be punished by:

1. For a first offense, a term of imprisonment, or by the imposition of a fine or by both, not exceeding twice that authorized by the

212

appropriate provision of this section and shall serve a minimum of fifty percent (50%) of the sentence received prior to becoming eligible for state correctional institution earned credits toward the completion of the sentence; or

2. For a second or subsequent offense, a term of imprisonment as provided for a habitual offender pursuant to Section 51.1 of Title 21 of the Oklahoma Statutes. In addition, the violator shall serve eighty-five percent (85%) of the sentence received prior to becoming eligible for state correctional institution earned credits toward the completion of the sentence or eligibility for parole.

G. 1. Except as authorized by the Uniform Controlled Dangerous Substances Act, it shall be unlawful for any person to manufacture or attempt to manufacture any controlled dangerous substance or possess any substance listed in Section 2-322 of this title or any substance containing any detectable amount of pseudoephedrine or its salts, optical isomers or salts of optical isomers, iodine or its salts, optical isomers or salts of optical isomers, hydriodic acid, sodium metal, lithium metal, anhydrous ammonia, phosphorus, or organic solvents with the intent to use that substance to manufacture a controlled dangerous substance.

2. Any person violating the provisions of this subsection with respect to the unlawful manufacturing or attempting to unlawfully manufacture any controlled dangerous substance, or possessing any substance listed in this subsection or Section 2-322 of this title, upon conviction, is guilty of a felony and shall be punished by imprisonment for not less than seven (7) years nor more than life and by a fine of not less than Fifty Thousand Dollars ($50,000.00), which shall be in addition to other punishment provided by law and shall not be imposed in lieu of other punishment. The possession of any amount of anhydrous ammonia in an unauthorized container shall be prima facie evidence of intent to use such substance to manufacture a controlled dangerous substance.

3. Any person violating the provisions of this subsection with respect to the unlawful manufacturing or attempting to unlawfully

manufacture any controlled dangerous substance in the following amounts:

a.   one (1) kilogram or more of a mixture or substance containing a detectable amount of heroin,

b.   five (5) kilograms or more of a mixture or substance containing a detectable amount of:

(1)   coca leaves, except coca leaves and extracts of coca leaves from which cocaine, ecgonine, and derivatives of ecgonine or their salts have been removed,

(2)   cocaine, its salts, optical and geometric isomers, and salts of isomers,

(3)   ecgonine, its derivatives, their salts, isomers, and salts of isomers, or

(4)   any compound, mixture, or preparation which contains any quantity of any of the substances referred to in divisions (1) through (3) of this subparagraph,

c.   fifty (50) grams or more of a mixture or substance described in division (2) of subparagraph b of this paragraph which contains cocaine base,

d.   one hundred (100) grams or more of phencyclidine (PCP) or 1 kilogram or more of a mixture or substance containing a detectable amount of phencyclidine (PCP),

e.   ten (10) grams or more of a mixture or substance containing a detectable amount of lysergic acid diethylamide (LSD),

f.   four hundred (400) grams or more of a mixture or substance containing a detectable amount of N-phenyl-N-[1-(2-pheylethy)-4-piperidinyl] propanamide or 100 grams or more of a mixture or substance containing a detectable amount of any analogue of N-phenyl-N-[1-(2-phenylethyl)-4-piperidinyl] propanamide,

g.   one thousand (1,000) kilograms or more of a mixture or substance containing a detectable amount of marihuana or one thousand (1000) or more marihuana plants regardless of weight, or

h.   fifty (50) grams or more of methamphetamine, its salts, isomers, and salts of its isomers or 500 grams or more of a mixture or substance containing a detectable amount of methamphetamine, its salts, isomers, or salts of its isomers, upon conviction, is guilty of aggravated manufacturing a controlled dangerous substance punishable by imprisonment for not less than twenty (20) years nor more than life and by a fine of not less than Fifty Thousand Dollars ($50,000.00), which shall be in addition to other punishment provided by law and shall not be imposed in lieu of other punishment. Any person convicted of a violation of the provisions of this paragraph shall be required to serve a minimum of eighty-five percent (85%) of the sentence received prior to becoming eligible for state correctional earned credits towards the completion of the sentence or eligible for parole.

4. Any sentence to the custody of the Department of Corrections for any violation of paragraph 3 of this subsection shall not be subject to statutory provisions for suspended sentences, deferred sentences, or probation. A person convicted of a second or subsequent violation of the provisions of paragraph 3 of this subsection shall be punished as a habitual offender pursuant to Section 51.1 of Title 21 of the Oklahoma Statutes and shall be required to serve a minimum of eighty-five percent (85%) of the sentence received prior to becoming eligible for state correctional earned credits or eligibility for parole.

5. Any person who has been convicted of manufacturing or attempting to manufacture methamphetamine pursuant to the provisions of this subsection and who, after such conviction,

purchases or attempts to purchase, receive or otherwise acquire any product, mixture, or preparation containing any detectable quantity of base pseudoephedrine or ephedrine shall, upon conviction, be guilty of a felony punishable by imprisonment in the custody of the Department of Corrections for a term in the range of twice the minimum term provided for in paragraph 2 of this subsection.

H. Any person convicted of any offense described in the Uniform Controlled Dangerous Substances Act may, in addition to the fine imposed, be assessed an amount not to exceed ten percent (10%) of the fine imposed. Such assessment shall be paid into a revolving fund for enforcement of controlled dangerous substances created pursuant to Section 2-506 of this title.

I.   Any person convicted of any offense described in this section shall, in addition to any fine imposed, pay a special assessment trauma-care fee of One Hundred Dollars ($100.00) to be deposited into the Trauma Care Assistance Revolving Fund created in Section 1-2522 of this title.

J. For purposes of this section, "public housing project" means any dwelling or accommodations operated as a state or federally subsidized multifamily housing project by any housing authority, nonprofit corporation or municipal developer or housing projects created pursuant to the Oklahoma Housing Authorities Act.

K. When a person is found guilty of a violation of the provisions of this section, the court shall order, in addition to any other penalty, the defendant to pay a one-hundred-dollar assessment to be deposited in the Drug Abuse Education and Treatment Revolving Fund created in Section 2-503.2 of this title, upon collection.

        Most of the above the average person probably never even heard of, which is quite natural. After all, this is only interesting for people, who actually either prosecute or defend accused people in a court of law. This section is titled "Prohibited Acts A – Penalties", there are several other sections, entitled the same, but instead "A", it goes "B", "C" and so on.

In addition to the crime category itself, the law provides for certain enhancements of the penalties described above. If you look at G 4 and 5 above for instance, a repeat offender needs to either serve 85% of the punishment imposed before he will be eligible for any credits or serve double the punishment to begin with. That can be a lot of time already. But it doesn't stop there. It is not done by simply doing your time, either. It continues with the punishments in form of enormous fines and penalties which can be imposed on him. You see this playing out in G 5 I and K. There is such a thing as the Trauma Care Assistance Revolving Fund and the Drugs Abuse Education and Treatment Revolving Fund. These two Funds are mentioned in Penalties A as quoted above, but I am sure there are other Funds as well, into which the convicted offender is ordered to pay into or can be ordered to pay into. The system of incarceration is not only a system of individual punishments, but one of payments into various funds, which were apparently designed to benefit the community.

If you didn't have the money to voluntarily pay into funds, which would benefit your community when you were a free man or woman, then the authorities can at last force you to pay into such funds when you get locked up. I think this is rather memorable. And for all intends and purposes, I don't think it is a bad thing. If you are a rather healthy individual, financially speaking, you should be able to use that wealth to your benefit, as most rich people already do. They can hire a good lawyer or a team of legal advocates rather to make them do what they must. Therefore, they can not only negate the severity of their punishments, they can also negotiate the length of their imprisonment by voluntarily paying huge sums into these organizations. But to make this system effective, the length of their imprisonment should be the less, the more money they will pay to those organizations, only then would it be effective.

217

Of course, that leaves the man and the woman, who are not rich to their own devices. If they can't wave around $ 2 000 000, they are subject to the full wrath of the legal system.

But that really is the case for any crime, but we are dealing with drug related crimes, so let's not lose our focus here.

I already mentioned the many drug-related categories for which someone can be locked up. We heard of the numerous enhancement categories, which the State puts into action in an attempt to quell further drug related crimes. If you don't want to look through the very detailed and lengthy Oklahoma Statutes to educate yourself on the various laws on the subject, I would like to recommend ODOC's own paperwork on this, which is covered in DOC policy OP-060211, starting at page 11. As any other policy of the agency, which is not deemed confidential, it can easily be found on their website. It details roughly which crime categories are excluded from credit levels achievements, which will cause an offender to discharge his sentence earlier than the Judge ordered, because he builds up a history of good behavior. But the DOC has put even more work into the subject of letting family members of inmates know, what is going on with their son, father or cousin. They produced an entire guide for family members, which I would like to recommend. It doesn't go into great details and quotes like I occasionally do in laying out the subject of incarceration, but it nevertheless does a decent job in providing some idea and explanations of why things are as they are. It is called the "Guide for Families & Friends of offenders" and of course is available from the website. My version is from 2013 and not much has changed since then which is why they didn't see a need to publish an updated version and I must agree.

The big question of this chapter is then: Should we legalize drugs or any part of the manufacturing, distribution and consumption of drugs? This chapter wouldn't be so long, if the question would be an easy one to answer, but with a combination of the right ingredients, I

218

think we can make a substantial difference for the better in the incarceration rate of the American public.

Why do I care if people take drugs in the first place? How is it any of my business what my neighbor or friends chose to put into their bodies? Why do we have to pay billions of dollars to the government for armies, who either go into foreign countries to fight drug operations or support other armies to do the same? Why should I care that thousands of people kill themselves every year because they overdose on drugs? As far as I can see, there are two main reasons for the entire war on drugs.

1.   We are afraid that it eventually will affect us personally. We don't want to be mugged, killed or bothered in any way because some addict needs money for his next fix.

2.   We want to protect the innocent, which is the children, either our own or the children who are raised in a drug environment, which means one of their relatives either takes drugs or deals in drugs or both.

I really can't see other reasons and I thought about this one long and hard. If you ask me, why I don't like drugs or why I don't like people who take drugs, it would be these two answers. As far as drugs are concerned, I would implement the following:

A. Let the citizens of this country make up their own mind if they want to take drugs, in other words, legalize them. This might be a hard point to swallow, because it hasn't been done in recent times. And when I say it hasn't been done in recent times, I mean there was a time, when drugs weren't an issue in this country and we just moved along fine. That doesn't mean that citizens didn't get high on something. It was either some naturally occurring plant material, poisons in small doses, Absinth and whatever else. People who wanted to get high did so no matter the times, because it was a free country and the people of this free country experimented with them just like they do today. It might

219

have been in smaller doses, but drug abuse existed nevertheless.

I don't know on what planet you live on, who your neighbors are or your family members, but I know a lot of people who take drugs and have easy access to drugs. I know that if you want to get drugs, you will be able to get them, no matter what the laws tell you or what the authorities tell you. The drug trade is well and alive in the United States of America like it is in any other country which calls itself a democracy. The battle against drugs is not won by demonizing them and ever increasing the penalties for drug offenses, it is won by education and setting an example. You can't keep telling people that they live in a free country and at the same time, try your hardest to restrict them and try to force them to do what you think is best. The promise of freedom comes not only with possibilities to do things and to become somebody, it also comes with responsibilities. And I think we fall a little short on that subject.   But before you call me all sorts of names and declare me insane, I invite you to read on and try to see the whole picture.

B. I would make it illegal for any individual to be intoxicated in public. That means, you leave your house and you are intoxicated, you are going down. The penalties for being intoxicated while in public would increase, the more responsibilities you have while in public. If you are just walking around and being disrespectful and mouthy towards other people, an officer should be able to perform a field sobriety test like they do at traffic stops. If you are found to be intoxicated, you would need to pay a fine, depending on the level of intoxication and the ruckus you caused.

The liabilities would increase the more harmful your intoxication would be for others. If you drive, you are obviously more dangerous to other people than if you just walk, thus the penalties would be higher. The same would account for operating machinery, like a truck or an amusement park ride. In other words, if your proven intoxication is potentially harmful to more people, the punishment would increase. In

220

this way, you can do what you want to do in your private life, but as soon as you are out in the public, your punishment for being drunk or drugged rises exponentially with the amount of people your intoxication affects or could affect.

Government and privately owned corporations could even conduct mandatory drug tests as they would see fit. If you work in a sensitive area, you would be drug tested more often than people who are not. If you are a truck or a bus driver, you would be drug tested every week. The same accounts for people who are in security related fields like being able to access private financial data or other relevant information. And if you are a bus driver for two years and never failed a drug test, the time frame for drug tests could be extended to monthly and so on, you get the idea.

Your drug test history could even be part of your next job application if you want it to. You could voluntarily add that information to your application for your next job, as part of your resume. What company wouldn't want an employee who hasn't taken drugs in 10 years?

Now what drugs would a company test for? Well, for starters, they could simply perform the same sobriety test as in current traffic stops and beyond that point, they pretty much can test for whatever they see fit.

C. Life insurance agencies already charge you a premium if you admit that you are a smoker. They just double your insurance payments because somebody determined that smoking can cause premature death and other serious health issues. That has become an accepted norm nowadays. If you ask anybody if smoking is a health risk, every single person will tell you, yes, it is. And why can't we do the same for drugs? If you are a drug user, as determined by your own admission, your life insurance payments are going to be high. How this works with life insurance agencies and smokers is pretty simple. They just ask you if you

221

smoke. If it comes to any kind of claim or payout and it is determined by interviewing witnesses or autopsies that you in fact were a smoker but didn't admit to it, fraud is assumed and no payments will be made. That is how it works with smokers and I don't see any reasons why it shouldn't be the same for drug users.

D. Government funded organization like the Food Stamp program, unemployment benefits and the lot could do the same thing. They would decrease payouts by 5% for a period of 6 month if the recipient was found being intoxicated by drugs. Thus it would be beneficial to be free of drugs, for you, for your family and for your kids. Being drug free would become a very beneficial thing to do. Before you decide to get high, you would think twice, or three times. You would think of the responsibilities and potential effects it would have, wouldn't you? You would still be able to get high, which is the great thing in my scenario. But the effects of you being high and irresponsible would not affect me, if I chose to stay drug free. As every politician will tell you, this is a free country and we should honor that promise of the founding fathers of this great nation.

In my scenario, we would be closer to the true meaning of that promise. We would also be able to empty the prisons, which is why this chapter is the first in the "Remedies" section, because undoubtedly it would have the most sweeping effect on the prison population.

E. Gang crimes would mostly be a thing of the past. Not only would there be no real reason to be in a gang, there would be no gang wars over territory. What are gangs doing, really? They sell illegal drugs on some corner or in some ominous location, where normal people not dare to go to. What would be left of a gang, if they couldn't dabble in the distribution of illegal drugs? What would happen to the drug lords, who ship the drugs to our continent? I don't know for sure, but I think they would have to find other ways to make money, maybe they would use their influence to farm corn or some other, useful activity. The United

States of America would save so much money, only thinking about it gives me the chills of excitement.

F. Courts and judges would be able to provide speedy trials to most offenders, because there wouldn't be any drug crimes to prosecute. They would be able to concentrate on real crimes, which is to say violent ones, or financial crimes or crimes against children and other, innocent people. They would be free of having to listen to any crook who got caught one too many times with a little bit of weed.

G. If a drug company wants to introduce a new type of drug or an enhanced version of an already existing drug for treatment of an ailment, they would have to file for approval just as they currently do. Nothing would have to change about that procedure. In actual fact, the Federal Government will still have to keep a drug schedule of sorts for that particular purpose. They want to keep track of things which are on the market already and want to be able to compare new substances with already existing once so they can determine a potential benefit and dabble in the procedure to trademark a new drug before it becomes readily available in the mass market.

H. Last but not least, the United States of America and every State in it should invest in a massive public education campaign targeting the harmful effects of drugs, similar to what is being done in the State of Oklahoma already with the use of tobacco products. Apparently, it proved to be pretty successful. One of these campaigns could look like the following:

The camera focusses on a truck, driving on some open road. The truck passes a big street sign on the side of the road. The sign says "US customs ahead – 10 miles". The camera angle focusses on the sign with the truck driving along the same road, slowly disappearing into the dark, only the red rear lights are still visible. The entire scene is maybe a minute long. After even the red rear lights of the truck vanish in the dark and only the road itself can be seen, a voice finally can be heard, saying:

"This is a man in his truck. Let's call him Mister X. He is on his way to enter the United States of America. Welded inside the frame rails of his truck are 15 Kilograms of pure heroin. The 15 kilo of 95 % pure heroin will be stretched into 400 kg of heroin, packaged for resale on the streets of a large, American city. This heroin will later cause a desperate drug addict to shoot your local gas station attendant to steal money for his heroin addiction. The same drug will cause a father to take his families savings of $ 15 000 out of his savings account to buy more of that same drug which Mister X just brought to our shores. Karen, your classmate for the last two years, will die in three years in her boyfriend's apartment, because he injected her with an overdose of that same heroin. He couldn't call for help, because he woke up four hours after Karen did her last breath. Two more people will die of an overdose of that same batch of heroin. One is a mother of two, who just started to take heroin, encouraged by her new friend who said, it is the best thing you ever tried. The other victim is a runaway you never even met." Out of the dark sight of the fading street, a shot of a young woman materializes. She doesn't have a name. While the camera slowly turns, a line of other people comes into focus and several houses also materialize, a scene of a neighborhood fills the screen, the voice says "Don't let drugs enter your neighborhood. Make sure that everybody knows where you stand. Just say no."

You know, something like that. With all that money saved on the justice system, we should be able to run a massive public education campaign. After a while, it would become totally unacceptable for anyone to even mention heroin, meth or even weed. People who take any sort of drugs would be completely confined to their own house, pretty much like it is with cigarettes today. I mean, I like my occasional cigarette, but you can't go anywhere where smoking is permitted anymore, provided you are not into gambling, because in Casinos you still can. But that is too much smoke even for me, so I avoid them. And what a public education campaign can do is evident by a chart provided by our statistical data gatherers in the CDC. Look at the following:

Trends in Current Cigarette Smoking Among High School Students and Adults, United States, 1965–2014

	Students* (%)	Adults** (%)
1965		42.4
1966		
1967		
1968		
1969		
1970		37.4
1971		
1972		
1973		
1974		37.1
1975		
1976		
1977		
1978		34.1
1979		

Year		
1980		33.2
1981		
1982		
1983		32.1
1984		
1985		30.1
1986		
1987		28.8
1988		
1989		
1990		25.5
1991	27.5	
1992		
1993	30.5	25
1994		
1995	34.8	24.7
1996		
1997	36.4	24.7
1998		
1999	34.8	23.5

2000		
2001	28.5	22.8
2002	22.5	
2003	21.9	21.6
2004	20.9	
2005	23	20.9
2006	20.8	
2007	20	19.8
2008	20.6	
2009	19.5	20.6
2010	19.3	
2011	18.1	19.0
2012	18.1	
2013	15.7	17.8
2014	16.8	

You can find the above chart on the Centers for Disease Control and Prevention website, chapter "Smoking and Tobacco Use". It will provide you with a bunch of other information as well, I just happen to pick up a page, which illustrates the decline of tobacco usage among students and adults in the United States in a time period from 1965 to 2014, whereby student data was not recorded before 1991 or couldn't be collected per the CDC. But even though, the main body of information is focused on the use of cigarettes over the years and how it declined. I don't see any reason, why this could not be done for drugs as well.

Per "Drugwafacts.org", the number of deaths attributed to tobacco smoking each year from 2005 through 2009 was at 480 320, whereby the total number of drug induced deaths for 2015 was at 55 403. Apparently, tobacco related death out-number drug related deaths by roughly 8.6 to 1. I mean, numbers are numbers and as I said, there is probably an enormous amount of data out there and information and accuracy might be slightly different depending on who is collecting the information, how it is collected and other parameters. However, it seemed really a little odd that we spend so much money on the war on drugs compared to the war on tobacco. Yet we are apparently much more successful reducing the use of tobacco by means of education than we are reducing the use of drugs through warfare and criminalizing drug use. Something seems to be odd here. We are spending billions of dollars to prevent drugs from entering the country and we are spending billions more on drug warfare by locking everybody up for using or possessing drugs. But it doesn't seem to be nowhere near as successful as simply educating the public on the disadvantages of smoking. I find this to be very interesting, think about it for a minute.

I mentioned above that one of the reasons for condemning drugs is, that we are afraid of the effects it might have on our own life and on our own environment. I really think with an approach like this, we can make significant progress in eliminating the effects which drug consumption has on our own life, I really do.

And if we empty prisons, we can put more money into things, we all benefit from, like playgrounds, books for schools and libraries, extending unemployment benefits, etc.

B. Protecting the innocent

There is however one more area we need to address. If we take all this serious, we must protect the ones, which can't protect themselves, our children. How are we going to shape our future? What kind of people are we raising? The subject of child care and child protection is actually pretty well covered already, we might have to pay a little more attention to it and maybe we even have to adjust the laws a little bit in that or the other direction, but generally speaking, a child in this State is a fairly well protected, human being.

If we lack in child protection, it probably would be in the department of personnel. I think the Department of Human Services needs more staff to follow up on Police Department Reports, School reports and other sources to hear about, investigate and act upon possible child neglect or child endangerment incidents. I would love to see some politician announce, that we are not going to build another aircraft carrier or we are not going to finance yet another jet fighter program for $ 40 Billion, instead we are going to increase the Department of Human Service's ability to follow up on reports of child neglect and child endangerment. And I would love to hear the State government or Federal government representative announce, that they will finance the building of campuses for children in abusive environments to go to and get a decent education, both on a High School level as well as on a University level. I don't know, what is so wrong with that idea.

That connection between remedies for our overcrowded prisons and the lack of services to protect and support children seems out of context and far-fetched. But I don't think it is as I already mentioned in point 2 above. I said, the second reason we are so afraid of drug related incidents and crimes is, that we fear for the future of our children and that they might have to grow up or could be affected in a negative way by drug environments. And if part of a solution is to legalize drugs as described in point 1 above, then the subject of increasing the protection of our children must be next and must be part of the solution as well.

If we allow citizens to do what they please within their own dwelling, which we already do to a certain degree, then we must protect the innocent from possible abuse of that freedom as well. To do only one thing and neglect to do the other would be a possible dangerous neglect, at least for some.

We already have laws in effect to protect children in their own homes. Anybody can file a report with the local Police Department if child neglect is assumed. It doesn't take the Police Department much to check on a home where such a report is submitted. All we have to do is to enforce the existing laws a little bit better and we would have point 2 covered, because the laws already exist, we just don't seem to have enough people in the Department of Human Services to enforce them. Here is what one section of our current law says. It is §21-843-5:

§21-843.5. Child abuse - Child neglect - Child sexual abuse - Child sexual exploitation - Enabling - Penalties.

A. Any parent or other person who shall willfully or maliciously engage in child abuse shall, upon conviction, be guilty of a felony punishable by imprisonment in the custody of the Department of Corrections not exceeding life imprisonment, or by imprisonment in a county jail not exceeding one (1) year, or by a fine of not less than Five Hundred Dollars ($500.00) nor more than Five Thousand Dollars ($5,000.00), or both such fine and imprisonment. As used in this subsection, "child abuse" means the willful or malicious harm or threatened harm or failure to protect from harm or threatened harm to the health, safety, or welfare of a child under eighteen (18) years of age by another, or the act of willfully or maliciously injuring, torturing or maiming a child under eighteen (18) years of age by another.

B.	Any parent or other person who shall willfully or maliciously engage in enabling child abuse shall, upon conviction, be punished by imprisonment in the custody of the Department of Corrections not exceeding life imprisonment, or by imprisonment in a county jail not exceeding one (1) year, or by a fine of not less than Five Hundred Dollars ($500.00) nor more than Five Thousand Dollars ($5,000.00) or both such fine and imprisonment. As used in this subsection, "enabling child abuse" means the causing, procuring or permitting of a willful or malicious act of harm or threatened harm or failure to protect from harm or threatened harm to the health, safety, or welfare of a child under eighteen (18) years of age by another. As used in this subsection, "permit" means to authorize or allow for the care of a child by an individual when the person authorizing or allowing such care knows or reasonably should know that the child will be placed at risk of abuse as proscribed by this subsection.

C.	Any parent or other person who shall willfully or maliciously engage in child neglect shall, upon conviction, be punished by imprisonment in the custody of the Department of Corrections not exceeding life imprisonment, or by imprisonment in a county jail not exceeding one (1) year, or by a fine of not less than Five Hundred Dollars ($500.00) nor more than Five Thousand Dollars ($5,000.00), or both such fine and imprisonment. As used in this subsection, "child neglect" means the willful or malicious neglect, as defined by paragraph 47 of Section 1-1-105 of Title 10A of the Oklahoma Statutes, of a child under eighteen (18) years of age by another.

D. Any parent or other person who shall willfully or maliciously engage in enabling child neglect shall, upon conviction, be punished by imprisonment in the custody of the Department of Corrections not exceeding life imprisonment, or by imprisonment in a county jail not exceeding one   (1) year, or by a fine of not less than Five Hundred Dollars ($500.00) nor more than Five Thousand Dollars ($5,000.00), or both such fine and imprisonment. As used in this subsection, "enabling child neglect" means the causing, procuring or permitting of a willful or malicious act of child neglect, as defined by paragraph 47 of Section 1-1-105 of Title 10A of the Oklahoma Statutes, of a child under eighteen (18) years of age by another. As used in this subsection, "permit" means to authorize or allow for the care of a child by an individual when the person authorizing or allowing such care knows or reasonably should know that the child will be placed at risk of neglect as   proscribed by this subsection.

The above only describes child abuse in general. In the same section of the law are a few other paragraphs which refer to child sexual abuse, child sexual endangerment and exploitation, which makes some differences in the age of a child. For instance, E. through H. states the following:

E. Any parent or other person who shall willfully or maliciously engage in child sexual abuse shall, upon conviction, be punished by imprisonment in the custody of the Department of Corrections not exceeding life imprisonment, or by imprisonment in a county jail not exceeding one (1) year, or by a fine of not less than Five Hundred Dollars ($500.00) nor more than Five Thousand Dollars ($5,000.00), or both such fine and imprisonment, except as provided in Section 51.1a of this title or as otherwise provided in subsection F of this section for a child victim under twelve (12) years of age. Except for persons sentenced to life or life without parole, any person sentenced to imprisonment for two (2) years or more for a violation of this subsection shall be required to serve a term of post-imprisonment supervision pursuant to subparagraph f of paragraph 1 of subsection A of Section 991a of Title 22 of the Oklahoma Statutes under conditions determined by the Department of Corrections. The jury shall be advised that the mandatory post-imprisonment supervision shall be in addition to the actual imprisonment. As used in this section, "child sexual abuse" means the willful or malicious sexual abuse, which includes but is not limited to rape, incest, and lewd or indecent acts or proposals, of a child under eighteen (18) years of age by another.

F. Any parent or other person who shall willfully or maliciously engage in sexual abuse to a child under twelve (12) years

232

of age shall, upon conviction, be punished by imprisonment in the custody of the Department of Corrections for not less than twenty-five (25) years nor more than life imprisonment, and by a fine of not less than Five Hundred Dollars ($500.00) nor more than Five Thousand Dollars ($5,000.00).

G. Any parent or other person who shall willfully or maliciously engage in enabling child sexual abuse shall, upon conviction, be punished by imprisonment in the custody of the Department of Corrections not exceeding life imprisonment, or by imprisonment in a county jail not exceeding one (1) year, or by a fine of not less than Five Hundred Dollars ($500.00) nor more than Five Thousand Dollars ($5,000.00), or both such fine and imprisonment. As used in this subsection, "enabling child sexual abuse" means the causing, procuring or permitting of a willful or malicious act of child sexual abuse, which includes but is not limited to rape, incest, and lewd or indecent acts or proposals, of a child under the age of eighteen (18) by another. As used in this subsection, "permit" means to authorize or allow for the care of a child by an individual when the person authorizing or allowing such care knows or reasonably should know that the child will be placed at risk of sexual abuse as proscribed by this subsection.

H. Any parent or other person who shall willfully or maliciously engage in child sexual exploitation shall, upon conviction, be punished by imprisonment in the custody of the Department of Corrections not exceeding life imprisonment, or by imprisonment in a county jail not exceeding one (1) year, or by a fine of not less than Five Hundred Dollars ($500.00) nor more than Five Thousand Dollars ($5,000.00), or both such fine and imprisonment except as provided in subsection I of this section for a child victim under twelve (12) years of age. Except for persons sentenced to life or life without parole, any person sentenced to imprisonment for two (2) years or more for a violation of this subsection shall be required to serve a term of post-imprisonment supervision pursuant to subparagraph f of paragraph 1 of subsection A of Section 991a of Title 22 of the Oklahoma Statutes under conditions determined by the Department of Corrections. The jury shall be advised that the mandatory post-imprisonment supervision shall be in addition to the actual imprisonment. As used in this subsection, "child sexual exploitation" means the willful or malicious sexual exploitation, which includes but is not limited to allowing, permitting, or encouraging a child under eighteen (18) years of age to engage in prostitution or allowing, permitting, encouraging or engaging in the lewd, obscene or pornographic photographing, filming, or depicting of a child under eighteen (18) years of age by another.

It is not the case, that this State or other States don't already have strict laws into place, which protects the innocent, we actually do. There is even another paragraph in the same section of the State law, which covers failure to provide for a child:

§21-852. Omission to provide for a child - Penalties.

A.   Unless otherwise provided for by law, any parent, guardian, or person having custody or control of a child as defined in Section 1-1-105 of Title 10A of the Oklahoma Statutes who willfully omits, without lawful excuse, to furnish necessary food, clothing, shelter, monetary child support, medical attendance, payment of court-ordered day care or payment of court-ordered medical insurance costs for such child which is imposed by law, upon conviction, is guilty of a misdemeanor; provided, any person obligated to make child support payments who willfully and without lawful excuse becomes delinquent in said child support payments after September 1, 1993, and such delinquent child support accrues without payment by the obligor for a period of one (1) year, or exceeds Five Thousand Dollars ($5,000.00) shall, upon conviction thereof, be guilty of a felony which is punishable in the same manner as any subsequent conviction pursuant to the provisions of this section. Any subsequent conviction pursuant to this section shall be a felony, punishable by imprisonment for not more than four (4) years in the custody of the Department of Corrections or by the imposition of a fine of not more than Five Thousand Dollars ($5,000.00), or by both such fine and imprisonment. As used in this section, the duty to furnish medical attendance shall mean that the parent or person having custody or control of a child must furnish medical treatment in such manner and on such occasions as an ordinarily prudent person, solicitous for the welfare of a child, would provide; such parent or person having custody or control of a child is not criminally liable for failure to furnish medical attendance for every minor or trivial complaint with which the child may be afflicted.

If we want to protect our children from abuse due to drugs, we already have the laws into place. There is no need to go on a "formulate, submit, get approved new legislation to protect our children" rampage. There is no need for all of this. And if you are still not completely and totally convinced, how this State and probably most other States already do the utmost to protect its children, let me refer you to §10A-1-2-101 of the Oklahoma Statutes. It is called the Child and Juvenile Code. Per this Code and thus per the laws of this State, you are obligated to report any real or suspicion of child abuse to the Department of Human Services Child Neglect hotline. Yes, you are. And you can be and hopefully will be prosecuted if you fail to do so.

Without further due, let me emphasize the above by quoting the below:

§10A-1-2-101. Establishment of statewide centralized hotline for reporting child abuse or neglect – Hotline requirements – Reporting abuse or neglect – Retaliation by employer - Violations.

A. 1. The Department of Human Services shall establish a statewide centralized hotline for the reporting of child abuse or neglect to the Department.

2. The Department shall provide hotline-specific training including, but not limited to, interviewing skills, customer service skills, narrative writing, necessary computer systems, making case determinations, and identifying priority situations.

3. The Department is authorized to contract with third parties in order to train hotline workers.

4. The Department shall develop a system to track the number of calls received, and of that number:

a.   the number of calls screened out,

b.   the number of referrals assigned,

c.   the number of calls received by persons unwilling to disclose basic personal information including, but not limited to, first and last name, and

d.   the number of calls in which the allegations were later found to be unsubstantiated or ruled out.

5. The Department shall electronically record each referral received by the hotline and establish a secure means of retaining the recordings for twelve (12) months. The recordings shall be confidential and subject to disclosure only if a court orders the disclosure of the referral. The Department shall redact any information identifying the reporting party unless otherwise ordered by the court.

B. 1. Every person having reason to believe that a child under the age of eighteen (18) years is a victim of abuse or neglect shall report the matter promptly to the Department of Human Services. Reports shall be made to the hotline provided for in subsection A of this section. Any allegation of abuse or neglect reported in any manner to a county office shall immediately be referred to the hotline by the Department. Provided, however, that in actions for custody by abandonment, provided for in Section 2-117 of Title 30 of the Oklahoma Statutes, there shall be no reporting requirement.

2. Every physician, surgeon, or other health care professional including doctors of medicine, licensed osteopathic physicians, residents and interns, or any other health care professional attending

the birth of a child who tests positive for alcohol or a controlled dangerous substance shall promptly report the matter to the Department.

3. No privilege or contract shall relieve any person from the requirement of reporting pursuant to this section.

4. The reporting obligations under this section are individual, and no employer, supervisor, administrator, governing body or entity shall interfere with the reporting obligations of any employee or other person or in any manner discriminate or retaliate against the employee or other person who in good faith reports suspected child abuse or neglect, or who provides testimony in any proceeding involving child abuse or neglect. Any employer, supervisor, administrator, governing body or entity who discharges, discriminates or retaliates against the employee or other person shall be liable for damages, costs and attorney fees. If a child who is the subject of the report or other child is harmed by the discharge, discrimination or retaliation described in this paragraph, the party harmed may file an action to recover damages, costs and attorney fees.

5. Every physician, surgeon, or other health care professional making a report of abuse or neglect as required by this subsection or examining a child to determine the likelihood of abuse or neglect and every hospital or related institution in which the child was examined or treated shall provide, upon request, copies of the results of the examination or copies of the examination on which the report was based and any other clinical notes, x-rays, photographs, and other previous or current records relevant to the case to law enforcement officers conducting a criminal investigation into the case and to employees of the Department of Human Services conducting an investigation of alleged abuse or neglect in the case.

C. Any person who knowingly and willfully fails to promptly report suspected child abuse or neglect or who interferes with the prompt reporting of suspected child abuse or neglect may be reported to local law enforcement for criminal investigation and, upon conviction thereof, shall be guilty of a misdemeanor. Any person with prolonged knowledge of ongoing child abuse or neglect who knowingly and willfully fails to promptly report such knowledge may be reported to local law enforcement for criminal investigation and, upon conviction thereof, shall be guilty of a felony. For the purposes of this paragraph, "prolonged knowledge" shall mean knowledge of at least six (6) months of child abuse or neglect.

D. 1. Any person who knowingly and willfully makes a false report pursuant to the provisions of this section or a report that the person knows lacks factual foundation may be reported to local law enforcement for criminal investigation and, upon conviction thereof, shall be guilty of a misdemeanor.

2. If a court determines that an accusation of child abuse or neglect made during a child custody proceeding is false and the person making the accusation knew it to be false at the time the accusation was made, the court may impose a fine, not to exceed Five Thousand Dollars ($5,000.00) and reasonable attorney fees incurred in recovering the sanctions, against the person making the accusation. The remedy provided by this paragraph is in addition to paragraph 1 of this subsection or to any other remedy provided by law.

E. Nothing contained in this section shall be construed to exempt or prohibit any person from reporting any suspected child abuse or neglect pursuant to subsection B of this section.

Now since we have that clear now, it should be evident to anybody who is reading this, that we have pretty darn good laws in this State to conquer the child abuse or child neglect issue.

I made this entire point as part of the subject of solving the issue of prison overcrowding, because if we were to move forward with legalizing drugs, I wanted to demonstrate that there is no need to fear for the kids. It might be a certain challenge to detect an environment in your neighborhood, which exposes children to drugs, but that would be no different than is the case currently. All that someone has to do is actually pick up the phone and dial that number to the Department of Human Services.

I don't think that the solution to our incarceration rate is a single one. I don't think that anybody can jump up on a stage and proclaim that he found the one thing, which could solve the mass incarceration problem in our country. And I never claimed that the solution to this problem would be an easy one, but it appears, that it is easier than anticipated. We don't have to reform society, we just have to make some adjustments to it.

C. The Plea Bargain, reform of

Plea Bargains is the bread and butter of the current justice system. It works to the benefit of some offenders and for other people it serves basically as a simple way of saying: I don't care whether or not you committed this crime beyond a reasonable doubt. I will charge you with it no matter what you say. If you don't have $ 2 000 000 to defend yourself, that is not my problem. I have done my job. But if you save us all a lot of time and money, I will talk to the DA to cut you a deal. Instead of 25 years in, I pretty much can guarantee 5 years in and 5 years deferred. With good conduct, you could be out in less than two. What do you say"?

Every lawyer and judge you talk to will tell you at once that plea bargains is the only hope of the justice system as it exists today. We have way too many people coming into the prison system to be able to supply a public and speedy trial to everyone. It is not going to happen. And as the system works today, they have a reasonable point. It is so funny how some parts of the constitution are so heavily defended like the right to Bear Arms, others are not more worth than a side note. Nobody seems to care a lot for the implementation for a public and speedy trial, even though it is one of the most important points in the amendments of the US Constitution. That is my own, personal opinion by the way. Others might not think so which is just fine.

But seriously, some within the justice system probably will argue, that offenders do get a public and speedy trial, because it is all a matter of definition and how you look at these things. If a person sits in jail and waits for his or her trial, you could argue that it is technically not the trial yet. The actual trial begins with the offender in a courtroom, either in front of a judge with his defense present, which would be called a bench trial or in front of the whole package as seen on TV, with jurors, visitors, the press and what have you. So theoretically one might say we do have public and speedy trials in this country, if you don't count the month and years an offender spends in jail before he gets a trial. After all, that is not what the amendment states. It doesn't say anything about jail time. It only talks about trials. And I guess, this is how the judiciary intends to get away with it. Their reasoning is time. Let's redefine the public and speedy trial moniker because we just don't have the time to give everybody a trial, it is as simple as that.

Let's see what the actual State law says about it:

§22-13. Right to speedy trial, counsel and witnesses.

In a criminal action the defendant is entitled:

1. To a speedy and public trial.

2. To be allowed counsel, as in civil actions, or to appear and defend in person and with counsel; and,

3. To produce witnesses on his behalf, and to be confronted with the witnesses against him in the presence of the court.

R.L.1910, § 5547.

If everyone has the right to a public and speedy trial, than everybody has the right. In my opinion, there is no if's and but's about it, there can't be. As it stands these days, both the public trial and the speedy trial are being butchered because too many offenders come into the justice system. Too many offenders are being circulated through the halls of the judiciary.

The public trial: A Plea Bargain is not public. It is a conversation the attorney has with his client and the District Attorney.

The speedy trial: If you sit in county jail for four months or two years, that hardly can be considered speedy.

If the argument of our current system is, that we don't have the time and the resources for a public and speedy trial, we might have to look at changing that.

I give you only one example out of my own life to demonstrate, how the current system works.

A person I know is locked up in jail since three month. This person was obviously charged with a crime, otherwise the person wouldn't be in jail, so far so good. If Person A, let's give this person a temporary name, will be eventually charged with the crime and if nothing changes in that direction, the time A spends in jail will hopefully get credited to the length of his potential prison sentence. If A gets five years for instance, these three months then will be deducted from these five years, bringing the final tally to four years and nine months. An option would have been to bail out of jail. But if the person doesn't have the money, than this is not an option. In the meantime, the justice system goes on with its life. And sometime down the road, A's case will be brought up and dealt with. But apparently there is no need to hurry anything.

If A is found to be innocent beyond a reasonable doubt, A will walk out of that jail free. A would have lost three month of his/her life, which A will never get back or get paid for.

As in so many other situations, the law already provides answers for these difficult tasks. The main problem seems to be, whether or not someone is guilty of a crime in the first place. If you are found to be innocent, the following applies:

§22-262. Discharge of defendant, when.

After hearing the proofs and the statement of the defendant, if he have one, or his testimony if he testifies if it appear either that a public offense has not been committed, or that a public offense has been committed, but there is not sufficient cause to believe the defendant guilty thereof, the magistrate must order the defendant to be discharged, by an endorsement on the complaint over his signature to the following effect:

There being no sufficient cause to believe the within named A. B. guilty of the offense within mentioned, I order him to be discharged.

R.L.1910, § 5678.

And if the judge determines, that the defendant is in fact guilty or to the least, that the State will charge the defendant with a crime, the following law goes into effect:

§22-264. Defendant held to answer.

If, however, it appear from the examination that any public offense has been committed, and that there is sufficient cause to believe the defendant guilty thereof, the magistrate must in like manner endorse on the complaint an order signed by him to the following effect:

It appearing to me that the offense named in the within complaint mentioned (or any other offense, according to the fact, stating generally the nature thereof), has been committed, and that there is

242

sufficient cause to believe the within named A. B. guilty thereof, I order that he be held to answer the same.

R.L.1910, § 5680.

Even if you are found to be guilty, the following applies or should apply in lieu of a speedy trial:

§22-812.2. Right to speedy trial – Review process.

A. Whenever the court finds that a case should be reviewed to determine if the right of an accused to a speedy trial is being protected, the court shall:

1. Issue notice to the District Attorney, the accused, and the attorney for the accused that the case will be reviewed by the court at a date and time which is not less than ten (10) days nor more than twenty (20) days from the date of the notice. Each party shall have the opportunity to present evidence or legal authority in support of its position; and

2. Take evidence from both parties regarding the appropriateness of the cause for the delay. At the hearing, the court shall consider whether the delay has occurred for any of the following reasons:

a.   the delay is the result of the application of the accused or an attorney on behalf of the accused,

b.   the delay is the result of the fault of the accused or the attorney for the accused,

c.   the accused is incompetent to stand trial,

d.   a proceeding to determine the competency of the accused to stand trial is pending and a determination cannot be completed within the time limitations fixed for trial,

e.   there is material evidence or a material witness which is unavailable and that reasonable efforts have been made to procure

243

such evidence or witness, and there are reasonable grounds to believe that such evidence or witness can be obtained and trial commenced within a reasonable time,

f.   the accused is charged as a codefendant or coconspirator and the court has determined that the codefendants or coconspirators must be tried before separate juries taken from separate jury panels,

g.   the court has other cases pending for trial that are for persons incarcerated prior to the case in question, and the court does not have sufficient time to commence the trial of the case within the time limitation fixed for trial,

h.   the court, state, accused, or the attorney for the accused is incapable of proceeding to trial due to illness or other reason and it is unreasonable to reassign the case, and

i.   due to other reasonable grounds the court does not have sufficient time to commence the trial of the case within the time limit fixed for trial.

B. If, after hearing all the evidence and the legal arguments properly submitted, the court finds by a preponderance of the evidence that the state is not proceeding with due diligence, that none of the exceptions set out in paragraph 2 of subsection A of this section justify additional delay and the right of the accused to a speedy trial has been violated, the court shall dismiss the case.

C. If a preliminary hearing has been held, the case may be refiled, unless the applicable statute of limitations has expired, upon a showing of newly discovered evidence which could not have been discovered prior to trial.

D. If a preliminary hearing has not been held, the case may be refiled, upon good cause shown, unless any applicable statute of limitations has expired.

E. If, after hearing all the evidence and the legal arguments properly submitted, the court finds that the right of the accused to a speedy trial has not been violated, the court shall set the case for review in four (4) months. If the case is still pending after the four-month period, the court shall conduct another review. The four-month review of pending cases shall be a continuing responsibility of the court until final disposition of the case.

Added by Laws 1999, 1st Ex.Sess., c. 6, § 2, eff. Nov. 1, 1999.

The State as the prosecutor in the form of the District Attorney, the Judge or the Jury thus already has an enormous number of tools at their disposal to deal with an offender or an offense. It all comes down to the actual application of the existing guidelines. I call them guidelines, because we already know that the prosecution team has a considerable amount of wiggle room in their proceedings. And the way these laws are applied and to what effect and the weight certain rules are given and their application is called Politics I guess.

At least that is what someone might think. As you can read in point "e", "g", "h" and "I" above, there are numerous reasons why a trial could be delayed. That is all good and great, but where does the public and speedy trial fit in here? As long as it gets to a trial, nobody could blame the court or the prosecutor or the DA to delay things, since the time and effort to get a trial going is considerable. We all understand that and that is not even the point. However, as you can also read in "B", a case can be easily dismissed as well. Yeah, that's right, in other words, empty our jails. I mean, let's be serious, but I think it is a good point. If somebody sits in jail for weeks or month and pleaded not guilty, the judge always has the option to dismiss the case as it stands because there is no reason why the DA cannot re-file the charge at a later point. As I mentioned above, it is all a matter of politics and the application of the law. It is not the case that an accused has to sit in jail forever before it is even determined, if he or she will get charged with the crime

245

discussed at the Preliminary hearing or with some other charges. But whatever might be the case, there is no point in keeping someone in jail and have the taxpayer pay for every single day, every single hour of his or her artificially prolonged room and board.

If you as the DA are dealing with a heinous or violent crime, we all understand the level of reluctance towards letting anybody go anywhere. That is understood and we are not talking about murder and rape and kidnapping cases here. We are talking about drug offenses, property charges, trespassing, failure to pay whatever official fine, child support cases, burglary in the second degree, traffic tickets and so on and so forth. We are talking about crimes or misdemeanors which were committed with no other person physically involved, which by the way is the majority of cases.

I don't know if it is a good idea to separate violent crimes against persons from other type of crimes as far as the public and speedy trial is concerned. After all, the DA bears a great responsibility to the public and to his oath. Luckily these crimes are not what causes our prisons to be overcrowded and luckily, as is the case with so many other aspects of the criminal justice system, the State already has a good law for situations such as this:

§22-234. Discretion to charge as misdemeanor.

When determining the appropriate charge for a person accused of committing a criminal offense, the district attorney shall have the discretion to file the charge as a misdemeanor offense rather than a felony offense after considering the following factors:

1. The criminal offense for which the person has been arrested is not listed as a criminal offense in Section 13.1 of Title 21 of the Oklahoma Statutes;

2. The nature of the criminal offense;

3. The age, background and criminal history of the person who committed the criminal offense;

4. The character and rehabilitation needs of the person who committed the criminal offense; and

5. Whether it is in the best interests of justice to file the charge as a misdemeanor offense rather than a felony offense.

Added by Laws 2016, c. 219, § 1, eff. Nov. 1, 2016.

If we compare §22-234 with the heading of this chapter, which is the reform of the Plea Bargain, it makes sense that I add the above, because many offenders don't even have to make a Plea Bargain with anybody if the crime is being charged as a misdemeanor. §22-234 tells us something else as well, which I think is crucial to the entire justice system in this State and in other States. The DA has an enormous amount of power as far as the future of a defendant is concerned. He has enormous power as far as an offender's liability is concerned. He has the power to rule over this person's future. Always bear in mind that a person doesn't have to put himself in that situation to begin with, but that is another story. If a DA wants to lock everybody up who jaywalks, he can do that. If the DA wants to be a ruthless person with no mercy, who tries to lock everyone up, he can interpret the law to this effect. It is all a question of how he looks at the law and the application of its many rules and regulations. On the other side, he doesn't really have to lock anybody up, who didn't commit a crime which includes physical harm to another person. The laws are there, ready for application and interpretation. After all, it is all a matter of politics. Where does the justice system want to go? How can the justice system best serve its people? The DA certainly can fill up the prison system in no time as we can see by looking at the above quotes, if he wanted to. Reversely he can do the exact opposite. Save us all billions of dollars and look at each crime individually. To make changes to the current "lock them up" attitude of course takes courage and determination because it means to challenge the status quo, which is always an uphill battle.

Another tool the prosecution can use to battle the Plea Bargain mantra is the Deferred Prosecution Program. It says that the DA doesn't have to charge the defendant if he qualifies to commit himself to be supervised by an agency and do a little bit of Community Service. There are no exact rules or names as in what exact type of Supervisory Agency the offender has to commit himself. The idea merely is instead of costing the State and the taxpayer money to house the offender in a prison or jail, he might as well pay a little fine for his supervision. In this way, the offender remains a taxpaying citizen, pay restitution, is supervised and could even provide services to the not-for-profit, local organizations instead of costing the taxpayer money. He remains free, but pays fines to be supervised. At least in this way, he is not taking out of the production cycle and is made to contribute instead of costing the taxpayer money. I think, this is another great idea, which is being used way too little by the prosecution. Here is the text of the law:

§22-305.1. Deferred prosecution programs - Guidelines - Factors considered.

Before the filing of any information against a person accused of committing a crime, the State of Oklahoma, through its district attorney, may agree with an accused to defer the filing of a criminal information for a period not to exceed three (3) years.

The State of Oklahoma may include any person in a deferred prosecution program if it is in the best interests of the accused and not contrary to the public interest. Each district attorney shall adopt and promulgate guidelines which shall indicate what factors shall be considered in including an accused in the deferred prosecution program. The guidelines shall insure that the State of Oklahoma considers in each case at least the following factors:

1. Whether the State of Oklahoma has sufficient evidence to achieve conviction;

2. The nature of the offense with priority given to first offenders and nonviolent crimes;

248

3. Any special characteristics of the accused;

4. Whether the accused will cooperate and benefit from a deferred prosecution program;

5. Whether available programs are appropriate to the accused person's needs;

6. Whether the services for the accused are more readily available from the community or from the corrections system;

7. Whether the accused constitutes a substantial danger to others;

8. The impact of the deferred prosecution on the community;

9. The recommendations of the law enforcement agency involved in the case;

10. The opinions of the victim; and

11. Any mitigating or aggravating circumstances.

Laws 1979, c. 226, § 1, eff. Oct. 1, 1979; Laws 2007, c. 358, § 5, eff. July 1, 2007.

§22-305.2. District attorney deferred prosecution.

A. If an accused qualifies for the deferred prosecution program, the accused and the State of Oklahoma, through the district attorney, may execute an agreement whereby the accused agrees to waive any rights to a speedy accusation, a speedy trial, and any statute of limitations, and agrees to fulfill such conditions to which the accused and the State of Oklahoma may agree including, but not limited to, restitution and community services.

B. The accused, as consideration for entering into a deferred prosecution agreement, consents and agrees to a full and complete photographic record of property which was to be used as evidence. The photographic record shall be competent evidence of the property and admissible in any criminal action or proceeding as the best evidence.

C. Property shall be returned to its owner only after the photographic record is made subject to the following conditions:

1. Property, except that which is prohibited by law, shall be returned to its owner after proper verification of title;

2. The return of property to the owner shall be without prejudice to the state or to any person who may have a claim against the property; and

3. When property is returned, the recipient shall sign, under penalty of perjury, a declaration of ownership which shall be retained by the police department or sheriff's office.

D. As additional consideration for the agreement, the State of Oklahoma shall agree not to file an information if the accused satisfactorily completes the conditions of the agreement.

E. The agreement between the accused and the State of Oklahoma may include provisions whereby the accused agrees to be supervised in the community. If the accused is required to be supervised pursuant to the terms of the agreement, the person shall be required to pay a supervision fee to be established by the supervisory agency. The supervision fee shall be paid to the supervisory agency as required by the rules of the supervisory agency. The supervisory agency shall monitor the person for compliance with the conditions of the agreement. The supervisory agency shall report to the district attorney on the progress of the accused, and shall report immediately if the accused fails to report or participate as required by the agreement.

F. The agreement between the parties may require the accused to participate or consult with local service providers, including the

Department of Human Services, the Department of Mental Health and Substance Abuse Services, the Employment Security Commission, federal services agencies, other state or local agencies, colleges, universities, technology center schools, and private or charitable service organizations. When the accused is required to participate or consult with any service provider, a program fee may be required unless the fee would impose an unnecessary hardship on the person. The program fee shall be established by the service provider based upon a sliding scale. Any state agency called upon for assistance in a deferred prosecution program by any district attorney shall render services and assistance as available. Any supervision fee or program fee authorized by this section may be waived in whole or in part when the accused is indigent. No person who is otherwise qualified for a deferred prosecution program shall be denied services or supervision based solely on the person's inability to pay a fee or fees.

G. The agreement between the parties may require the accused to pay a victim compensation assessment pursuant to the provisions of Section 142.18 of Title 21 of the Oklahoma Statutes. The amount of the assessment shall be agreed to by the parties and shall be within the amounts specified in Section 142.18 of Title 21 of the Oklahoma Statutes for the offense charged.

H. Any deferred prosecution agreement including, but not limited to, any fee, sliding scale fee, compensation, contract, assessment, or other financial agreement charged or waived by the accused or the State of Oklahoma shall be a record open to the public.

I. 1. On or after the effective date of this act, each office of the district attorney shall, upon request and within a reasonable time, provide the name and other identifying information of an accused entering into a deferred prosecution agreement.

2. A deferred prosecution agreement entered into prior to the effective date of this act shall not be a record open to the public, unless confidentiality was waived as a condition of the agreement.

251

I think especially points 7-11 are of great interest, just look at the wording and the language. I suspect where most of these things in mitigating punishments break down is in the time involved and general attitude towards offenders. A District Attorney actually has to pick up the phone or get in his car and talk to some people. He needs to talk to the victim. Is the victim even interested in a conviction? Does the victim really want to see this offender behind bars for the next five years? Based on the history of the offender, was he ever or will he potentially be a danger to the general public? And if you look at point 11, what are the mitigating or aggravating circumstances in his particular case?

There is a lot of reading to do and a lot of education to be gained if you strive to understand the current justice system. As for me, it seems that at least the State of Oklahoma doesn't have to have the highest female incarceration rate in the nation and doesn't have to be amongst the top five States with the highest male incarceration rate. All the laws are in place to turn this around on a dime, if we are willing to look at these laws.

Instead of locking everybody up and paying for it, we need to take a closer look at alternatives, of which there are plenty. We don't even have to change much in the current laws, if anything at all. It turns out, that the DA and the defendant as well as his attorney have an enormous arsenal of tools at hand to completely challenge and change the current system of incarceration. From a "lock them all up" mentality to the idea, that every locked-up citizen cost me money, so let's try to find alternatives to locking people up.

If you talk about Deferred Sentencing, you also need to mention the Community Sentencing Act, which basically work hand in hand. They are not the same, but Community Sentencing can be part of a Deferred Sentencing Program. The Community Sentencing Act starts at §22.988, if you want to look at it and see what it is all about. It is designed to establish a community service program for felony offenders. The idea again is to lighten the burden on the taxpayer to pay for someone's incarceration and instead have him do some work in the community he is sentenced in. It is very easy and very simple.

Let's quickly look how this works. In §22.988.6 you can look at the duties of the planning council, which consists of judges, district attorneys and local citizens. The Planning Council finds ways to put an offender to work. The Community Sentencing System is part of the Department of Corrections and as such needs to be funded by it. So the question we need to ask ourselves is this: Is it better to lock somebody up for a number of years and pay for it or is it better to sentence somebody to Community Service and have this person serve his sentence by serving his community? You make up your own mind about this. But since all this is part of the Plea Bargain solution, let me at least say this. I much rather prefer somebody who cleans the streets, repairs the streets and helps built buildings for my community than to spend millions of dollars for some outside company who won the bid to build the next fire station. The great thing about this is that we can have it both. General labor workers might as well come out of our prisons instead out of Mexico. And some of these offenders are actually highly skilled professionals already.

The Community Sentencing Act is fairly extensive and I didn't want to include it all in this text, but I would like to quote one section of it:

§22-988.8. Community services and sentencing options.

A. A community sentencing system established pursuant to the provisions of the Oklahoma Community Sentencing Act shall include those community punishments and programs and services enumerated and funded in the annual plan submitted to the Community Sentencing Division within the Department of Corrections and any other services or punishments subsequently added and funded during a plan year. The options may not be utilized for

offenders not meeting the eligibility criteria of programs and score requirements for the Level of Services Inventory (LSI) or other approved assessment. Each local system shall strive to have available to the court all of the following services for eligible offenders:

1. Community service with or without compensation to the offender;

2. Substance abuse treatment and availability for periodic drug testing of offenders following treatment;

3. Varying levels of supervision by the Department of Corrections probation officers or another qualified supervision source;

4. Education and literacy provided by the State Department of Education, the county library system, the local school board, or another qualified source;

5. Employment opportunities and job skills training provided by the Oklahoma Department of Career and Technology Education or another qualified source;

6. Enforced collections provided by the local court clerk, or another state agency; and

7. The availability of county jail or another restrictive housing facility for limited disciplinary sanctions.

B. The court may order as a community punishment for an eligible offender any condition listed as a condition available for a suspended sentence.

C. In all cases in which an offender is sentenced to a community punishment, the offender shall be ordered as part of the terms and conditions of the sentence to pay for the court ordered sanction, based upon ability to pay. Payments may be as provided by court order or pursuant to periodic payment schedules established by the service provider. If the offender does not have the financial ability to

254

pay for the court ordered sanction, payment shall be made from funds budgeted for the local community sentencing system.

Some of the options in the above referenced text are currently not feasible. They are not feasible because the States already spend too much on incarceration itself. Point 3 and 5 are worth looking at for instance. Varying levels of supervision which hints at possible alternative sources for supervising offenders besides the Pardon and Parole officer employed by the Department of Corrections. What these possible other sources could be didn't seem to have been fully explored. For now, it is just a side note. The same accounts for point 5. It mentions the Oklahoma Department of Career and Technology Education, but doesn't fail to leave the door open for "other qualified sources".

Once again, the opportunities and options the justice system has to empty our prisons are abound and beautiful. It just needs to be done. So please, dear justice system, build more playgrounds instead of building more prisons.

To conclude the Plea Bargain section, the following should be applied. Besides utilizing all the tools the justice system has already as laid out above, a fairly simple process could be implemented, which could look as follows:

a. For non-violent offenses, utilize the tools already provided by law. Instead of always going for a Plea Bargain, employ all the other tools there are for non-violent offenders, of which there are a lot. From Deferred Sentencing, Community Sentencing, choices to charge many offenses as Misdemeanors, the tools an attorney has at its disposal are numerous.

b. The Preliminary Hearing should be held no longer than one week after arrest. The criminal history of the accused, if any, is already at the judge's disposal. He can decide in no time, if the accused follows a pattern of past behavior or if he is looking at someone, who has been arrested for the first time. This serves the due diligence necessities the judge has as well as the rights of the accused if found innocent beyond a reasonable doubt.

c. All non-violent offenses or misdemeanors can be handled right there, one week after the arrest, at the latest. The judge can issue fines, community service, restitution and even deferred sentences or a combination of them all. There is no need for any other hearings beyond this point.

d. Depending on the size of the municipality, the Courthouse should employ at least one public defense attorney for indigent offenders, which should all be present at the Preliminary Hearing which per b. should be held within a week of the arrest. If no attorney can be present within the time frame, the DA and judge, which represent the State, could schedule the Preliminary Hearing within two weeks after the arrest, which should be the latest time frame such hearing should be held. Beyond that, cases must be dismissed without prejudice for all non-violent offenses.

e. The Preliminary Hearing for violent offenses and other offenses for which no resolution could be found could be extended to four to eight weeks.

f. At the Preliminary Hearing, which in this scenario really already takes the role of a trial and is the trial, the parties come to one of the following conclusions:

1. The charges are being upheld and a Judgment and Sentence is issued

2. The charges are being amended and a Judgment and Sentence is being issued

g. In all other cases where a Judgement cannot be issued for whatever reasons and circumstances, a trial must be scheduled within four to eight weeks of the Preliminary Hearing. After considering all the above points mentioned in a, the number of offenders who will demand a trial should be quite low and mostly consist of violent offenses and other offenses, for which a judgment could not be issued.

Up to this point, nobody even mentioned a Plea Bargain, because everything was handled within a time frame of two weeks. No offender, rightfully accused or a victim of sorts, stayed in jail for more than two weeks.

h. If it was decided that a later trial must be conducted, the Court Clerk, the defense attorney and the accused himself must get to work, because it is on now. Every party has now the opportunity to schedule persons for the trial, who will bring aggravating circumstances to the trial or who will bring mitigating materiel to the party. The Court Clerk or an assigned deputy keeps an eye on the amount of people who are scheduled for the trial and also keeps all paperwork in order, carefully filed into the good and the bad.

i. The trial as laid out in h is the one and only trial, but as also mentioned, it should bring everything to the table which could help the accused on the side of the defense and in reverse, the DA can dig out anything and everything in the interest of the public, which could further the accused's conviction.

j. It stands without reason that the accused should have all opportunities at the pre-trial stage to access his attorney and contact anybody he wants to for the purpose of mounting mitigating evidence. Full access to pen, paper, stamps, telephone privileges and such must be granted and should not be restricted. If need be, the accused could be charged for the materiel, if the State needs to provide it for the accused, who are indigent. At this point the accused must have the opportunity to choose any weaponry he can to defend his life and to defend his freedom. He must have the same opportunities as the DA, who can call, meet and contact anybody in this country and in any other country if he deems it necessary and proper for the sake of public safety.

257

k. The public and speedy trial is served, the accused can defend himself in a proper way and the judiciary cannot keep him in jail forever.

l. After the trial, the defendant is freed immediately or sentenced immediately and must be transferred to a prison within four weeks. End of story.

The above is only a rough draft as far as a Plea Bargain is concerned. I think however that no matter the exact circumstances, people involved, time frames, etc. it will be closer to justice than is currently the case. We might need a few more people in the courtroom if you look at the scenario in its totality, because there could be lot going on in there at the same time since now there is a need to give the accused a public and speedy trial. On the other hand, we could lose a lot of positions in the prison or jail system, because offenders will not sit in there for weeks and month, just waiting for their turn.

I haven't even provided any statistical data or other information what effects the overcrowding of the prison has on our society as a whole. It is clear that people will lose their jobs if they are being held in the jail for month before it is even decided if they are guilty or innocent. That for instance would not be the case any longer. For first time offenders with non-violent crimes, it could be a fairly short brush with the justice system. After a week or two, the offenders theoretically could get back to work, which is a good idea, because only people who work pay taxes and contribute to the society, we should not forget that. Every inmate is a burden to a democracy or to any other political system for that matter.

Some time ago, the influx of offenders into the prison system has given us the Plea Bargain, which was the justice system's answer to overcrowding, because nobody had the financial resources or the personnel needed to handle all this. And few were even willing to look in that direction. This notion in itself was understandable and you can't really blame anybody for that. But over the years it has gotten so bad, that we are finally at a point, where we need to do something about it. It however needs to work and needs to be financially viable. I think the above can work and will be viable.

D. Enhancements of Crime Categories

This is another procedure law makers put into action to follow up on the "hard on crime" idea, which was probably started by former President Nixon. The long and the short of it basically is, "if you can't behave yourself, we will lock you up until you die. We don't care about where you come from, what your particular circumstances might have been or are; we don't care about none of that. We will give you one chance and one chance only. If you can't follow suit, you are done."

Per this philosophy, the punishment for your crime varies. If you commit a felony offense for the first time, you will be eligible for credits within the prison system as described in "The current prison system". If you commit the same type of crime a second time, you are only eligible for such credits after you serve let's say 50% of the time the judge gave you. This is to let you know, that the law makers are not playing around. You are no kid no more. You ought to learn at one point in time and if you won't we have one more thing for you. If you happen to commit the same crime again, after you already got two warning shots, or any other crime fitting certain categories, you will have to serve up to 90% of the time the judge gave you before you will become eligible for credits. At this stage of the game, 10 years in prison really means 9 years in prison, whereby for first time offenders, 10 years in prison can mean 3 years served and two more years on probation.

The DOC in its policy letter OP-060211 breaks it down for you.

c. Pursuant to Title 63, Section 2-402, effective September 1,1992, inmates convicted of possessing or purchasing a controlled dangerous substance within 1,000 feet of a public or private elementary or secondary school, public vocational school, public or private college or university or other institution of higher education,

recreation center, or public park, including state parks and recreation areas must serve fifty percent (50%) of the sentence received prior to becoming eligible for state correctional institutional earned credits toward the completion of said sentence. Inmates convicted a second or subsequent time under this statute must serve ninety percent (90%%) of the sentence prior to becoming eligible for state correctional institutional earned credits toward completion of said sentence.

(1) Effective June 7, 1993, 63 O.S. Section 2-402, was amended to include the Possession or Purchase of a Controlled Dangerous Substance in the Presence of any Child Under 12 Years of Age.

You will find this section on pages 14 and 15. This is one example, but there is also an entire list of crimes, where the offender has to serve at least 85% of the time adjudicated by the judge before he can even thing about release. These types of crimes were mentioned earlier in this book and mainly consist of crimes where the injury of another person is involved or the danger of injury to another person. This is however slightly different than what I am talking about here. As far as the 85% crimes are concerned, that is how an offender starts his term in prison after being convicted. The enhanced crime categories on the other hand come into effect, if the offender commits the same type of crime again.

Let's say he committed a crime which is not part of the 85% crime category. For his first offense, he gets away with 3 years and gets released on probation after 18 months. If he gets caught doing the same thing again, he will have to serve at least 50% of the entire time. He gets five years this time around and thus needs to physically be incarcerated 2 and a half years. That is quite a difference to the 18 month he needed to do the first time.

And this is the entire idea. The lawmakers wanted to address recidivism, meaning people who can't restrain themselves from doing the wrong thing over and over again. And the ways and means they addressed this was by multiplying the punishment. Their idea was if the offender doesn't "learn" from his first prison experience, you just have to hit him harder, like you do with a spoiled kid, which is not listening. You start with phone restrictions and after the third time you have to give the kid two weeks house arrest or whatever.

And now the taxpayers pay and pay and pay. Because you have to look at the people to whom these laws apply to. If somebody is hooked on drugs, he or she has already made peace with the fact, that the family is gone for the most part. He is on his own and if he doesn't have help from family and friends, there is nothing to stop him from keep using drugs, thus he will find himself back in prison. And the sad part of it all is that prison doesn't help to keep him off drugs. Drugs are closer to him in prison than they are in the outside world.

The other category is the drug dealer and gang member. And it is pretty much the same story here. If you were raised with drugs and gangs, it is more likely than not that you become part of this world as well and no law in this country, severe or lax, can or will change that. Ergo the prisons kept filling up with more and more offenders, who get harsher and harsher punishments because for some of them the alternatives aren't even visible. And for some of them there are no treatment options or places to go to. It is just not an option. As sad as this is, it is the real world. And the more gang members are being locked up, the more gang activity there is inside these walls, because the need for drugs is still there, nothing has changed, except now you can't just move to your grandmother across the State lines if you want to get out of this live. It is already too late for you. In prison you either play your role or not. If you don't want to serve the gang any longer, you better get yourself into protective custody and hope for the best; that is all you can do.

Does this system work? That is anybody's guess. I am not the judge here, but if I would be allowed to furnish an opinion along this line, then my opinion would be that it didn't work.

Besides the fact, that it just fills the prison with more long-term offenders and the taxpayer has to pay for it, I think it is not justice.

Below is the State law, or part of the State law which deals with such penalties:

§21-51.1. Second and subsequent offenses after conviction of offense punishable by imprisonment in the State Penitentiary.

A. Except as otherwise provided in the Elderly and Incapacitated Victim's Protection Program and Section 3 of this act, every person who, having been convicted of any offense punishable by imprisonment in the State Penitentiary, commits any crime after such conviction, within ten (10) years of the date following the completion of the execution of the sentence, and against whom the District Attorney seeks to enhance punishment pursuant to this section of law, is punishable therefor as follows:

1. If the offense for which the person is subsequently convicted is an offense enumerated in Section 571 of Title 57 of the Oklahoma Statutes and the offense is punishable by imprisonment in the State Penitentiary for a term exceeding five (5) years, such person is punishable by imprisonment in the State Penitentiary for a term in the range of ten (10) years to life imprisonment.

2. If the offense of which such person is subsequently convicted is such that upon a first conviction an offender would be punishable by imprisonment in the State Penitentiary for any term exceeding five (5) years, such person is punishable by imprisonment in the State Penitentiary for a term in the range of twice the minimum term for a first time offender to life imprisonment. If the subsequent felony offense does not carry a minimum sentence as a first time offender, such person is punishable by imprisonment in the State Penitentiary for a term in the range of two (2) years to life imprisonment.

3. If such subsequent offense is such that upon a first conviction the offender would be punishable by imprisonment in the State Penitentiary for five (5) years, or any less term, then the person

262

convicted of such subsequent offense is punishable by imprisonment in the State Penitentiary for a term not exceeding ten (10) years.

4. If such subsequent conviction is for petit larceny, the person convicted of such subsequent offense is punishable by imprisonment in the State Penitentiary for a term not exceeding five (5) years.

B. Every person who, having been twice convicted of felony offenses, commits a subsequent felony offense which is an offense enumerated in Section 571 of Title 57 of the Oklahoma Statutes, within ten (10) years of the date following the completion of the execution of the sentence, and against whom the District Attorney seeks to enhance punishment pursuant to this section of law, is punishable by imprisonment in the State Penitentiary for a term in the range of twenty (20) years to life imprisonment. Felony offenses relied upon shall not have arisen out of the same transaction or occurrence or series of events closely related in time and location. Nothing in this section shall abrogate or affect the punishment by death in all crimes now or hereafter made punishable by death.

C. Every person who, having been twice convicted of felony offenses, commits a subsequent felony offense within ten (10) years of the date following the completion of the execution of the sentence, and against whom the District Attorney seeks to enhance punishment pursuant to this section of law, is punishable by imprisonment in the State Penitentiary for a term in the range of three times the minimum term for a first time offender to life imprisonment. If the subsequent felony offense does not carry a minimum sentence as a first time offender, the person is punishable by imprisonment in the State Penitentiary for a term in the range of four (4) years to life imprisonment. Felony offenses relied upon shall not have arisen out of the same transaction or occurrence or series of events closely related in time and location. Nothing in this section shall abrogate or affect the punishment by death in all crimes now or hereafter made punishable by death.

This is the reality. The above is also referred in many discussions as the Three Strikes law. If you commit certain types of crimes three times in a row, you are done. You will go to prison for life and that is the end of that. This is all great and all, but I do have my problems with that.

For starters, these laws were not passed by sheer necessity, but came into effect because of the shock effect the lawmakers envisioned they will have. They figured that nobody wants to be locked up behind bars for the rest of his life because of some stupid drug trafficking that he was doing. They figured there ought to be some sort of thinking process being triggered in offender's mind's which made them stop selling and dealing drugs. If a DA had the power to lock somebody up behind bars for the rest of his life because he was repeatedly charged with drug trafficking, they figured, drug trafficking would be stymied. That seems to be what the whole idea was, except it didn't work as evidenced by the number of offenders in prisons today. And I think one of the reasons it didn't work was, because they didn't visit the low-income areas of the country, they didn't interview the people who were born and raised in a drug infused environment, they didn't look at the real problem and thus, they couldn't develop and come up with a real solution. The only thing they probably saw was the real possibility to look really good in the eyes of the voter. Stomp out the drug trafficking and thus stomp out the drug use. If anything is true today than it is that: It didn't work. It did not work as a deterrent and I think it is time that people realize that and find another approach.

Besides the fact however that it didn't work, I would like to point out one more factor, one more reason I think the Three Strikes laws should be abolished, or maybe three of them:

First, the taxpayer must come up with the money to pay for all these extended stays in the penal institutions and I personally don't like it. If it would have been an effective tool, by all means, I am all for it, no

264

questions asked. But it is not, so don't spend billions of dollars on keeping these offenders behind bars forever.

Second, I think it is arbitrary justice, because the only difference between somebody behind bars who got locked up for the first time and somebody who got locked up under these provisions is time. If an offender is found committing the same crime a certain time after his first offense, he will receive or can receive a tougher punishment. That seems to be the only factor involved.

It is injustice because what about the finance shark who committed financial fraud on 150 customers of his? Let's go over this for an example. He was charged with fraud in one form or the other in 150 cases, well enough. After spending some time in prison, he finally gets charged with 150 counts of whatever the exact, financial crime was. If the particular crime calls for a fine and imprisonment of up to 5 years but no less than one year imprisonment, he should be going to prison for 150 years. But because he was charged with the 150 crimes all at the same time, he won't go to prison for 150 years, he will go to prison for 20 years and will be able to receive parole after 10. It is not the case that he committed these crimes all at once. It took him 10 years to fraud all these people, but since he didn't get charged earlier with a similar crime, these 150 crimes get bundled into one. My point is, only because he didn't have an extensive record of his crimes in the court system and he wasn't charged with a crime prior to this conviction, he still committed the crimes over the last 10 years. Thus he should receive similar charges as offenders under the Three Strikes Laws, except he won't . And that is exactly my point. If you get charged with multiple crimes at once, you don't fall under the enhanced punishment rules, but if you get charged with multiple crimes over a period of time, you can be charged with enhanced punishments. That is why I think it is not justice. In an attempt to quell drug consumption and another number of violent crimes, somebody introduced the factor of time into the way people can get punished. This basically means, that you have different punishments for the same crime out of the box so to speak. Besides all other factors

265

which both the prosecutor and the defense can throw at the case, these time factors are in effect and can be used. I think it is arbitrary justice, which is just another way of saying, it is no justice at all.

Third reason why these Three Strikes Laws must be abolished is because they don't get applied across the criminal or civil code. It looks more like a fashion statement to me, let me emphasize. The people and law makers got made because the death toll of drug abuse was rising and the drug trafficking seems to be getting out of control. They didn't like that, which is understandable. If one of my children would have died of drug overdose, I might have voted for the same I must assume. But besides the fact that drug death and drug consumption didn't change because of that, these laws were only applied to certain categories of crimes, mostly the violent type. At first glance, this seemed to be a noble idea, who would not agree with locking up people for a longer period of time if they commit violent acts more than once? That is human nature and even logical. Ignoring for a second the fact that these crime statutes didn't work out as we hoped they would, I still wonder, why these enhancements weren't applied to non-violent crimes as well. If I don't deal in drugs, if I don't consume drugs, if I am not part of a gang or know or support someone who is, there are other types of crimes which affect my life. And to me, they could appear to be even more important, because they affect my life and the quality of my life even more than any drugs or drug related crime. If the justice system need to apply these Three Strikes Laws, I want them applied to companies who pollute the air I breathe, I want them applied to any company who swipes my credit card without even telling me for amounts of money no one agreed to in the first place, I want them applied to companies who just rise their fees without ever telling me, I want them applied to any car mechanic who fraudulently claims he installed a new alternator but used a polished up, old one, I want them applied to any doctor's office who tells me that my insurance covers the procedure only to send me an enormous bill after the operation with the explanation that they didn't know, I want them applied to any used car dealer who darn well knows what is wrong with a car but didn't tell me, I want them applied to any construction company

266

who messes up my hardwood floors and gets away with it. These are the things, Mr. and Ms. Normalo deal with on a daily basis. If you want the Three Strikes law so bad, apply them to cases, which affect my personal life and which bother the heck out of me or let them go. That would be a real life, public service, which is after all, what the justice system should be used for, to protect your productive citizens. That means of course, protect them from violent offenders as well, but if you apply justice, don't pick and choose.

E. Become a citizen again, barriers to

I run into this subject all the time. People who spent time behind bars are not done with their punishment upon release. Their punishment continues long after they walk out that door. A few of the main reasons for this is as follows:

1. Offenders cannot vote until they fully discharge their sentence. What does that mean exactly? The judge issues to the Department of Corrections a Judgment and Sentence document. It lays out the amount of time someone needs to spend behind bars and any possible stipulations. Sometimes that sentence is a combination of time spent inside a prison and time spent under supervision outside of the prison walls. As we now know, 10 years doesn't have to mean 10 years, since the offender can earn credits for good behavior, for programs attended and other things. He cuts his sentence dramatically. The voting right however is only reinstated after the full length of the sentence as laid out in the Judgment and Sentencing document is fulfilled. If he gets 10 years, he cannot vote before the time has elapsed. I consider this injustice simply because the offender's punishment ends with the discharge of the sentence. Even if there are parole stipulations in play after he leaves the prison itself, he nevertheless becomes part of the

society again. He might have to see the Probation and Parole officer every once in a while for drug testing or other things, but he works, he walks the streets of his home town, he pays cable fees, he pays taxes again, he utilizes the local power company and his kids might even go to school, if he has any children. Yet he has no saying in any decision the municipality makes. As far as anybody in his family is concerned, he is a free man. As far as all his friends and co-workers are concerned, he is a free man. If he goes to the car dealer and buys a car, he is considered a free man, yet he isn't. I think that constitutes punishment beyond the punishment he was handed by the judge. And it is a sweeping rule. It applies to all crimes and all sentences in the realm of felonies, which of course it should if we look at it with the eyes of the justice system. That still doesn't make it fair or just. The motivation behind this rule strikes me as odd as well. What is the idea behind such an arbitrary law? What could anybody gain by this ruling? I couldn't find a good reason why prisoners can't vote and I sure can't find a good reason why ex-prisoners can't vote for a certain time. It is just something very odd.

2. The sentence on job applications "Have you ever been convicted of a crime", or "Did you ever commit a felony crime in this State or any other State within the continental US" is one of the hallmarks on any job application. It makes getting a job with a lot of employers a little bit more complex if not impossible. Since this seems to be an idea within the private job community, there is probably hardly anything you or anybody can do about it. It is something employers do for good measure it seems.

For one reason or the other, people in this country like to file lawsuits. I am sorry this sounds a little general and all, but I can't help myself noticing this fact since I moved here. Monitor the news coverage for a few days and look at recent events of any kind and you will read, how this or that person intends to file, plans to file or filed a lawsuit for whatever reason against this or that person or organization. It is a cancer really which permeates the society. And if you look at this background and put yourself in the shoes of the employer, you begin to understand where they are coming from. It is just another measure of protection

Employers use. The idea seems to be that if there is going to be a lawsuit against this company, we want to cut down on the possible motives for one. And that includes ex-inmates. If they do anything wrong which is repulsive to the customer and provides grounds for a lawsuit, the employer could potentially be in a worse spot than having employed somebody, who doesn't have a criminal history. If they employ someone without a criminal history, they have a better defense because they always can point to the fact, that there is only so much they can do to pre-qualify an applicant for a job. They did the best they could so to speak. They can't say that for an ex-inmate because the lawsuit could allege that they should have known that this employee with a criminal background will do something detrimental to good health and good conduct, which he already displayed in the past which was the reason he got locked up in the first place. It is thus a simple exercise in choice. You cannot officially discriminate for reasons of nationality, age, gender, religion and so on, but there is no law that you cannot discriminate against former inmates.

For better or for worse, this is the current state of affairs and we could lament over this forever. The real question is whether or not it should be changed. Well, you can't change it because of fear and money. Employers are afraid to lose money in lawsuits. It is better to go the safer route.

A remedy would be to not make the above question part of a job application, there is nothing more to this than that. That is it. Just do it.

Maybe I wasn't diligent enough in my search, but I couldn't find any law regarding this subject. It seems more like an idea. It seems to come out of the Human Resources Department Training handbook. Everybody who gets trained in Human Services and has anything to do with the hiring procedure of a company, seems to come across a section in this handbook which reads: "Don't hire ex inmates. Sure, they could be just as qualified as anybody else. They could even be better workers

269

because they already know what life looks like if you don't follow the rules of life. But please, just don't do it, trust me on this. You don't want to get suit by a customer who had a negative encounter with one of your employees who is an ex-inmate. It is bad news all over the place. So, if you learn nothing else from this section of your training, learn this: Don't hire ex inmates."

I never read the handbook for Human Resources Training but you go ahead, prove me wrong.

The question of this point is, does anyone gain or lose anything by putting this sentence or similar sentences in job applications? I think it ultimately comes down to any single company who needs to hire workers and what they chose to do. I don't think it is a good idea if we implement a law or any laws for that matter, which have the purpose or intend to limit a company's ability and freedom to hire whoever they want to hire. The current, existing laws on Equal Employment Opportunity are already nullified by the personal or professional choices of the hiring official. If you want a good job is already more a question of who you know than what you can do or what you did in the past. The hiring of workers in any field is and always will be guesswork at best. You hope for the best choice but really don't know. And that is true in the hiring process for any ex- inmate. As far as a company is concerned, he should be just another applicant. The perception of the company could be, that he did his time and that would be the end of that. Companies could do that. But it shouldn't be enforced by any laws or regulations. The owner of the company should not be forced to ignore certain aspects of the applicants past if he chooses to do so. The hiring official already does that anyway, no matter any laws of the State.

I think it is best to leave that one alone. There is nothing we can gain from implementing any such laws. Time will tell and maybe the one or the other study in the process, if there are any benefits or disadvantages in hiring ex inmates compared to workers without a criminal history of any kind.

One area where improvement is possible however should be mentioned. Whether an inmate answers the question of criminal history to the positive or to the negative, he still needs to account for the time he spent in prison. He can't just delete the last two or five years and expect the hiring official not to notice it. The question will come sooner or later and if the former inmate prepares himself, the better he will be. I think the best thing an inmate can do to prepare himself for this moment is to be prepared. What did the inmate do in the prison facility itself? Did he engage himself in some sort of activity or was he just a lazy sleazo, only interested in doing nothing and blaming other people for his situation? What you do in prison does have an effect. If you keep yourself busy and get up in the morning on a regular basis prepares you for the upcoming life with a job. If you are assigned to a specific job in the facility you are incarcerated, make the best of it. This is where prison life can actually help an inmate get prepared for real life.

And this is also the stage in the game, where the career criminals separate themselves from the inmates who came to prison once and already have enough of it. You see this in their attitudes.

A guy is assigned to keep the hallways clean. Nothing is particular difficult or demanding about this type of job. From Monday through Friday, from 0900 to 1600, you get up, get yourself a broom and a mop bucket and every two hours, you sweep and mop this hallway. The most compelling aspect of this simple job is that it counts as a program, and if you are part of a program, you get credits on a monthly basis. The prison administration doesn't pay you a lot of money to do this job, but they certainly will give you a lot of credits so you can get out of prison that much sooner.

Now certain types of inmates just do their job. They might not like it a lot, but they will do it because they also realize, if they continuously refuse to do it, they will potentially see some sort of disciplinary actions against them and they don't want that to happen either.

271

The other type of inmate just doesn't care. They don't care about their life after prison, if they plan to have one, they don't care about their family, they don't care about girl friends or wives, they don't care about their children. The only thing they care about is themselves. Their motivation to get to a lower security prison simply is that it is easier and cheaper to get contraband like drugs and cigarettes. If they are part of a gang, it is easier to advance the selfish and stupid goals of the gang in a lower security setting. Here you have the type of inmate, who is on his own, more so than other types of inmates, because he is trapped in his selfish cage with no thoughts for anybody. It is a sad story for these types of people, but they do exist. And for them, nothing anybody tries to do for them is of any avail, it doesn't work. They do what they do inside a prison or in the outside world.

Unfortunately for many of us, in Corrections or outside of Corrections, the system is geared towards the latter type of inmates. Like is the case with most laws, which are trying to regulate the life of people in a more pronounced way as opposed to general terms, it exists because somebody messed it up for all of us. Common sense does get you a long way in life, but if somebody messes up, you pay for it from her on out. Why is it necessary to show my driver's license to a cop when he stops me as opposed to just telling him that I have my license in my night stand drawer at home? Because somebody lied to a cop about his driver license. That is how many laws came into effect and will be created in the future. It is the malady of the honest man or woman.

F. Simplify the Prison Security System

There are minimum, medium and maximum level prison facilities. The decision where an inmate is to be housed is determined by a wide range of factors. The main idea is, the more security points an inmate has, the higher his security level will be. The overall scale is covered in DOC policy OP-060102 (M) which reads as follows on page 7:

272

C. Scale Summary and Recommendations

1. Custody Level Indicated by Scale

Enter the assessed custody level indicated by the following scale:

a. Minimum: 9 or fewer points on items 1-7

b. Medium: 10-16 points on items 1-7

c. Maximum: 9 or more points on items 1-3

d. Maximum: 17 or more points on items 1-7

If you read the above, they talk about points on a number of items. The easy version of this rather long and detailed policy is, the more security points an inmate has, the higher his security level will be. You can't be assigned to a minimum-security facility if you have more than 9 security points, but only if these points were calculated from items 1-7. Let me give you a little idea, what they mean when they talk about points and some of the criteria. Remember, I am still quoting the same reference:

5. Prior Felony Convictions

Prior felony convictions are to be considered during the past ten years from the date of discharge, excluding charges on the current incarceration.

All prior adult or juvenile felony convictions/dispositions or periods of incarceration for the past ten years are to be included. Inmates who have had a prior incarceration on a delayed sentence will be considered to have had a prior incarceration unless the sentence has been deferred and expunged.

a. Enter 2 points if the inmate has one felony conviction in the past ten years.

b. Enter 4 points if the inmate has two or more felony convictions in the past ten years.

The above is item number 5.

6. Disciplinary History

The inmate's entire disciplinary history is to be considered.

Escapes are addressed in the escape section.

a. Enter 0 points if the inmate has received no disciplinary convictions; or

b. Enter 1 point if the inmate has received three or more class

B disciplinary convictions within the past year; or

c. Enter 2 points if the inmate has received one or more class

274

A disciplinary conviction within the past two years.

d. Enter 3 points if the inmate has received one or more non predatory class X disciplinary convictions within the past two years.

This obviously talks about item number 6. If you are not familiar with the disciplinary procedure of the DOC, I can't blame you, normally only people who work within the Department of Corrections will ever even hear about it. And inmates don't want to talk about it to their family and friends, because it shines a light on them and tells anybody, that they couldn't behave as they actually promised to their mothers, fathers and spouses. Whenever they talk to anybody in their family, they mostly paint this picture of pure goodness and remorse to coerce money out of them for food and telephone privileges. They don't want anybody to hear about their rude behavior to Corrections staff or why they are on restrictions. It doesn't fit the picture they try so hard creating.

But it does exist, inmates face so called Misconduct Reports for a number of infractions. Class B infractions are the lowest category, Class A is sort of medium infractions and Class X is a report written on an inmate, who was really bad. These are mostly internal measurements, which are being handled within the DOC itself. The resulting punishments can be anything from telephone restrictions, restriction on the stuff you can buy from the commissary, loss of credits for a month or longer, etc. However, it sometimes will lead or contribute to charges by the DA of that county, because the infraction was a violation of the law of the State. Most fights within a prison will be handled internally by the DOC. Most drug violations will be handled by the DOC internally. Only if it becomes a matter of public interest will the prison administrator call upon the local police department to come in and investigate the crime scene. Then a Misconduct Report will become part of the materiel the DA will use to build his case against an inmate. If an inmate stabs someone to death, it will obviously be a Class X Misconduct, but it will also become a Murder I charge in the local DA office. If a drug bust in a

275

prison is big enough to be noticed, the drug possession charge will not only be in the form of a Misconduct Report with the resulting, internal disciplinary infractions by the prison itself, it will be a "Possession of a Controlled, Dangerous Substance with Intent to Distribute" charge by the DA of this county, if he chooses to do so.

So quite a number of factors go into the Security points assessment of each offender. Even the age of an offender plays a role:

7. Current Age

Enter the appropriate score based on the inmate's age at the time

of the initial classification review.

a. Enter 4 points if the inmate's age is 28 or less.

b. Enter 3 points if the inmate's age is 29 to 36.

c. Enter 2 points if the inmate's age is 37 to 42.

d. Enter 1 point if the inmate's age is 43 to 50.

e. Enter 0 points if the inmate's age is 51 or over.

Apparently even the DOC thinks that people get wiser with age. In my own, personal experience, that is not always the case, but generally speaking, it is the case more often than it is not.

The Case Manager looks over the Field File of the inmate and tries his or her best to determine, what to do with this guy, where to send him and so on. And he isn't quite sure yet, because some inmates might have the same charge, but their circumstances of the crime itself was totally different. Or it might be the case, that there was a factual attempted murder, but in one case, the perpetrator was a house wife, who was drunk and mistakenly thought her husband was an intruder and shot him and the other case was a gang banging idiot, who followed an order by his gang boss to shoot up the other drug dealer's car. Factually they are the same crimes, but the circumstances are completely different. And of course, the DOC accounts for that as well, hardly anything the DOC doesn't account for. For circumstances such as this the following applies

3. Discretionary Overrides for Higher Custody Level

The following items do not affect the inmate's assessed custody level, but are factors which may affect the custody level assignment and subsequent transfer to specific facilities. All requests must be documented regarding the reason for the override on the initial custody assessment and the chronological record.

a. Circumstances of the Offense

If the current score undervalues the actual severity of the crime, an override may be necessary. Staff must document the aggravating characteristics of the crime being used for the override decision. The District Attorney's Narrative or Information Sheet are examples of documentation that may explain aggravating characteristics.

b. History of Violence

An inmate who has a documented history of violent conduct, such as murder, rape, domestic abuse, assault, or arson that is not fully captured in the serious offense history score may require assignment to a higher security facility.

c. Documented STG (Security Threat Group) and/or perpetrator of STG related violence (4-4312-1)

If the inmate is known to be a major leader within a gang or security threat group that causes management problems and uses violence to achieve its goals within a correctional setting and/or in the community; this affiliation may be considered to be a management issue in the facility. Gang membership alone is not sufficient to score this category. Such individuals should be identified as major gang or security threat group members validated through reliable documentation and/or disciplinary convictions for gang/security threat group activity.

Case Management may look at the DA's paperwork to determine what the story is on this particular inmate. As it says in the heading, the last three points apply to inmates with aggravating circumstances. In other words, it might be the same crime, but this inmate still needs to serve time in higher custody because he is a gang banger or he doesn't seem to be able to contain his violent behavior. In the real world of Corrections, we need to keep an eye out for rival gangs, if we like to or not. After all, we are still responsible for the safety and security of every single inmate and to house feuding gangs in the same housing unit is not a good idea as far as safety and security is concerned.

And if there are aggravating circumstances, there should be mitigating circumstances as well and there are.

4. Discretionary Overrides for Lower Custody Level

The following items do not affect the inmate's assessed custody level, but are factors that could affect the custody level assignment and subsequent transfer to specific facilities. All requests must be documented regarding the reason for the override on the initial custody assessment and the chronological record.

a. Circumstances of the Offense

The score does not reflect the true nature of the crime. Staff must document the mitigating characteristics of the crime being used for the override decision.

b. Time Left to Serve

An inmate serving a high or highest category crime with 330 days of projected discharge may be considered for lower custody for the purpose of reintegration. Mandatory overrides will not be considered for this item.

c. Intermediate Revocation Facility

d. Other

Any other attributes associated with the inmate that justifies an override to lower custody level. Complete documentation of this factor must be contained in the inmate's file or other ODOC records

The physical health and vulnerability of an inmate are important factors as well. And so is the crime the inmate committed. Very old people which are fragile and can easily be extorted or preyed upon need special consideration as well as sex offenders. Inmates who committed sex crimes don't fare well in a relatively open prison setting because other inmates will try to kill them one way or the other. You can't even house a sex offender with somebody with no violent history. The inmate code demands from everybody incarcerated to attack and possibly kill a sex offender. And if the sex crime was committed against a child, you better try very hard to kill this guy or otherwise be killed yourself. In cases such as this, security points don't matter, violent history doesn't matter, misconduct history doesn't matter or if this person is incarcerated for the first time or for the third time. Nothing can contribute to this guy's labeling as a sex offender and as such the only option he has is to be assigned to Protective Custody.

279

Which brings us right to the main point of this chapter. The Custody Level Assessment procedure isn't necessarily complex or time consuming. Administrators seem to be doing their best to get the job done, which is following the law and the judge to keep a person imprisoned for a certain amount of time and at the same time, do this in a safe and somewhat efficient manner. Can this whole procedure be made easier? I think it can.

Inmates are made of two types. One group has the intention to move on with their lives and the other group doesn't care about anything. In my humble opinion it is most important to the System of Incarceration to do its best separating these two types. The inmates who don't care about anything know that they will not change their attitude, which is quite all right. They probably will continue to lead a miserable life and probably will come back to prison until they die or stay behind walls and locked doors forever, whichever comes first. The problem I see with the current system is that these two groups are mixed and the DOC doesn't have any system in place to address this.

If you are thrown into a pack of wolfs, you need to become a wolf in order to survive. If you are thrown into a prison housing pod which has a high number of gang members in it, you are forced to become a gang member yourself. A prison is a very confined area, you can't go anywhere. Your only option is to become part of the environment, voluntarily or by force, which amounts to the same thing. I look at prison violence as some sort of cancer. It penetrates the walls and activity of a prison and everybody who is locked up within these walls.

Someone serves time for check fraud or falling behind paying child support or any bill for that matter. His payment plan fell to pieces when he lost his job or whatever might be the reason. The point is, he has no history of violence, he has a history of not paying bills in time. Yet he finds himself in a medium facility with all sorts and kinds of vicious criminals. And he is in that facility because there wasn't space anywhere else. Now he can try his best to find the right mixture of doing his time and become part of that system and not extending his stay in the process by participating in gang activity, extortion or smuggling. But his existing is not determined by anybody's good behavior, it is determined by the worst behavior, if he likes it or not. A prison administration tends to try to keep the peace. A prison tries to eliminate everything which doesn't contribute to a calm and safe environment. Yet they need to act fast and furious if anything goes wrong. If there is a fight, they need to lock everything down, do their investigation and find out what went wrong. Only then can they hope to return to normal operation. And that is a constant struggle.

I think the recidivism rate would dramatically improve if we were to separate the two groups. The inmates who never change and the inmates who need another chance or at the least, will be able to demonstrate good behavior.

The prison security system could be divided into the following facilities:

1. Stage 1 facility:

   a. Death Row Unit

   b. Protective Custody Unit

   c. Medical Unit

   d. Anybody with a violent crime against another person which resulted in bodily harm or the attempt thereof

   e. Anybody who violated Stage 2 facility conditions as a disciplinary and temporary measure

2. Stage 2 facility:

   a. Work Center

b. Preparation Unit for Work Center

3. Stage 3 facility:

Home supervision

a. Confined to a home

b. Monitored

At the initial Assessment Center each inmate who doesn't automatically qualifies for Stage 1 due to his crime or physical condition, will get a chance at a Stage 2 facility. He even can sign an affidavit to that effect. "I swear that I will adhere to the conditions and responsibilities which I will incur by being assigned to a Stage 2 facility. I will do nothing to compromise my ability to qualify for the Work Center. I understand the rules and regulations of the Work Center."

In order to understand and sign for the conditions of the Work Center, the DOC must introduce such a thing of course. That includes but shall not be limited to understand the entirety of the Misconduct policy as laid out in DOC policy OP-060125.

ACTS CONSTITUTING RULE VIOLATION

Class X

X-1 Banding together for purposes of inciting others in a course of disorderly conduct

(e.g., demonstration; work stoppage; hunger strike; to commit or facilitate commission of a felony or misdemeanor; to prevent or coerce official action; when the actor or any other participant to the knowledge of the actor uses or plans to use a firearm or other deadly

weapon; involvement in writing, circulating, or signing a petition that poses a threat to the security of the facility).

X-2 Riot or taking over a part of the physical plant. May only be used when the director declares an emergency status in writing.

X-3 Killing another person(s) or participating in an activity that directly results in the intentional death of another person. Includes any attempt to cause grave injury to another person rendering that person brain dead or left with the loss of a limb or organ.

X-4 Inmate-on-staff/civilian assaults with serious injury to staff/civilian – required urgent and immediate medical treatment and restricted the person's usual activity and/or required medical treatment beyond first aid. Examples of treatment beyond first aid include stitches, setting of broken bones, treatment of concussion, loss of consciousness, etc.

X-5 Inmate-on-staff/civilian completed non-consensual sexual acts – includes one or more of the following: (a) Contact between the penis and vagina or the penis and the anus involving penetration, however slight. It does not include kicking, grabbing or punching genitals when the intent is to harm or debilitate rather than to sexually exploit. (b) Contact between the mouth and the penis, vagina or anus. (c) Penetration of the anal or genital opening of another person by a hand, finger, or other object

X-6 Inmate-on-staff/civilian attempted non-consensual sexual acts – includes one or more of the following: (a) Attempted contact between the penis and vagina or the penis and the anus. It does not include kicking, grabbing or punching genitals when the intent is to harm or debilitate rather than to sexually exploit.

(b) Attempted contact between the mouth and the penis, vagina or anus.

(c) Attempted penetration of the anal or genital opening of another person by a hand, finger, or other object.

X-7 Kidnapping or taking another person as a hostage.

X-8 Inmate-on-Inmate completed non-consensual sexual acts –
includes one or more of the following: (a) Contact between the penis
and vagina or the penis and the anus involving penetration, however
slight. It does not include kicking, grabbing or punching genitals when
the intent is to harm or debilitate rather than to sexually exploit. (b)
Contact between the mouth and the penis, vagina or anus. (c)
Penetration of the anal or genital opening of another person by a
hand, finger, or other object.

X-9 Inmate-on-inmate assault/fight with serious injury and/or assault
with a weapon –required urgent and immediate medical treatment
and restricted the inmate/victim's usual activity and required
medical treatment beyond first aid. Examples of treatment beyond
first aid include stitches, setting of broken bones, treatment of
concussion, loss of consciousness, etc.

X-10 Possession/introduction/attempt to introduce any explosive,
combustible substance, fireworks, gun, firearm, weapon,
ammunition, knife, sharpened instrument, Class A tool, keys or
security equipment.

X-11 Maximum or Medium Custody Escape, or a documented
attempt to escape (e.g., possession of maps, staff uniforms), or
aiding or abetting an escape for any period of time from the custody
of the Department of Corrections while housed at a maximum or
medium security facility.

X-12 Inmate-on-staff/civilian assaults that did not involve serious
injury - assault did not result in injuries requiring medical treatment
beyond first aid (for example, application of bandages to wounds).
Note: Excludes all verbal assaults and assaults by throwing liquid,
waste, chemicals or urine.

X-13 Inmate-on-staff/civilian assaults and attempts by throwing
substances – includes assaults by throwing or spitting liquid, blood,

waste, chemicals, urine, etc., that did not result in non-serious or serious injury.

X-14 Inmate-on-staff/civilian abusive sexual contact - includes one or more of the following: (a) Sexual contact without consent or when the victim was unable to consent or refuse. (b) Intentional touching, either directly or through the clothing of the genitalia, anus, groin, breast, inner thigh, or buttocks of the victim. It does not include kicking, grabbing or punching genitals when the intent is to harm or debilitate rather than to sexually exploit.

X-15 Inmate-on-inmate attempted non-consensual sexual acts – includes one or more of the following: (a) Attempted contact between the penis and vagina or the penis and the anus. It does not include kicking, grabbing or punching genitals when the intent is to harm or debilitate rather than to sexually exploit. (b) Attempted contact between the mouth and the penis, vagina or anus. (c) Attempted penetration of the anal or genital opening of another person by a hand, finger, or other object.

X-16 Minimum Custody Escape or Community Corrections Walk Away, or a documented attempt to escape/walkaway (e.g., possession of maps, staff uniforms), or aiding or abetting an escape/walkaway for any period of time from the custody of the Department of Corrections while housed at a minimum security facility or Community Corrections Center, Community Work Center, Halfway House, or Community Corrections Program (GPS). This does not include itinerary violations.

X17 Setting a fire.

X-18 Tampering with or blocking any lock, locking device, fire suppression equipment or other security equipment.

X-19 Selling, trading, bartering, receiving or giving prescribed medication/drugs to another person. Possession/introduction or attempt to introduce/manufacture or attempt to manufacture any intoxicant/drug/illegal substance or possession of any drug paraphernalia.

X-20 Possession/utilization/attempt to introduce a cell phone, cell phone paraphernalia, electronic communication device, computer, camera or video equipment or engaging in electronic communication (e.g., texting, accessing or posting to an internet site) while incarcerated at a minimum, medium or maximum security facility or contracted county jails.

X-21 Adulteration of any foods or drinks.

X-22 Violation of State or Federal law (does not require conviction in a state or federal court).

X-23 Running from or resisting apprehension, refusal to submit to restraints or removing restraints within facility, to include hiding within the facility to avoid detection or with the intent to escape.

X-24 Inmate-on-inmate abusive sexual contact – includes one or more of the following: (a) Sexual contact without consent or when the victim was unable to consent or refuse. (b) Intentional touching, either directly or through the clothing of the genitalia, anus, groin, breast, inner thigh, or buttocks of the victim. It does not include kicking, grabbing or punching genitals when the intent is to harm or debilitate rather than to sexually exploit.

X-25 Inmate on staff/civilian sexual harassment, menacing or stalking. Includes verbal statements, questions or comments of a sexual nature. May include profane or obscene language or gestures of a sexual nature. Physical or verbal threatening, intimidation, bullying or menacing.

Class A

A-1 Work, school or program misconduct. Includes, but is not limited to, unexcused absence, quitting without prior approval, getting fired/expelled/removed, tardiness, shirking of duties, failure to notify staff when too ill to work, refusal to participate, cheating on tests or possession/passing of stolen tests or answer keys.

A-2 Inmate-on-inmate assault/fight without serious injury – assault did not result in injuries requiring medical treatment beyond first aid (for example, application of bandages to wounds). Note: Excludes all verbal assaults, assaults by throwing liquid, waste, chemicals or urine.

A-3 Inmate-on-inmate assaults and attempts by throwing substances – includes assaults by throwing or spitting liquid, blood, waste, chemicals, urine, etc., that did not result in serious injury.

A-4 Destruction of evidence. Includes but is not limited to flushing or swallowing evidence.

A-5 Physical or verbal threatening, intimidation, bullying or menacing of another inmate.

A-6 Demanding/receiving money or favors or anything of value in return for protection against others, to avoid bodily harm, or under threat of informing.

A-7 Fraternizing with staff or carrying out any action designed to coerce administration with the exception of sexual activity.

A-8 Inmate-on-inmate sexual harassment. Includes verbal statements or comments of a sexual nature. May include profane or obscene language or gestures when clearly of a sexual nature.

A-9 Engaging in sexual activity with another consenting inmate. Indecent exposure, to include urinating or defecating in any location other than a toilet, or masturbating in view of others.

A-10 Bestiality.

A-11 Outside defined boundaries of a facility as defined by facility or present in a restricted area.

A-12 Under the influence of and/or any use of illegal drugs, alcohol, intoxicating substances and/or refusal to submit to substance abuse testing and/or an attempt to alter or destroy a substance abuse testing specimen. Testing is not mandatory when it is evident the inmate has used an intoxicating substance. If the inmate alleges inability to produce a specimen, a two hour delay under observation will be allowed. Includes use of any medication in an unauthorized manner and/or misrepresenting to staff that medication was taken as ordered (e.g., cheeking, palming).

A-13 Possession or attempt/use/introduction of any tobacco, tobacco-like products, electronic cigarette, matches or lighter at a maximum, medium or minimum security facility. Does not include Community Corrections Centers, Community Work Centers or Halfway Houses.

A-14 Counterfeiting, forging, or unauthorized reproductions of any document, article of identification, money, security, or official paper. Includes altering, mutilating or attempting to destroy.

A-15 Destruction/mutilation/malicious alteration of state/private/public property to include the intentional blocking of any drain in any manner which causes flooding.

A-16 Possession/introduction or attempt to introduce any item not authorized by the facility; includes but is not limited to unauthorized identification, unauthorized tool, money or other contraband.

A-17 Breaking into an office, room/locker or taking/destroying the property of another person.

A-18 Tattooing or possession of tattoo paraphernalia/self-mutilation; to include body piercings or any attempt to inflict self-injury or ingest any harmful or poisonous substance.

A-19 Refusal of medical care/appointment after transportation to an outside medical facility.

A-20 Failure to cooperate in any investigation. Does not include disciplinary procedures investigations.

A-21 Disrespect to staff/civilians. Includes, but is not limited to, using abusive/obscene language, making profane/obscene gestures, insolence, lying to staff, making allegations to staff the inmate knows to be false and malingering.

A-22 Failure to obey verbal and/or written orders, policies or rules.

Class B

B-1 Unauthorized contact/conduct with anyone (e.g., public, visitor) by means of mail or telephone to include passing unauthorized messages or conducting unauthorized activities. Includes violations of OP-030117 entitled "Correspondence, Publication, and Audio/Video Media Guidelines."

B-3 Any attempt to send or receive money or property in any form from another inmate. This includes attempting to conceal the transfer through a third party. This also includes possessing, receiving, trading, selling, giving, or loaning of any property regardless of value as well as attempting to give, giving, or receiving money or anything of value as a bribe or inducement.

B-4 Preparing or conducting a gambling operation or participating in games of chance for gain/profit. Possession of gambling paraphernalia that is not specifically authorized property as specified by OP-030120.

B-5 Failure to comply with rules and conditions of community-based placement (e.g., accountability plan, itinerary, failure to successfully complete required telephone contact, failure to follow sign-in/sign-out procedures or outside the defined boundaries of the facility without permission). Applies to Community Corrections Centers,

Community Work Centers or Halfway Houses or Community Programs (e.g., GPS) only.

B-6 Aiding or abetting in the commission of any rule violation.

B-7 Possession/utilization/attempt to introduce a cell phone, cell phone paraphernalia, electronic communication device, computer, camera or video equipment or engaging in electronic communication (e.g., texting, accessing or posting to an internet site) while incarcerated at a community corrections center, community work center or halfway house.

B-8 Possession or attempt/use/introduction of any tobacco, tobacco-like products, electronic cigarette, matches or lighter at a Community Corrections Center, Community Work Center or Halfway House.

B-9 Unauthorized use of state/private/public property/supplies.

You would be surprised how few inmates actually know or care to know the above rule violations. They of course know the main rules. They know they cannot abuse another inmate sexually or otherwise, throw liquids on anybody, smoke or use drugs and these things. Especially if you live within the system for a number of years, it becomes pretty clear to you, what you can't or can do. After all, the rule violations above are mainly based on common sense. DOC has to make specific rules for the same reason why courts and lawmakers need to make very specific rules. People and inmates are bound to use any lack of clear language or definition to their selfish advantage.

A lot of the above fits into the current system and I added these rule violations to give the reader a clear view of the fine nuances and differences of rule violation. Not every violation is the same in every facility. A Community Corrections Center is naturally less restrictive than a Medium or Maximum-Security level facility. A Class X misconduct can be a Class A misconduct in another prison, which has a lower security level.

290

All these rules would have to be re-written obviously, but the main idea remains. The lower your security level is, the less the restrictions will be. The idea needs to be, that citizens who want nothing more than to get out of prison and to be re-joined with their families, are going to get that exact chance. Many people have drinking problems and get caught one too many times driving while under the influence of alcohol. That is unfortunate but the truth. Now they are going to be locked up for a while after they got caught drunk driving for the 5th time. If at all possible, I want them to keep their job to be able to support themselves and their families. In fact, if they are not convicted of a violent crime against another person or an attempt to do so, I want an offender to have the least restrictions. And the reason for that is, I don't want to pay for it. I don't want to pay for overcrowding and more and more prisons. I want to pay for more schoolbooks and support for single parents. I want to pay for better pay for teachers and better books for schools. I want to pay for things which help to create a future. I am even willing to pay for cheaper colleges, so more people can enjoy a decent education after High School.

In other words, it doesn't help my future or the future of this country or anybody in it, if we keep locking more people up for longer periods of time.

If somebody commits a non-violent crime like being in the possession of stolen property, nobody really cares about that except the person involved. The person involved has a vested interest to get his property back, thus he is very interested in this whole subject. But does that crime affect anybody else? Does this crime have such a sweeping effect on our society that the guy who kept the property for a buddy of his needs to be locked up for five years? Where is the public interest in locking this guy up for five years? These and similar crimes should be mandatorily recommended for Stage 3, which in my scenario would be Home Supervision. There is nobody affected. Like you drive two drunken friends from a bar to their house, except one of them still has an open bottle of booze in the pocket of his jacket. When the cop stops the car because one of your tail lights doesn't work, this all comes to light. Oh yeah, big, fat crime. He had an open container in the car. There you go again, prove that our country goes down and goes down fast, big freaking deal. A passenger in a car is drunk, oh my God, call the infantry and the SWAT team, this is serious.

These and other "crimes" within the network of our society are minor infractions in my eyes, which does not warrant the need to have the taxpayer pay for a three month long stay in a county jail. If the cost to house an inmate in a jail cost about $ 45 a day, that amounts to $ 4 000. And why do I have to pay $ 4 000 for this guy? Aren't there better things the county can do with this money?

If that was a first-time offense, have him pay a fine instead which he can pay based on his income and ability to pay, make up a payment plan and be done with it. If an offender does the same thing repeatedly, add Community Service to the punishment. And if he still can't adhere to the rules and regulations of the society, think about Stage 3 imprisonment, which is Home Arrest or Monitored Supervision. In the case of Home Arrest, he can't leave his house. He would have to take a leave from his job, can't go to the Basketball game of his son and so on. In the case of Monitored Supervision, he can go to his job and buy food from the closest grocery store, but that is it. He can't take vacations with his wife and kids or visit his grandmother in Florida for four months to talk her into co-signing for a car loan.

The funny thing is most of these tools are already in place. We have Monitored Supervision, we have fines and Community Service. A lot of these things already exist, we just don't use them that often it seems. If someone doesn't listen, we apparently tend to lock him up and hope for the best. To lock somebody up for drunk driving is one thing. But to lock him up with gang banging morons and career criminals doesn't do anybody any good, honestly.

All right then, the Case Management of the DOC goes by Security Points, which helps them to classify an offender to determine, for what level of confinement he qualifies. I just don't think the Security Points system is very accurate and is a great tool to determine, where the offender needs to be placed. For instance, a sex offender doesn't need an assessment in that regard. For a case like this, it doesn't matter, how little or how many Security points he has because he can only be housed in Protective Custody and that is the end of that. There is just no alternative. The same accounts for gang members. For safety reasons, they can only be housed in certain environments which do not include being housed alongside rivaling gang members. Again, Security points are not a major consideration to make a decision where to place this guy.

After a while, many Security points fall off again. If you receive a Misconduct while incarcerated, you will possibly get three additional Security points. After a year or whatever might be the measurement, you will lose these points again. And once again, for some offenders like the two examples above, none of these matters, because they can't be moved. They have to stay put in that specific prison because it can guarantee the highest level of security. If they theoretically qualify for Lower Security placement because they only have 6 Security points, the Case Manger needs to override that potential disaster to happen to keep them in Medium Security facility or Protective Custody.

The Security Points system works best as a motivation for offenders who want to get to lower Security level facilities because they are less restrictive and as far as Community Corrections and Halfway Houses go, they can even enjoy the possibility to find a job and start working again. But it doesn't work for all offenders, which brings up the question, why it exists.

I would like to propose to replace this system, because I already mentioned how this system is obsolete for certain crime categories. The biggest problem we Corrections Officers have is the behavior of inmates. And this goes back what I wrote earlier on already.

293

There are these offenders, who are responsive to rules and regulations and who make it a priority to get out of prison and there are those, who simply put, don't care what happens to them. No Security Points system is going to change that. What we can do is give the ones who do care a fair chance, that is, what we can do. We need to separate these two groups.

If an offender is assigned to a Stage 3 or Stage 2 prison, his future should be determined by his behavior. The good part of being assigned to either one of these Stages is, that he is already separated from the most violent and destructive inmates, which would be incarcerated in Stage 1 facilities.

Since he already made it to the lower security level facilities, all he has to do is follow the rules and regulations of this facility. If he can't do that, he will get re-assigned to a Stage 1 facility, even if only temporarily. And that should be all. He receives a Misconduct or even two or three Incidence Reports regarding rule violations, and he is out of there. An Incident Report is a rule violation which gets handled by the facility itself. It doesn't affect the time he needs to serve; he might have to do some extra work or cannot have a visitor for two weeks. All these disciplinary actions are handled on a local level. However, if these incidents add up to the level of a disturbance to the facility, he would have to go to a Stage 1 facility for some time. But he wouldn't need Security points. He would have received a Misconduct Report or several Incident Reports, which would be the determining factor where he goes.

There is no need for a Security Points system as it exists today. Offenders with certain crime categories already have no choice but to go to higher Security or as I called it here, Stage 1. All other offender's placement should be based on their portrayed behavior. The driving motivation in Case Management should be, to spend as little money on offenders as possible. Talk about a public interest, here it is.

We seem to have lost the focus of this aspect of corrections some time ago. Some lawmakers seem to be perfectly content with the fact, that we pour so much money into the prison system to keep as many offenders locked up for as long as possible. Maybe they got frustrated, because they couldn't think of better solutions. I don't want to turn this into a society of ex-inmates. I want us taxpayers to pay as little as possible for corrections and pay as much as possible for education, because I think this is where our future lies. And believe it or not, I think educated people do better to begin with. I am certain there are some good studies on this subject.

G. Enhance the level system

Next up on the many improvements we can make is the Level system. This would be not as sweeping as some other points. It is not affecting any major laws, it is just another way to separate good behavior from those people who just don't care, which in my estimate is a vital part of corrections.

As I said earlier, it doesn't make a lot of sense to throw every single inmate in a big pot and let them figure it out for themselves. We are doing this for 50 years and maybe it is time to try another approach.

It is correct that inmates can earn credits for good behavior. I quoted some references to that effect in the earlier part of this book, relating to advantages inmates have while incarcerated. If they stay out of trouble, they will have the chance to get promoted from Level 1 to Level 4, all in a due and timely fashion. The higher their level, the more days they will get credited on their sentence. In the reverse, if they are found to be guilty of misconduct or other, disciplinary actions, they can lose their earned level again. It is basically a back-and-forth thing for some, because as I mentioned, it is always a struggle to stay out of trouble, especially in an environment like a prison. Many decisions an

295

inmate has to make are not up to him but are motivated by the pressure of gangs and other interest groups.

The Level system was put into effect by the lawmakers and the DOC oversees its execution. Since it is a system based on good behavior and staying out of trouble, it is the DOC which has the final say in who gets promoted, who stays promoted and who gets demoted. The law provides the tools, the DOC uses these tools; this is basically how it works.

I think the current system is as good as it should get because the amount of credits inmate can earn is already substantial. The number of days they get credited is already a good chunk of their sentence. To shorten their sentence even further by earning more credits and thus days is not part of this proposal. It is merely another step in a direction which promotes good behavior.

Level 5:

-For Stage 2 and 1 facilities

-Gaming console plus not more than 30 discs containing Gaming software (provided inmate has flat screen TV)

-Clothing with their choice of color and make

-No restrictions on the purchase of food items which doesn't need refrigeration except storage capacity limitations

-No strip searches

Level 6:

-For Stage 2 facilities

-WIFI access

-Cell phone

-Access to on site computer and printer for job applications

-e-mail account for family contacts and job applications

-Choice of TV size up to 50" (flat screen only) if space limitations allow

-Membership access to internet content providers if paid by a third party

-No restrictions on food items if refrigerator is available

-Refrigerator if facility space allows

If an inmate has to move from a Stage 2 facility to a Stage 1 facility, he of course loses Level 6 privileges and as is the case with other property an inmate cannot have any longer, he has 30 days to have the items mailed or picked up by somebody.

The intention behind the enhanced Level system is to further separate inmates who can and will appreciate being treated as a human being as opposed to a caged animal. It is also designed to keep families intact. If family is a major contribution to the motivation of an inmate, then it makes sense to involve family in his time of confinement.

This can be applied retroactively as well. If we were to designate facilities in such a manner, a way needs to be determined how current Level system inmates could qualify for these levels. When the Level system was introduced, there were a number of lawsuits connected with the implementation of this system compared to older versions. Inmate who felt they were all of a sudden disadvantaged by the new order of things filed suit to keep their older system going or at least adjusted. This is among the biggest hurdles when lawmakers want to introduce new policies into the prison system. Even if a new system benefits 99 % of the prison population and only a few come up short, there are going to be lawsuits, because some inmates have nothing but time and need something to do.

In this entire level scenario, inmates who qualify for Stage 2 facilities from the get go would start their sentence on Level 6 and would lose privileges as they violate rules and regulations, pretty much as it already is designed to work with the current levels. Not much would effectively change as far as promotions and reductions of levels are concerned, it would just be adjusted.

However, there is one major difference in the thinking process. Qualified offenders who are incarcerated in Stage 2 facilities have to earn their privileges to stay on Level 6, where they would start to begin with as opposed to starting on Level 1 or Level 2 and earn their way up. They would have to show from the start that they intend to get out as fast as they can, they would have to show that they are not here because they are career criminals. Their punishment is confinement, not the total loss of dignity and humanity. This hopefully creates an atmosphere in which someone who goes through a difficult time in his life still has a chance of redemption. It could contribute to separating the real criminals from those people who want to do better. I theorized earlier that one of the big problems in the current prison system is, that every offender no matter his crime, can wind up in an environment which can make it extremely difficult to stay human. The current system doesn't account for the intentions behind a crime, it doesn't differentiate between someone who has no intentions to change his life or get out of prison and the ones which do. Assigning qualifying offenders to Stage 2 prisons and letting them start on Level 6 would do that, I think, because an offender starts his sentence in an environment which attempts to mimic his current living situation. He is still confined but it is now up to him to show that he can do better and will do better. And he can do so on his own terms. He is not forced to join gangs or other interest groups.

He is not forced to live with violent offenders who might or might not care if they live or die or how long they need to spend behind bars.

For certain crimes, there are no alternatives to Stage 1 facilities due to the violent and/or heinous nature of the crime. But our prisons are not overcrowded because of these offenders. They are filled with offenders who are charged with drug offenses, property offenses, failure to pay offenses, driving under the influence, being under the influence and so on.

H. Training

As discussed earlier, training is a major point in Corrections. It is not a major point because the training is abundant and prolific, but because it does not exist.

A Corrections Officer is hired. Depending whether he works in a State owned, privately owned or even a federal prison facility, the training procedure varies greatly, both in depth and quality. I experienced a private prison facility and a State-owned facility, so I only feel comfortable writing about these two.

The training in the private prison was two weeks, the training in the State facility was six weeks. In this time, you get to be acquainted with two things. The basic policies and procedures of the Department of Corrections and very basic self- defense techniques. You also have weapons training in the State facility, because in cases of Emergency, they have the right to re-assign you to a facility, where carrying weapons might be part of your job. This apparently is not the case in private facilities, but that might vary from State to State. So in this time, you get to find out about what you can do as a CO and what you can't do, you learn to defend yourself and you get somewhat proficient to restrain an offender who got out of control. As is the case in other fields, what you learn is what you get. So CO's know little about anything what is going on in the system of incarceration than what their job assignment requires. Changes in policy and procedures are made known via sign- up sheets. Your supervisors are supposed to make sure that you read and understand the changes which take place, but that is anybody's guess. It might work on some facilities where supervisors actually care about their subordinates, on other facilities you just sign a piece of paper and go back to your job. In many cases there is no time slot allotted for more than that. The Department of Corrections as it currently exists is already so stretched, that COs can't just take a week off to get trained. Even a weekly training within a year's time seems to be a difficult task for some facility administrators. So, there is not only hardly any time available to stay up to date as a CO, there is even less time provided to advance in your job. If you want to take courses within the DOC to avail yourself for higher positions, you are looking for the needle in a haystack. It is basically up to you to advance your training. It is up to you to make the time, to pay for it and fit it all in your schedule of work and family to get any enhanced training. I was told that at one point in time, the DOC actually helped pay for college courses, like the Army still does. That of course went down the drain, it was sacrificed on the altar of prison overcrowding.

It is easy to get discouraged in the current prison system, especially if you are a Corrections Officer. You have to work whatever shift your supervisor puts you on, no matter your circumstances. You have to work on holidays and on weekends. All other staff take weekends off. All other staff get to take holidays off. If you as a Corrections Officer want to take a weekend off to take your family to a water park, you basically have to use your leave, which cuts into your summer or Christmas holidays. You have to deal with erratic behavior on an almost daily basis because you are the one person the inmate has access to every hour, every day. If anything goes wrong, you have to fix it. Everybody else comes in after the fact. You get hit with the full frustration inmates feel for various reasons. You are the one who is responsible to keep the inmates in line and following rules and regulations. All other staff just read the reports you write and act on it, lowering someone's level or promoting good behavior, whatever might be the case.

Administrative staff in Corrections have a fixed schedule. No matter what happens on the facility, they go home in time and come to work when they are supposed to. Security staff don't have that luxury. They have to be on site 24/7 and if a situation requires it, will be called in to work in the middle of the night because something happens, which needs attention and people to fix.

In a perfect world, an inmate is compliant, courteous, respectful and follows the rules. In the real world, people get locked up, because they did something which violated the law. This attitude is carried into the prison or jail. Some inmates are in prison because they were too lazy to get a real job, some are in prison because they never knew that to make it in this world, you have to get a real job. In some cases, nobody ever told them, in some cases they just didn't listen. Many inmates are not very intelligent, their ability to distinguish right from wrong, good from bad is limited.

My point is a Corrections Officer's job can be very hard and mentally draining. You are being tried all the time. As the main person every inmate talks to and has contact with, a Corrections Officer bears the full brunt of the frustration and sadness of every inmate, all the time.

And the Corrections Officer is also expected to make the perfect decision every time. Does an inmate have a real issue with another group of inmates or is he just trying to gain a personal advantage? Is there going to be a fight or is it just noise? Does the inmate have a viable, medical issue or is he just complaining of an upset stomach?

Good training will help a Corrections Officer distinguish noise from real problems. Good training will help a CO make good decisions

301

because he knows the rules and policies. Good training helps the CO understand not only the rules of the DOC, but the laws of the State.

If you know everything about a subject matter, you can't be the negative effect of it, because you know. If a mechanic knows what he is doing, there will be no surprises after he repairs a car. If a baker knows all about his ingredients and knows how they react with each other and how they will behave in the oven, he will have a perfect cake every time.

It is the same with a CO. If he would know all there is to know about Corrections, he will be a calm, competent professional and every inmate will know it, too. There would be no attempts to coerce any CO to do something which is not covered by the law or DOC policy. The inmate would know that the CO knows and he wouldn't be able to convince him otherwise. He wouldn't be able to complain about anything which is already covered by policy. COs would do the same thing every time and inmates would stop trying to make a CO do things which are not policy, because the CO would know policy. And better yet, the CO could do everything which is now divided into several jobs.

In my years as a Corrections Officer and working in prison settings, it works as follows:

You have the Corrections Officer. You have the Case Managers, which take care of the programmatic needs of the offenders and are responsible to calculate their remaining time. They also accompany inmates to get various chores done, like acquiring ID's and certificates, depending what the Security Level of the facility is. Then you have the Case Manager Supervisor or Unit Manager, who oversees the work of Case Managers. You have the entire Records Department, which file all paperwork and put it together and submit it to the Populations Office for approval. If you want to know, how much time you have left on your sentence, these are the woman and man who will be able to tell you. Here is a little excerpt from the DOC policy OP-030101:

A. Unit Manager

The unit manager is in charge of the unit and oversees all unit programs and activities. The unit manager is a member of senior facility staff, maintains a close working relationship with other departments, chairs the unit team classification meetings, reviews all team decisions and ensures quality assurance of inmates' records and classification to include reentry planning in accordance with OP-060901 entitled "Pre-Release Planning."

The unit manager reviews inmate transfer eligibility, inmate program eligibility rosters, and ensures the quality of other on-unit programs. Additionally, the unit manager oversees sanitation and maintenance of the unit.

1. Unit managers will conduct case management audits as outlined in Section V. of this procedure.

2. Unit managers provide direct supervision to case managers and correctional unit assistants assigned to their housing unit.

B. Case Manager

1. The case manager is responsible for all casework and many social services functions, preparation of classification actions and parole reports, ensures consistent reviews of inmates regarding their special needs, security and/or level assignment changes, and

enters the required data and other pertinent information into the Offender Management System (OMS). The required information to be entered into OMS includes, at a minimum, the inmate's progress toward meeting the developed case plan, the inmate's overall adjustment (unit and work), any requests made by the inmate and other significant issues or serious incidents.

2. Case managers provide social services such as cognitive program provision, counseling and guidance for the inmates on the unit in areas of individual conduct, personal difficulties, social skill development, to include guidance to those with physical and developmental disabilities, crisis intervention, interpersonal communications, and planning for the future. (4-4429-1, 4-4435) In accordance with OP-060104 entitled "Community Corrections Assessment" and OP-060204 entitled "Inmate Transfers," the case manager maintains inmate transfer eligibility and program needs, assists inmates with pre-release plans and reentry preparation, and processes inmate-related correspondence and other materials relating to the inmate's commitment. The case manager serves as the primary contact point between the inmate, the administration, and the community. (4-4435)

The following is taken right from the horse's mouth, from DOC policy 060101 entitled "Overview of Case Management"

Overview of Case Management

Case manager functions within the Department of Corrections (ODOC) include appropriate and timely classification of all inmates, providing crisis intervention, work assignments, programmatic activities, managing behavior, developing open communication between staff and inmates, assistance with reentry, and assisting with facility operations and inmate development. Other functions consist of documenting and communicating any behavior that would present a risk to the facility, staff, other inmates or the public to ensure appropriate action is taken to safeguard the department's mission.

I. Inmate Accessibility to Case Management Staff

Facilities will have scheduled case management coverage a minimum of five days per week.

Case managers will be assigned work hours as determined by the facility head/ administrator to allow for inmate accessibility compatible with the role of case management and facility need, in accordance with OP-030101 entitled "Unit Management Overview and Major Objectives."

II. Responsibilities of Case Management Staff

Case manager responsibilities/duties will include:

A. Developing individualized accountability plans, as documented on the "Adjustment Review" form (DOC 060203A) to address identified needs of the inmates on their assigned caseloads

B. Responding to all inquiries in regard to those inmates on their assigned caseloads.

C. Participating in the facility and unit orientations of newly assigned inmates and ensuring inmate awareness of available programs.

D. Maintaining a current list of inmates assigned to their caseload. The listing will include information critical for the proper classification and management of the inmate in accordance with this procedure. This will be submitted monthly to the unit manager.

E. Participating in the inmate disciplinary process.

F. Encouraging active participation in programmatic activities and ensuring appropriate referrals for all programs noted on the inmate's case plan. Case managers may function as program providers as a means of ensuring a variety of programmatic opportunities are available to the inmate population

G. Appropriate classification of inmates on their caseload.

H. Awareness and knowledge of classification procedure revisions, additions, or deletions, and implementation of revised procedures as they become effective.

I. Ensuring inmates are appropriately classified and appropriate transfer packets are submitted in accordance with OP-060104 entitled "Community Corrections Assessment", OP-060204 entitled "Offender Transfers", OP060102(F)(M) entitled "Female/Male Initial Custody Assessment

Procedures" and OP-060103(F) (M) entitled "Female/Male Custody Assessment Procedures."

J. Reviewing inmate progress at least once a month and documenting the review in the case notes section of the Offender Management System

K. Facilitating inmate reentry according to procedures outlined in OP-060901 entitled "Pre-Release Planning and Reentry Process."

So where am I getting with all this? Well, just hold on for a minute. I want to show you one more thing which is fascinating. This piece of administration in the DOC is 100 years old and never changed, at least so I think.

You know, when you hear in the news how corporations merge or buy each other out and that kind of stuff? You probably think there is a lot of paperwork connected with this and there probably is. After all, there are a lot of bits and pieces which need to be re-aligned and re-organized to make it work. If you buy a house, there is also a lot of paperwork connected to that transaction. You need to sign a lot of papers which the Title company tries it's best to explain to you. The result of all that is a fairly sized chunk of papers, all neatly organized in a thick folder. And I think as far as the private person with a regular job is concerned, that chunk of papers is as much as it gets in someone's private life.

Everything else these days is accomplished with one or two pieces of paper and the rest is stored in electronic form on a server with two backups. And that is the end of that. I don't care much where you look these days and what type of organization we are talking about. Everything is stored electronically and backed up for all intends and purposes to keep everything safe and secure. You open bank accounts, you open a power supply company account, you apply for a new job, you buy a new or a used car, you put your kids into a new school etc. The most physical paperwork you encounter is one or two pieces of paper, ready to be signed. All other information is stored electronically, for better or for worse.

For some reason DOC doesn't work that way. The moment an offender enters the world of the DOC, he will carry around with him a folder with his name on it, filled with an enormous number of papers. Of course, having accurate information which is available to anyone at a moment's notice doesn't have to be a bad thing, not really. Well, yes and no. It is good to have all information in one place, if it would be all information in one place to begin with. It probably still could be done better these days, but at least you can see a purpose in that folder. Except there is a computer system as well, which is called the Offender Management System or OMS for short.

Now look at the poor Case Manager or anybody who deals with that inmate and ask him for an accurate assessment of that inmate. He would have to go through and read a thousand pages of paper and 50 screens online to fully understand what is going on. That is the extent of the work. Compare that with the ever-increasing prison population and the lack of funds and you can begin to understand, that only a fraction of that wealth of information is accessed because time alone prevents to go any deeper. And for the most part, that is good enough. Which raises the major question, why isn't it simplified? Well, I don't know, but here is what the DOC needs to have in anybody's Field File. It is taken from DOC policy 060212 called "Maintenance and Access of Offender Records":

III. Creation of the Record

A. Field Record

1. Upon reception of an offender, either for supervision or incarceration, the receiving district or facility will ask the Closed

Records Unit for an existing closed field record. The Closed Records Unit will search DOC files for any record of previous periods of supervision or incarceration. Within one working day, the appropriate district or facility will be advised by the Closed Records Unit of the existence or nonexistence of prior records.

2. In instances in which a prior record is located, the Closed Records Unit will send the record to the appropriate district or facility within two working days. In instances in which no prior record exists, the district or facility will create a field record for the newly received offender.

IV. Organization of Field

A. Field Record

The following materials (when applicable) will be placed in the record sections as indicated and will be maintained in chronological order, the most recent material on top. All materials will have the appropriate signatures and dates prior to placement in the field record.

Section One—Legal, Institutions and CCC's

Acknowledgment of Release to

Deportation Order

Court Minutes

Death Warrants

Death Certificate

Detainers

Designation for Disposition of

 Personal Property

District Attorney's Information

Executive Leave

Extradition Paperwork

Fingerprint Card

Identification Packet

Interstate Agreement on Detainers

Forms

Jail Time Statement

Judgment and Sentence

Mandates and Opinions

NCIC Search

Notice of Court Cost Hearing

Notice of Transportation Costs

Copies of Offender Identification and

Re-Entry Envelope

Order Revoking Parole/Probation

Parole Certificate

Pardon Certificate

Property Inventory Form

Photo Packet

Rap Sheet

Reception Intake Form

Receipt for Prisoner/Documents/

 Detainer

Requests for Notification

Sheriff's Receipt

Specialized Offender Accountability

 Plan

Stay of Execution

Warrants

Writs

Related Correspondence

Section One—Legal, Probation and Parole

Application to Accelerate Parole Certificate

Application to Revoke

Court Minutes

Death Certificate

District Attorney's Information

Judgment and Sentence

Mandates and Opinions

Motion to Dismiss

NCIC Search

Copies of Offender Identification and

Re-Entry Envelope

Rap Sheet

Requests for Notification

Restitution Schedule

Rules and Conditions

Specialized Offender Accountability Plan

Summary of Facts

Warrants

Writs

Related Correspondence

Section Two—Credit and Sentence Information, Institutions and CCC's

Certificate of Release

Consolidated Record Card (Copy only, original in commitment folder)

Earned Credit Class Report

Eligibility for Enhanced Level 3 and 4 Credits

Escape Reports

Final Disposition Report

In-Processing &Time Calculation Audit Form

Intra-facility Assignment Form (if used to award credits)

Monthly Earned Credit Report

Rebill Form

Release Checkout Sheet

Reporting Instructions & Acknowledgments

Section Two—Credit and Sentence Information, Probation and Parole

Deferred Evaluation Summaries

Discharge Notices

Final Disposition Report

Information Acknowledgment

Summary of Supervision

Termination Summary

Transmittals Regarding Openings and Closure

Verification of Closure

Related Correspondence

Section Three- Assessment and Intake Information, Institutions and CCC's

Assessment of Protective Measure Need

Case Plan

Cell Assessment Form

Classification Audit Form

Custody Assessment Scale

District Attorney's Narrative

Family/Employment History

Facility Assignment Form

Housing Assignment Form

Initial Custody Assessment/Facility Assignment Form

Offender Profile Screening

Interstate Investigation

Intra-Facility Assignment

Juvenile Criminal Records

Assessment Instruments

Offender Case History

Offender Accountability Plan

Physical Description

Protective Custody Review

Reassessment of Protective Measure Need

Reception/Intake Form

Record of Chemical Abuse Testing (If positive)

Reintegration Assessment Referral Form

Related Correspondence

Request for Protective Measures

Separatee/Medical Flag

Test Results

Verifications

Section Three-Assessment and Intake Information, Probation and Parole

Interstate Investigations (Plus Forms III & V)

LSI/ASUS

Mediation Report

Offender Accountability Plan

Personal History Summary

Pre-Pardon Investigation

Pre-Parole Investigation

Pre-Sentence Investigation

Screening Information

Verifications

Related Correspondence

Section Four-Programs/Case Management, Institutions and CCC's

Adjustment Review

Administrative Segregation Hearing

Administrative Special Management

Offender Notice

Chronological Record

Education and Vo-Tech Information

Escorted Leave Forms

Halfway House/GPS/EMP Screening Form

New Arrival Review

Offender Financial Responsibility

Pre-Release Checklist

Program/Work Referral

Related Case Material or Correspondence

Release of Information Authorization

Request for Review of Individual Department of Corrections Record

Segregation Housing Order

Segregation Review

Substance Abuse Information

Visiting and Telephone Information

Section Four-Programs/Case Management, Probation and Parole

Assessment of Needs

Assessment of Risk

Chronological Record

Reassessment of Needs

Reassessment of Risks

Release of Information Authorization

Request for Review of Individual Department of Corrections Record

Special Reports

Substance Abuse

Related Memos & Correspondence

Section Five-Parole Consideration/Probation and Parole, Supervision, Institutions and CCCs

Notice of Pardon and Parole Board

Hearing Results

Pardon and Parole Board Investigator Report

Parole Matrix Assessment

Parole Stipulation Report

Parole Waiver

Parole Status Report

Related Memos & Correspondence

Section Five–Parole Consideration/Probation and Parole Supervision,

Probation and Parole

Court Cost Receipts

Delinquent Notices

Notice of Change of Address

Probation Fee Receipts and Notices

Restitution Receipts and Notices

Travel Permits

Written Reports

Section Six–Misconducts and Revocations, Institutions and CCCs

Administrative Review Authority

Correspondence

Incident Reports

Misconducts Section Six–Misconducts and Revocations, Probation and Parole

Arrest Reports

Notice of Executive Revocation Hearing

Notice of Probable Cause Hearing

Parole Revocation Documentation

317

Supplemental Reports

Violation Reports

Waiver of Executive Hearing

B. Commitment Document Folder (Legal File)

The following documents for all incarcerated offenders will be maintained in a manila folder separate from the field record:

1. Certified commitment documents; parole revocation certificates;

2. Consolidated Record Cards (CRC's) for all closed sentences and for any unrevoked or consecutive parole violation sentences;

3. Original copy of the "Disciplinary Hearing Report" and all attachments; and

4. Jail time statements.

5. All original forms of personal identification will be maintained in a sealed envelope and stored in the commitment document folder (legal file). Personal identification items include: a certified copy of the Birth Certificate, Social Security, state issued identification card, state issued driver license, United States passport, military records (DD214),

Certificate of Degree of Indian Blood (CDIB), Oklahoma tribal photo ID card, or photo identification issued by an Oklahoma technology center school.

a. When an offender discharges or paroles, they are to be given all forms of identification contained in the envelope.

b. When an offender discharges or paroles, the commitment document folder will be retained in Section 2 of the file.

C. Offender Identification and Reentry Envelope

A copy of the forms of personal identification in the commitment folder and original offender identification (ID) cards will be maintained in Section 1 of the field record in an envelope no larger than 8 ½ x 11. The contents will be documented on the cover of the envelope.

If you even glance at that list, especially if you are not familiar with the subject matter, you might get a headache. But for the sake of argument let's just say, it is a lot. And this file is carried around wherever the offender goes.

The Oklahoma DOC currently manages about 65 000 offenders, which are either incarcerated or on some sort of supervision. What does it take to keep the information of 65 000 people on a server? Not very much. We are not talking about 15 million people; we are talking about a fraction of that number. It takes very little actually. My own, personal home computer could manage 1000 documents for 65 000 people, no sweat.

Let's simplify this procedure. The most important document is the Judgment and Sentence. What did the court papers say, what type of punishment did the judge hand down and how many days and what was the crime? This determines placement and classification level of the inmate, because the Judgment and Sentence also tells you if any program stipulations are included in his term. What is wrong with a running day count? Well, actually the DOC software already does that so it would be a simple task to update that in a new computer program. Since you have a running count of the days remaining, the only thing which is necessary to do is to adjust the running count to the Level the offender is on. For each Level promotion or demotion, the days remaining change, because the offender gets more days credited as he moves up a level. He also gets credits for program completions and various, other accomplishments. This could all be included in the calculation parameters. For each program completed, the offender gets

319

credited 30 days. Boom, one stroke of a button and it's done, the days remaining automatically adjust. He receives a Misconduct for bad behavior and one stroke of a button adds 30 days or a drop in Level causes him to lose 30 days in that fashion.

Based on the nature of the crime, the program can incorporate other parameters as well. After the offender has a certain number of days left, he qualifies for a lower-level facility. The program triggers a date two month in advance, letting everyone know, who looks at this offender's file that he needs to be shipped to a lower security facility on this date latest.

And the list goes on. The entire point of this is, that there is currently a lot of paperwork to go through and if one person has to go through 1000 pages of documents and information about just one, single offender, it invites mistakes. One document which is filed in the wrong section can invite misjudgment and lack of vital pieces of information. More importantly, nobody is going to look at the entire field file of the offender, because most of the information is available online anyway, at least the type of information he needs to know, which is basically, how many days does the offender has left to serve.

There is a need to update the offender tracking and information system. I don't' think it is very expensive, the main cost stemming from the fact that you have to pay a bunch of people for four years to enter the vital pieces of the information packet into the new computer system. Or you pay a computer programming company to convert all information from one old system into a new system, if that is possible. It is possible, but it still remains a question of cost. It comes down to the question, what conversion system is cheaper, but that shouldn't deter the DOC from doing it.

The rewards would be less human error, more clarity even for the uninitiated and even the offender himself could actually understand for the first time in his life, what the Case Manager is talking about. Right now, the offender basically has to trust the Case Manager in doing the right thing.

In the years I worked in the world of DOC, I personally witnessed numerous instances of miscalculation of time served and other factors which affect the release date of an inmate. Sometimes people got released in the middle of the night because somebody found out that they are not supposed to be incarcerated any more. Of course, mistakes like these are not broadly publicized, but they do happen more often than you think.

The following is a simplified approach and proposal to offender management and tracking:

A. At the Reception center, which is the first location the offender goes to after entering the World of DOC, all original paperwork is completed and kept in a secure location.

B. The days remaining are entered into the Days To Serve (DTS) tracking system. It provides a continuous account to the offender and everybody who cares to know and find out, mainly Case Managers and Administrators. A print out can be handed to the offender.

C. Every instance, event, promotion, demotion, program completion, disciplinary action and what have you is completed and scanned into the offenders program. It can even be completed online with no need to scan anything but for the sake of argument, it can be an option.

D. Since the Days remaining will change due to C. above, every instance which causes change will be bookmarked at the day the change occurs. Everybody can now easily look up the event which caused the days remaining to change by clicking on the bookmark. Who has done it, when it occurred and so on.

E. This in my humble opinion minimizes errors. Every single person is on the same page, literally and figuratively, all the time.

This of course is just one simple idea to rework the Offender Management Tracking system. But I have personally witnessed too many errors and miscalculations to ignore the need to overhaul the current system. It needs to be done.

Besides the fact, that the management of an offender is unnecessarily complex and opens the doors for errors and miscalculations, I see one more problem with the system as it exists today.

The Management of the inmates is divided into several levels as I mentioned earlier already. There is the Corrections Officer, the Central Transportation Unit, the Case Manager, the Case Manger Supervisor, the Unit Manager, the Chief of Security, the Records Clerk, the Records Department Supervisor, the Captain, the Major, the Programs Director, the Teacher, the Mail Clerk, the Mail Clerk Supervisor, the Misconduct/Grievance Supervisor, the Law Library Supervisor, etc.

The amount of personnel necessary to manage a prison is based on its size of course. The fewer inmates the facility holds, the more people take over more functions at the same time.

I think it is worthwhile to look at bundling these functions, which leads us back to the Training of Corrections Officers.

As is currently the case, the Corrections Officer is the enemy of the inmate, whereby the Case Manager, Chief of Security and Facility Administrator are his "friends", or persons he has to be nice to, because they are the ones who can determine, when he goes home. They are the ones who can determine if any restrictions are placed on him. The CO is their enemy because they are the ones who enforce the rules. They take their illegal cellphones from them, they catch them in the act when they smoke on State property, they are the ones who tell them what to do

322

and when to do it. In the minds of the inmate, the CO's are the ones who restrict them in their movement and in their daily decisions.

A Corrections Officer doesn't know the particular circumstances of each inmate. He certainly can find out, but it is not part of his job description. If he sits on the Case Manager's computer for five hours like the Case Mangers do and tries to do a Case Manager's job, he will not be able to do the tasks his particular job requires, which is supervising inmates.

You don't need to know much if you are a Corrections Officer as is evidenced by the amount of training a CO receives before he gets thrown into the cage. You need to know a little bit more if you are a Case Manager. This knowledge can be easily acquired, but it is basically up to you since the DOC can't help you. They have no resources to train Corrections Officer or really to train anybody for that matter. There are no courses you can take to advance your skills and knowledge, there is no financial or time support if you want to enroll in a few subject matter related college classes. There is really nothing much the DOC can or will do to support the advancement of a Corrections Officer. Or anybody else for that matter who is on their payroll.

If knowledge is power, the Corrections Officer is not that different from somebody who prepares burgers at a Fast-Food restaurant. The learning curve and the amount of time it requires to learn the ins and outs of making burgers and coffee specialties can't be that different from what a Corrections Officer needs to learn to get his job done. Of course, everybody who sits above a Corrections Officer in the food chain will tell you in an instant, what a great job you do and all that. And maybe some people even mean that, after all we do the dirty work. We deal with irate, crazy, lazy and irrational inmates all day long which is something they don't have to do. Maybe that is where the appreciation comes in, who knows.

I envision a system, where everybody is on the same page.

323

I think the management of the inmate can be put into one person.

A Corrections Officer should not be just a Corrections Officer, he should be the Corrections Manager. We can work on the name of course, but here is how a prison could be run:

1. Facility Manager

-Oversees the facility operation. Determines the amount of personnel necessary to provide services to all inmates and staff

2. Human Resources

-Depending on the size of the facility, this function can be either centrally run by Headquarters or from the facility itself

3. Deputy Manager for Re-Entry

-Oversees the Corrections Mangers both in terms of validity and amount needed

-Makes the schedules for all Corrections Managers

-Creates a Rotational schedule for his subordinates, whereby the Corrections Managers rotate to either one of two positions: Security and Case Management. This will depend on the size and type of the facility. In Stage 2 facilities the CM (Corrections Manager) will mostly be able to hold both positions at the same time, whereby in higher level security prisons, a rotational schedule will become more relevant due to the nature of the inmates.

4. Deputy Manager for Discipline

-Oversees the disciplinary measures for inmates and ensures they align with policy and State law

-Ensures justice by verifying each disciplinary actions taken and the presence of both an accuser as well as a proper opportunity for defense

5. Deputy Manager for Liaison

-Contracts with outside sources for programs, courses and education

4. Corrections Manager

-Is in close contact with the inmates and is every inmate's manager.

-Has access to the Offender Management system and enters all relevant data

-Liaises with Pardon & Parole

-Handles all Pre-release planning procedures

-Audits the inmate's file before release or parole for any detainers, fees etc

-Does a week in Security and a week in Case Management on a rotational schedule. This depends on the size of the facility. Smaller prisons don't need a rotational schedule.

In very large facilities, you might need to have several Deputies of the same type or more human resources personnel. But the basic layout stays the same, whereby the Corrections Manager handles and is responsible for all inmate needs.

Pardon & Parole operations can stay as they are. They might have to adjust a little bit here and there, but the main idea remains that they supervise and look over offenders who have stipulations connected to their release.

This proposal elevates the Corrections Officer to the level of Corrections Manager. It also means that the new position needs more training. It means that two weeks of quickly going through some basic policies is not going to cut it. The Corrections Manager needs to be a professional in the full sense of the word. He needs to be sufficient in all security related matters. He needs to be able to defend and detain. He needs to know Case Management and he needs to know the family situation of each inmate. He needs to know what his crime is and what his criminal history is, if any.

That all means that a Corrections Manager needs to be trained sufficiently. It might take six months; it might take a year. Competence doesn't come over night, it needs to be developed. And if we hope cut down on recidivism and if we hope to successfully integrate former inmates back into a productive society, we better get going.

I. Disciplinary Procedures and Justice

This is going to be a short one.

If an inmate messed up, he is subject to disciplinary measures. These measures come in at least two different flavors. One version is less severe than the other. The facility itself has the option to impose its own discipline upon the offender, which is done for little infractions. A report is written which provides a hopefully accurate account of what happened. It provides the time, the day, the people involved and tells the reader exactly what took place, accompanied by a recommendation of how this situation should be dealt with. These reports are normally done by the people who deal with the offender on a daily basis, the Corrections Officer and other staff like Kitchen Supervisors, Volunteers, Work Crew foremen and the lot. Depending on what facility it is and what the Security level is, recommended sanctions can be loss of visitation privileges, loss of the ability to buy goods from the canteen or to leave the facility for programs or church services. These sanctions would ordinarily have a time limit. If an offender is caught smoking for instance and he has been observed smoking more than once, the sanctions for the second offense could mean that he loses certain privileges for a longer time or sanctions imposed are added.

If the violation is more serious or the offender has shown that the informal sanctions have no effect on an individual's behavior, a Misconduct Report is drawn up. This means he can lose a Level for a certain amount of time which will result in more time he has to spend behind bars. Let's assume he is punished by the loss of Level 4 for 30 days, which is fairly common practice. If he gets 45 days credit on Level 4, but only 15 on Level 1, he needs to spend 30 more days behind bars. This time frame can also be extended which will result in more time he has to do. Along with the loss of time come normally one or two other restrictions. This Misconduct Report becomes part of the inmate's disciplinary history and thus is prone to become a bargaining tool when the offender gets closer to a possible Parole date or even Probation. An inmate with no disciplinary sanctions is generally easier paroled than one with two or three Misconduct Reports.

The entire subject of Misconduct is covered in OP-060125 "Inmate/Offender Disciplinary Procedures". Since it can be a serious matter, it is very formal and structured. The list of possible offenses is already covered in the last section called "Training", so I don't' have to mention that again.

Where I would like to propose a change is in the disciplinary procedures, no matter if you talk about incident reports with resulting punishments or various kind, which is conducted by the specific facility or an actual Misconduct Report which will follow the offender no matter where he goes.

Justice however needs to be applied to both types of discipline. If there is going to be justice of any kind, we cannot just propose justice for one type of discipline and no justice for the other type of discipline. If the word justice means "just behavior or treatment" and the word "just" is defined as "morally right and fair", then we need to apply it universally.

An incident report on some facility at first glance doesn't sound like much to anybody. And it probably isn't if looked at as an individual infraction. The offender did something wrong, truthfully or allegedly so and is being punished for it. That sounds simple enough and reasonable. It goes into his file. It becomes part of his record, at least on the facility he is. The next infraction could be another incident report or a misconduct report, which could be or could not be influenced by the previous incident report. And that is my whole point. Every incident will reflect on the offender no matter in what form and in what color it is being served.

Is this a wrong thing? Of course not, it is part of the system and there is absolutely nothing wrong with it. If you have done wrong, you will get punished, outside or inside a prison or jail. If you just follow the rules and regulations of the network within society you are currently living in, you will be all right, just like most of us.

So why do I have to make an article about it which is part of remedies for overcrowded prisons?

Because Incident Reports and Misconduct Reports can lead to an offender doing more time, which I have to pay for, which is fine if it is justified. If the alleged offense is imaginary or only half true and the offender is still convicted, then I respectfully like to pronounce: I am not ok with that.

The problem as it currently exists is simple. You can even read it in OP 060125:

F. Standard of Proof

In order for an inmate to be found guilty of a rule violation, the trier of fact must find that that there is some or any evidence that the inmate committed the rule violation charged.

The language is extremely vague. What does that even mean? And there is more:

4. Reasonable attempts will be made to locate all identified witnesses; however, it is the inmate's responsibility to provide sufficient information to properly identify a witness. If witnesses cannot be located, the disciplinary coordinator must document the efforts made to locate the witnesses on the "Witness Discretionary Action Record." If an inmate refuses to identify a witness it will be the inmate's responsibility to gather any statements and provide them to the disciplinary coordinator. Such statements must be verifiable or will not be considered credible.

In his defense, the inmate can snitch on other inmates or at the least put other inmates in harm's way, subjecting them to the scrutiny of the facility security staff. Well, good luck with that. In all my years in Corrections, I have never seen one instance where an inmate calls upon another inmate to testify on his behalf. It just never happens because Corrections Officers and other staff of the facility are the natural enemies of the inmate. It's like a deer which is being hunted by a pack of lions is asking another deer to assist in his defense. I don't say it never happened, but I have never seen it and it doesn't make a lot of sense.

Then there is the staff representative who is or can be appointed to assist the inmate understanding the charges against him and what he can or can't do. I have seen this happening on several occasions because some people can't read. It is a very rare occurrence but it does happen. The following explains what a staff representative can do:

B. Responsibilities of the Staff Representative

1. The staff representative will attend the disciplinary hearing/disposition with the inmate.

2. The staff representative will be impartial in the roles and responsibilities as defined:

a. Will consult with the inmate before the hearing/disposition;

b. Will explain the charge against the inmate and the potential sanctions;

c. Will explain the ramifications of a guilty plea;

d. Will assist the inmate in understanding the disciplinary process including the process for appeal;

e. Will assist the inmate in understanding the process of presenting their version of the charges;

f. Will attend the hearing/disposition with the inmate; and

g. When required, will assist the inmate in communicating with the disciplinary coordinator and/or the disciplinary hearing officer

It is already embarrassing enough to not be able to read or write. And if you are not able to read or write, what makes anybody think that he will be capable to understand any part of the procedure he is facing? Yes, he might hear what the staff representative is trying to explain to him, but really understand what is going on? I don't think so. On top that, realize where the inmate finds himself. He is sitting or standing in a confined space, surrounded by senior staff of the facility since the Disciplinary Officer is required to be pay band H or above, which is mentioned on page 4. That is generally not an entry level pay grade, thus this Officer is already employed for a little time or at the least is familiar with many aspects of the subject matter.

The offender is already in a weak spot. He doesn't want to be there, he wants to get out as soon as possible, because in some facilities which are medium or above, even talking to an officer for an extended period of time can get you in trouble with some parts of the inmate population. The inmate rule is, that you don't talk to a staff member, unless you try to coerce that staff member to bring you some contraband or conduct other, illegal favors. That would be the only instance where prolonged conversations could be acceptable.

Many hearings also include threats and intimidation. The staff members don't have all the time in the world to deal with that problem which the inmate caused to begin with. The perception basically is that due to his stupidity and lack of willingness to behave appropriately, he is stealing our time. If he wouldn't have done what he did, we didn't need to sit around here, doing paperwork and listening to this guy. We would be doing something else, preferably something more pleasant. It is all his fault; how dare he commit a rule violation and force me to spend my time with something I would rather not spend my time with.

Hearings like this can probably be compared with a similar situation in real life. If you were to be charged with a felony and walk into a court room to meet with the judge and the prosecutor, you would find yourself in a similar situation. There is no defense attorney, provided by the court or paid by you. They talk a whole bunch of legal terms and rattle off numbers of sections of the law and its paragraphs. Since they do this for a while, they also use abbreviations and shortcuts. And you would be right in the middle of all this. You try to understand what is going on but can't really get a hold of anything, which makes sense, since this is not your world. The only thing you can recognize is that there is going to be a charge leveled against you. And since they are friendly people and don't want to waste their precious time any more than necessary, they offer you a deal. Accept these terms and conditions and we will let you go. Take this deal and you will be on your way. And ever so subtly they make it clear that if you are not willing to accept these terms and conditions, you will keep wasting our time, because we didn't do the crime, you did. And we will make you pay for it.

That kind of is the situation an inmate finds himself in, just on a slightly smaller scale. And to be honest with you, many inmates don't care enough to have it any other way. They probably know, they got away with way more than with what they are being charged with so they will gladly accept that punishment. That is especially true for offenders who do so much time, that one month or six month more doesn't even face them.

But it is still no justice and if we as a society tell our children that justice is important and the Constitution says that justice is important and we turn around and only provide justice to a select few, then we are nothing more than Hippocrates.

One remedy of the situation would be to have other people than security personnel deal with the hearing and the whole disciplinary process.

Security personnel are an interest group, just like used car dealer salesmen are an interest group or to stay with the subject matter, police and prosecutors are an interest group. If a Corporal, Sergeant or above in a prison is part of the disciplinary process, as a Hearing Officer or as an Investigative Officer, he is also part of a specific interest group. If he spends too much time with an offender, his supervisor might not like it a lot. If he even follows the OP 060125 policy to the letter and takes the side of an inmate, because he realizes he doesn't really understand what is going on, he might or might not attract the wrath of one of his supervisors. If he is too lenient with the imposition of sanctions more than once because he feels there is not enough evidence, his supervisors might look at him differently as far as future possibilities for promotions are concerned. If the tone of his specific facility is that they always punish offenders the hardest way possible and he diverts from that "policy", he might find himself in a situation where he is being passed up for promotions. If he rebels against his own interest group in other words by trying to do his job properly and by policy, he might be leveling a disservice to himself.

It is also not feasible to create an entire new section within the Department of Corrections for the sole purpose of conducting unbiased hearings. I for myself already don't want to pay for prisons and paying a bunch of more people to conduct hearings and such wouldn't add to that purpose of reducing costs in the prison system.

But the DOC can do the following instead:

1. If an offender is charged with a disciplinary infraction, the report must be submitted to a staff member in a section of the prison, who is not part of the chain of command of the officer or staff member, who submitted the report.

2. No staff who receives a disciplinary report can be involved in any part of the incident in question

3. Every staff member of the DOC who received an incident or misconduct report from the facility head or a designee must submit the recommendations within 7 business days to the facility head or designee who will submit the recommendations to Security and Case Management and other sources if necessary

4. The facility head or a designee has the authority to choose a staff member to handle a report

5. The reports must be evenly distributed amongst all full-time staff member

6. The investigative staff member handling the report must be granted full access to all files, camera footage, statements of both staff and

offenders relating to any part of the incident as he/she sees fit and appropriate

7. The offender must be given the opportunity to appoint a defense person on his behalf. This person shall be of assistance in the disciplinary proceedings the inmate may face and can be any one of the following: another inmate, any person appointed by the inmate who was not involved with the incident itself and who is not a staff member of the DOC or law enforcement entities

8. The staff member investigating the misconduct and submitting the recommendations must grant the offender the opportunity to use a telephone or writing utensils to contact witnesses on his behalf and the staff member has the explicit authority to provide such

9. The facility security or any other department of the prison has the authority to detain the accused in a properly secured location for the length of the investigation as facility security measurements dictate

10. All materiel and paperwork pertaining to the incident are to be kept on the facility where the incident occurred until the accused either declined an Appeal or the Appeal process has been completed.

11. After a possible Appeal to the Director of the DOC or his designee or the expressed denial by the accused to file an appeal will all related documents be sent to the offender's field file to become a permanent record of the offender's field file

12. If the offender is found not guilty, all relevant documents must be destroyed

I think the above will provide both justice and a streamlined disciplinary procedure. If there is to be an Appeal procedure, it could be handled in a similar manner, except it would preferably be done from a senior facility which in this case could be DOC headquarters.

334

J. Construction Division

Ever since the inception of the Department of Corrections in its various forms since the last 200 years, the idea always has been that the inmate should be put to work to not only contribute to the cost of incarceration, but to prevent him from idling around uselessly.

This has always been a hallmark of the Corrections Department which is why when you look at old movies depicting prison life, you more often than not see people dressed in striped clothing working at one place or the other, accomplishing various chores. This has been the case but for the most violent and heinous criminals, who were incarcerated within a much more restricted confinement.

For some reason this has come a little bit out of fashion. These days, the favorite idea of society and Corrections seem to be to lock everybody up and forget about it.

I regret that new approach to incarceration. I regret not only having to pay for the incarceration of inmates, but also for the upkeep and the construction of new prison facilities and various, related sites and buildings, which would include officer training facilities and such.

The law of the State of Oklahoma has the following to say about this subject:

§57-58. Employment of prisoners.

Wherever any person shall be confined in any jail pursuant to the sentence of any court, if such sentence or any part thereof shall be that he be confined at hard labor, the sheriff of the county in which such person shall be confined shall furnish such convict with suitable tools and materials to work with, if, in the opinion of the said sheriff, the said convict can be profitably employed either in the jail or yard thereof, and the expense of said tools and materials shall be defrayed by the county in which said convict shall be confined, and said county shall be entitled to his earnings. And it shall be the duty

of said sheriff, if in his opinion the said convict can be more profitably employed outside of said jail or yard, either for the county or for any municipality in said county, so to employ said convict, either in work on public streets or highways or otherwise; and in so doing he shall take all necessary precaution to prevent said convict's escape, by ball and chain or otherwise, and fifty percent (50%) of the profits of such employment, after paying all expenses incident thereto, may be retained by said sheriff as his fees therefor, the balance to be paid into the treasury of the proper county to the credit of the general fund; and when a convict is imprisoned in the county jail for nonpayment of a fine he may be employed by said sheriff as provided in this chapter; and in case any convict employed outside of the jail yard shall escape, he shall be deemed as having escaped from the jail proper.

R.L. 1910, § 4596

The idea of the above text and other State law on the subject has been successfully converted by the Department of Corrections. It is covered and regulated by DOC policy 090106. Inmates do work in their respective municipalities and counties. They are not dressed in striped clothing any longer but instead wear grey outfits but nevertheless are easily recognizable as inmates. They help maintain highways, public roads and publicly financed facilities.

Here is a short list of eligible inmates:

D. Community/Work Center Programs

The following will be considered when determining inmate assignments to a community/work center program:

1. Inmates Assignment to Non-Departmental Supervised Work Crews– Community

a. Earned credit level – preferably earned credit class level three or four. Earned credit class level one and two inmates will be considered

336

on a case-by-case basis for assignment to this type of work supervision;

b. Excellent to outstanding work evaluation;

c. Excellent to outstanding personal hygiene and appearance;

d. No recent misconduct history of a serious nature;

e. Good to excellent attitude, behavior, and emotional stability; and

f. Excellent to outstanding interaction with staff, other inmates, and visitors.

2. The agency will contact the facility when requesting inmate services. The facility will ensure the inmate population is reviewed by the facility classification team for suitable candidates that meet the following criteria:

a. No class "A" or "X" misconducts in the proceeding 60 days;

b. Not in one of the exclusionary categories listed in Section IV. item B.; and

c. Inmates will be screened for any medical conditions that would preclude assignment to the program and will be approved by medical staff prior to assignment.

3. Contracting agencies may interview eligible inmates prior to assignment. Such interviews will be conducted through the designated staff member.

Of course, only inmates from certain type of facilities can participate in the Public Works Program:

IV. Selection and Assignment of Inmates

A. Inmate Criteria

1. All inmates must be assigned minimum or community security.

2. The facility classification committee will determine participation.

3. Prior to an inmate being assigned to a crew, staff will review the "Activity/Housing Summary" (DOC 140113C) for any work related restrictions. A copy of the "Activity/Housing Summary" will be provided by the medical unit within five working days of the request by facility staff.

4. Facility staff will complete the "PWP Screening Form" (Attachment D, attached) for inclusion in the PWP packet

There are a lot of inmates assigned to Minimum and Community Corrections facilities. It always can be better of course, but inmates do work for the people so to speak. But for the sake of saving money, we could go much further than just that. And apparently somebody else already had a similar idea. Let me introduce the forgotten State law §57-508.3. It is called "Construction Division"

§57-508.3. Construction Division.

A. There is hereby created the Construction Division within the Department of Corrections. The purpose of the division shall be to provide inmate construction crews for construction projects of the Department of Corrections.

B. The Director of the Department of Corrections shall adopt and promulgate such rules as may be necessary to carry out the duties of the Construction Division and shall appoint a Director of the division who shall administer the activities of the division.

C.   1. An inmate working for the Construction Division of the Department of Corrections shall be subject to all rules established for inmate work by the State Board of Corrections and subject to all statutes governing the operation of the Construction Division of the Department of Corrections.

2. Inmates working for the Construction Division are not state employees, and are specifically forbidden from organizing into unions or other associations in connection with their work or from engaging in any strike, work stoppage, slowdown or collective bargaining process. This prohibition applies to any inmates forming a union local or similar organization at any Construction Division project or location; provided, however, it shall not prohibit any inmate from otherwise achieving or retaining status as a union member.

3. The claims of the state against an inmate to cover the costs of incarceration of an inmate shall be prior to the unsecured claims of any creditor.

4. The authorization for an inmate to work for the Construction Division is a privilege granted to the inmate by the state which may be revoked by the Director of the Department of Corrections.

5. As used in paragraph 3 of this subsection, "costs of incarceration" shall include all costs associated with maintaining an inmate in the custody of the Department of Corrections and shall include costs paid by the state for medical care for the inmate.

Added by Laws 1996, c. 166, § 1, eff. July 1, 1996.

I don't know how much of this is currently in effect, if anything, I just couldn't find DOC policy which would relate to such a thing as the Construction Division. We do of course have inmates in our facilities who take care of the upgrade of the buildings. They install walls, doors, handle any and all plumbing issues and so on and so forth. Prison facilities would normally only pay for the materiel needed to get something fixed. Inmate crews wouldn't help to build the prison, but they would keep it up and in good condition as funds allow, so far so good.

But why stop there? You hardly hear of cities and counties which don't have minor or major, financial issues. This might have to do in part with the simple fact that news agencies are quick to point out bad news but would hardly consider it worthwhile reporting how great some cities and counties are doing.

There is however room for improvement. If there is a Construction Division within the Department of Corrections, then the Department of Corrections should use it to its full potential. The only thing the DOC has to do is formulate rules and regulations regarding the above like they already did with the Public Works Program. The same qualifications could even be applied for eligible inmates. The same policy could even be applied, it just would need some minor additions. The above referenced DOC policy further says:

B. Supervision

1. ODOC security will be provided for all inmates assigned to institutional (Warden's Crew) public works crews for the custody and control of inmates. Crews will not exceed one departmental staff member for each 10 inmates.

2. Any public agency employee may supervise an inmate crew following completion of a favorable criminal background check and with required training as outlined in VII. D. below. The inmates will be checked out to the agency employee by the supervising ODOC staff person.

3. Supervision and security counts of all public works crew inmates will be in accordance with OP-040101 entitled "Facility Security Standards."

4. Transportation of the inmate to the work site will be coordinated between the agency and the designated staff member as specified in the contract agreement.

5. The host facility coordinator will ensure that inmates assigned to the program have read and signed "Inmate Guidelines and Rules for Public Works Program" (Attachment F, attached). The original will be placed in the inmate's field file.

Nothing in this policy says that inmates can't do construction. Right now, they are mainly used to clean up highways and streets, do maintenance and yard work around public buildings and such. What a world it would be if cities and counties could use inmate crews to actually build something. Why can't a crew consisting of 80% inmates not build a school, or a school Baseball field, a track, a gymnasium, anything? Why shouldn't they be able to build a highway, a turnpike, anything which would benefit the citizens of the county and every taxpayer in it? I would very much vote for it. Why should we pay $ 30 Million for a new building if we can safe $ 10 Million by using inmate labor? The Fire Department needs a new facility, because the city limits expanded in the last 25 years which necessitates an expanded fire department. Well, let's get to work then. The inmates can dig the holes, route the plumbing, build the walls and the roof, paint the whole joint and install all fixtures. And if it is too time consuming to drive the inmates back to the prison every night, the Construction Division can even provide trailers which can be hauled around the countryside and put to use wherever needed. The supervision requirements don't change. In these times you can even hook up every inmate with a GPS based monitoring system, which causes an alarm to go off if an inmate moves outside a defined parameter. These units already exist for inmates on supervised probation, it wouldn't be too much of a stretch to expand on that technology.

To conclude this chapter, I would like to make a case for the Construction Division of the Department of Corrections and its implementation. The policies of the DOC as far as Public Works Programs go, already exist in sufficient clarity. It just seems that nobody uses it. I say, let's put them to use and save us all a lot of money.

I understand the need of the private sector to get contracts from the city and county. But as far as the construction of new buildings is concerned, it very often is dismissed due to the availability of funds. And if a private company finishes a big building project for a state agency, they let half of their workers go again anyway so I can't quite follow the argument of protecting the private building industry.

And we haven't even taken into consideration the amount of clean-up projects inmates could accomplish. There is an enormous amount of clean-up to do all over the country. The demolition of old factories to make space for new projects could be entirely in the hands of inmates. The cleaning of streets, forests, cities, lakes and rivers across the country has to be an enormous amount of work waiting to happen.

We basically have the laws to put all these tasks into effect with little cost to the community itself. We just have to do it.

And if supervision is an issue, I am the first one to volunteer for half a day to watch a group of 20 inmates clean up a river. I am the first one to volunteer to watch inmates install a filter system on some old factory so the fumes would not pollute the nearby vacation spot. And I will be among the first volunteers to watch a group of inmate's repair and paint houses in a run-down neighborhood to increase my own quality of live and the quality of life of my neighbors and fellow citizens.

EPILOGUE

If we were to change anything and everything per the "Remedies" section of this book, we really would not have to change a lot.

It seems that we have maneuvered ourselves into a rather critical situation, which puts not only inmates but staff who work within the correctional setting at risk.

We cannot expect for any inmate who is thrown into such a situation to come out the other end a changed or even rehabilitated man. The word "Corrections" itself is sacrificed on the altar of overcrowding and lack of funds. Many prisons in this country have no alternative but to house people in ever more confined areas. The resulting tension is like a pressure tank with no release valve, the next catastrophic failure only a matter of time.

As our own failure to work on solutions continues to haunt us, we tend to get more and more agitated. We want to be left alone, any one of us has to deal with his/her own problems. After a while, we don't even want to look anymore, the ability to have compassion for our fellow citizen gets lost. Why is it, we tell ourselves, that people do stupid things and end up in prison? And why is this any of my concern?

As for me, the answer is simple. I know how to do it better. I read it in many laws of this State and in many policy letters of the Department of Corrections. It doesn't need much and what it needs can be accomplished without spending another Billion Dollar on top of a budget which is already behind.

Why would anybody else care?

Because we continue to build an Army of people who hate and we create this Army within our own borders. If you look at the current prison situation, there is little anybody can gain. Do you need to get punished for crimes committed? Absolutely. It is any democracy's tool to remind its members to do the right thing. The notion however to increase punishment beyond the necessity to confine a person for committed crimes has gone too far.

Inhumane conditions, gang warfare, the lack of speedy and public trials, the need to look over your shoulder at any given time, the mark on your forehead telling every potential employer that he should not hire you, financial ruin, loss of dignity and self- respect. This is the reality for many people who leave the prison system.

We are fighting an Army of hate and we continue to pay for this Army by creating the situation in which such an Army can be indoctrinated and thrive. And we don't need to, because the cost to our society goes way beyond the cost to keep someone incarcerated.

I think in most respects, we already have the solution. Many laws and policies in this State already exist to improve the current conditions as I tried to demonstrate in the previous pages. For reasons not known to me, it was decided to worsen the conditions and to apply the laws in such a way to create ever more offenders and prisons.

I think it is worthwhile to remedy this.

I didn't try to paint a vibrant, colorful picture of no prisons and no punishments, I simply tried to mark a way out of this situation without calling for a revolution.

The current prison system can be improved with little, if any investments in time and money. And I hope I was somewhat successful in showing how and why it would be a good thing to do.

The Author

Questions/Comments

boma2002@aol.com

© 2024 Martin Bolt
Production and publishing:
BoD – Books on Demand, Norderstedt
ISBN: 9783759766694